THE TREMBLAY REPORT

THE
TREMBLAY
REPORT

*Report of the Royal Commission of Inquiry
on Constitutional Problems*

Edited and with an Introduction by

DAVID KWAVNICK

The Carleton Library No. 64

McClelland and Stewart Limited

THE CARLETON LIBRARY

A series of Canadian reprints and new collections of source material relating to Canada, issued under the editorial supervision of the Institute of Canadian Studies of Carleton University, Ottawa.

The Canadian Publishers
McClelland and Stewart Limited
25 Hollinger Road, Toronto

Printed and bound in Canada by
T. H. Best Printing Company Limited

TABLE OF CONTENTS

NOTE ON THE EDITOR
David Kwavnick's fields are French-Canadian politics and Canadian interest groups. He graduated from McGill University (B.A.) and from Carleton (M.A., Ph.D.), and has taught at the University of Saskatchewan (Saskatoon) and Carleton. He has published articles in the *Canadian Journal of Economics and Political Science, Canadian Public Administration,* and the *Canadian Journal of Political Science,* and recently published a book, *Organized Labour and Pressure Politics: The Canadian Labour Congress 1956-1968.*

EDITOR'S INTRODUCTION

THE TREMBLAY REPORT AND FRENCH CANADA

On February 12, 1953, the Lieutenant-Governor of Quebec gave royal assent to a bill establishing a royal commission to inquire into constitutional problems. In particular, the commission was charged with examining fiscal relations between the Government of Canada and the provincial governments.

The commission's immediate objective was to justify the proposition that the authors of the British North America Act had intended the provincial legislatures to have exclusive access to all forms of direct taxation. Section 92(2) gives the provincial legislatures exclusive jurisdiction over "Direct Taxation within the Province in order to the raising of a Revenue for Provincial Purposes." Section 91(3) gives to Parliament the power of "Raising of Money by any Mode or System of Taxation." The reconciliation of Sections 91(3) and 92(2) has, over the years, aroused a good deal of controversy.

The premier of Quebec, the Hon. Maurice Duplessis, no doubt regarded the establishment of the commission as little more than the addition of another arrow to his quiver. The Act establishing the commission provided that it was to report on or before March 1, 1954, leaving barely more than one year in which to complete its work. A consolidation of the old familiar arguments supplemented by some up-to-date documentation was all that could realistically have been expected.

Instead, the Tremblay Commission, as it came to be known, produced one of the most remarkable government documents in Canadian history to that time. The Report was nothing less than an examination in depth of the philosophical and moral basis of French-Canadian society and a restatement of its *raison d'etre*.

There have been many royal commissions, both federal and provincial, in Canada. They investigated the problems confided to them by their terms of reference and made recommendations. What is unique about the Tremblay Commission is that it undertook to expound the unarticulated major premises of a society's existence and to justify those premises by reference to what it believed to be absolute and immutable standards of eternal verity. The Tremblay Commission raised questions the answers to which most people simply take for granted. The surgeon about to enter the operating theatre does not engage in a philosophical debate on the value of human life or attempt to find in absolute morality a basis for saving the life of his patient. But this, by analogy, is precisely what the Tremblay Commission did. And it is the moral and philosophical inquiry into the justification for the existence of French-Canadian society which ensures that the Tremblay Report will be indispensable to scholars for as long as Canadian history and Canadian politics are studied.

The immediate objective of the Tremblay Commission was to shore up the claim of the Quebec provincial government to provincial primacy in the field of direct taxation. Since this claim could not be supported in law it was necessary to turn to other arguments, namely, the historical and the sociological. The gist of these arguments was that the Fathers of Confederation had opted for a federal union in order to ensure to each of the various communities in British North America the means to pursue its development in accordance with its own particular values and outlook. The provincial legislatures had been given exclusive jurisdiction over those areas of legislation which were deemed to be necessary to carry out this intention and they were given the necessary financial resources to do so in the form of direct taxation and statutory federal grants. Over the years the range of government activities increased dramatically and direct taxation became the major source of government revenues. But these developments should not have caused any difficulties. The expensive new governmental activities have been primarily in the field of welfare which, according to the Commission, had been assigned in its entirety to the provinces while the direct taxes needed to pay for them had likewise been assigned to the provinces. The problem, said the Commission, resulted from the fact that the Federal Government had created a vicious circle; using the excuse of war, it had taken the lion's share of direct taxes, to justify these revenues in peacetime it usurped provincial responsibilities and, finally, it uses these heavy responsibilities to justify its continued fiscal dominance.

This argument can be debated at length, but the debate would probably prove sterile since it is not the argument itself which would be at issue but the basic assumptions of the participants in the debate. The basic assumptions of the Tremblay Commission, the premises underlying its historical and sociological position, are the vital part of its report. It is to them that we now turn.

History, beyond a few established and indisputable dates and events, does not exist in any concrete or absolute sense. But a mere catalogue of dates and events is not history any more than a skeleton is a person. The work of the historian is to put the flesh of meaning on the bones of fact. The historian provides the interpretations, traces the trends, draws the themes and attempts to find some meaning in it all. In short, the work of the historian is to make history. But different historians draw different themes and place different interpretations on the same facts. The result is that there are different schools of historical interpretation.

The historical perspective of the Tremblay Commission belongs to the conservative nationalist school; at its base is the so-called Compact Theory of Confederation. In its most popular form, the compact theory asserts that the agreements upon which the Confederation settlement was based were in the nature of a compact or treaty between the original four provinces, that each of these provinces entered Confederation on certain conditions and after having received certain guarantees. Quoting with approval from the writings of Judge Loranger, the Commission sketched the principles of the compact theory in the following terms:

1. The Confederation of the British Provinces was the result of a compact entered into by the provinces and the Imperial Parliament which, in enacting the British North America Act, simply ratified it.

2. The provinces entered into the federal union, with their corporate identity, former constitution, and all their legislative powers, part of which they ceded to the federal parliament, to exercise them in their common interest and for purposes of general utility, keeping the rest which they left to be exercised by their legislatures, acting in their provincial sphere, according to their former constitutions, under certain modifications of form, established by the federal compact.

3. Far from having been conferred upon them by the federal government these are the residue of the old powers, and far from having been created by it, it was the fruit of their association and of their compact, and it was created by them.

4. The parliament has no legislative powers beyond those which were conferred upon it by the provinces, and which are recognized by section 91 of the British North America

Act, which conferred it, only the powers therein mentioned or those of a similar nature, *ejusdem generis*.

5. In addition to the powers conferred upon the legislatures by section 91 and section 92, their legislative jurisdiction extends to all matters of a local or private nature, and all omitted cases fall within the provincial jurisdiction, if they touch the local or private interests of one or some of the provinces only; on the other hand, if they interest all the provinces, they belong to parliament.

6. In case it be doubtful whether any special matter touches all or one, or a few provinces only, that is to say, if it be of general or local interest, such doubt must be given in favor of the provinces, which preserved all their powers not conferred upon parliament.

7. In the reciprocal sphere of their authority thus acknowledged there exists no superiority in favor of parliament over the provinces, but subject to imperial sovereignty, these provinces are sovereign within their respective spheres, and there is absolute equality between them." (Vol. I, p. 65-66)

Thus, according to the compact theory, Confederation was made by the provinces acting *qua* provinces and was an act of provincial policy. The provinces created the Federal government as an act of provincial policy the better to enable them to pursue provincial policies. The provinces, subject only to the sovereignty of the Imperial Parliament, are the repositories of all legislative powers some of which they ceded to the new level of government. In summary, the Government of Canada is little more than an inter-provincial agency. The provincial governments are the senior governments. They maintain a permanent position *in loco parentis* vis-a-vis the Federal government even to the extent that the Parliament of Canada is denied the authority to alter the quorum of the House of Commons without provincial consent.

The compact theory, once it is accepted as the premise, yields the logical conclusion that no changes can be made in the original agreement without the unanimous consent of all the parties to that agreement. It goes without saying that the protagonists of the compact theory intended that this principle apply to those parts of the compact enshrined in formal legal documents such as the British North America Act. But does the BNA Act contain the whole of the compact? Are all of the conditions and guarantees upon which Confederation is supposedly based contained within the four corners of the BNA Act? The Tremblay Commission took the view that the BNA Act is merely a starting point, that the guarantees and conditions set out therein cannot be understood except by reference to the reality to which they were intended to apply and, therefore, all of the essential elements of that reality come within the protection of the compact theory.

But what are these essential elements? An attempt to answer this question must eventually come to grips with two other extremely interesting questions implicit in it. First, if the nature of Confederation was determined by certain essential elements, those elements can be understood through an understanding of the nature of Confederation. Into what kind of an arrangement, seen in retrospect, did the Quebec leaders believe they were entering? In short, in the conservative nationalist French-Canadian view, what is Canada?

Second, what was the reality which the conditions and guarantees of the Confederation settlement were intended to protect? Obviously, in general terms, they were intended to protect French Canada, to ensure its survival. But what does this mean in terms of specifics? What aspects of the human existence are essential to the preservation of French Canada, or, to phrase the question differently, by what aspects of the human existence is French Canada defined? In short, in the conservative nationalist French-Canadian view, what is French Canada? A thorough examination of these two questions is beyond the scope of this introduction. But an understanding of the Tremblay Report requires at least a partial answer.

What is Canada? What is Confederation? In the conservative nationalist French-Canadian view the purpose of Confederation was to establish a political framework within which the various "communities" (for want of a better term) of Canada could live their own collective lives unimpeded by the others. If the word "country" means a piece of territory and a government to manage certain of the affairs of the people inhabiting that territory, then one of the purposes of Confederation was to establish a new country. But if the word "nation" means a community holding the same, or similar, values and loyalties then it was certainly not intended that Confederation establish a new nation. On the contrary, a new nation would have meant the negation of what, in the conservative-nationalist, French-Canadian view, was one of the primary aims of Confederation; it would have meant the destruction of the very particularities, communities and local elites which Confederation was intended to preserve.

The provinces were not seen as the building blocks of Canada. They were seen as complete and natural entities in themselves, claiming the loyalty of their inhabitants and ministering to all the immediate needs of those inhabitants. In the words of the Tremblay Commission:

> To sum up, the central government was entrusted with the main general, military, administrative and technical services but there was reserved to the provinces all . . . that concerned social, civil, family, school and municipal organization; everything which touched the human side most nearly [closely] and which influenced the Canadian citizen's manner of living. (Vol. I, p. 38)

It follows that any attempt by the government of Canada to concern itself with the day-to-day life of Canadians would be regarded as a usurpation of provincial responsibilities. Similarly, any attempt on the part of the government of Canada to win the loyalty of Canadians or to be accepted by them as a national government would be regarded as a contravention of one of the primary purposes and conditions of Confederation.

Confederation was regarded as the work of the several local elites of British North America, intended to preserve both the distinct communities which those elites represented and the elites themselves. The pursuit of national unity, as that term was understood, meant the creation of conditions conducive to co-operation for the common good among those elites. It meant not undermining the position of the local elites by going over their heads and appealing directly to their constituencies. It meant allowing each of the provincial communities to pursue its own way of life unhindered by the differing attitudes, values and social institutions of its neighbours and thus reassuring these communities, and especially their leaders, of the efficacy of the Confederation settlement. Canada, in the Commission's view, was intended to be an affair of the head among the local elites not an affair of the heart among the masses.

What is French Canada? This is a difficult question to answer because it can be approached on several planes. What is beyond question, however, is that French Canada was not merely a community of Canadians distinguished from their compatriots by virtue only of the fact that they spoke French as their mother tongue. French Canada was distinguished not only by its language but also by its way of life, its institutions, its social structure and, above all, by its value system and goals.

The French Canada idealized by the conservative nationalist elite was essentially a medieval society: rural and agrarian with a self-sufficiency based on subsistence agriculture, unchanging, with sharp distinctions between the social classes and little movement between them. The social philosophy and values were those of the Roman Catholic Church while the goals of the society (i.e., its notion of progress) was apocalyptic and messianic. The central institution of this society was, beyond doubt the Church which, according to the Tremblay Report "supplied French Canada with its thought, its way of life and the majority of its social institutions." (Volume II, p. 33)

The factors which led to the dominance of the Roman Catholic Church are complex and a detailed discussion of them lies beyond the scope of this introduction, but an understanding of what this dominance meant in terms of values, outlook and life style is essential.

In a rapidly changing world it is likely that large organizations, especially those which have been successful, will face crises of identity. Their leaders will be obliged to choose between reaffirming the validity of the conditions and doctrines which enabled their organization to be successful in the past and abandoning those conditions and doctrines in favour of others which will enable the organization to succeed in the future. But the abandonment of formulae which have proven their effectiveness in the past is not an easy task, especially when the future appears uncertain. As a result, the leaders of such organizations often exhibit the tendency to idealize the conditions and doctrines of the past, to regard the decline of those conditions as signs of decadence or straying and, to continue to insist on the validity of the old doctrines regardless of the evidence of reality. Alvin Toffler has described this reaction to change as "obsessive reversion to previously successful adaptive routines that are now irrelevant and inappropriate. . . . The Reversionist sticks to his previously programmed decisions and habits with dogmatic desperation. The more change threatens from without, the more meticulously he repeats past modes of action. His social outlook is regressive."[1]

For the Roman Catholic Church, the crisis came in the mid-nineteenth century. The Europe envisaged by the Congress of Vienna, a Europe whose unarticulated major premises would

[1] Alvin Toffler, *Future Shock* (New York, 1970), pp. 359-360.

be medieval and pre-industrial, had disintegrated beyond recall. The Church, like the classes represented by the leaders who met at Vienna, had enjoyed its greatest successes during the medieval period. It now faced the task of abandoning the doctrines which had been successful in the past or re-affirming them. It appeared at first that the Church might attempt to come to terms with the modern world; it chose a young pope who was known to favour reform: Pius IX.

But the revolutions of 1848 and the political conditions in Italy frightened the new pope and he sought refuge in the tried and tested doctrines, he became a "reversionist" and a reactionary. Ensconced in the Vatican he thundered anathemas upon a world he did not understand, he compiled a Syllabus of Errors which proscribed that world, he condemned modernism and he set the Jesuits loose again upon a world that already had enough problems. When his reactionary views began to meet with opposition he foisted upon the Church the doctrine of papal infallibility; saying, in effect, that if his views and reality did not coincide the fault lay with reality. The Catholic Church has not yet recovered from the panic-stricken reaction of Pope Pius IX.

What were the outstanding characteristics of the world-view to which Pius IX committed the Church? They were the characteristics of Western Europe during the period in which the Church attained the peak of its secular power, the characteristics of medieval Europe.

In general terms, it was a world whose economy was dominated by a peasant-based agriculture with a leavening of tightly organized craft guilds in the towns. The dominant characteristics of day-to-day life were security and stability. The peasantry and the landed classes lived in a timeless world exactly as had their fathers and grandfathers before them. In the towns, the guild craftsmen used their organizations to oppose any change in their traditional and uncompetitive way of doing business. Security and stability extended to the social structure which was rigid, had well defined social classes and little mobility.

The intellectual tone of that age was set by the scholastics who started with the assumption that everything which ought to be known by man was already known. If God in his wisdom decided that additional truths should be revealed to man, He would reveal them. The learned man was he who had learned the truths contained in the ancient and accepted sources.

Research, as Roger Bacon discovered, was blasphemy; an attempt to seize by force or cunning the secrets that it had not yet pleased God to reveal. Moreover, God in his wisdom may have deemed it necessary to conceal certain things from man in order not to weaken faith. For the fruits of scholarship were not judged in terms of their truth or falsehood but, as Copernicus discovered, in terms of their effect on faith. It is here that we come to the keystone of the entire age.

That keystone is the doctrine that the material world and man's earthly existence are of little importance in themselves. The life of the body in this world is but a momentary preliminary to the eternal life of the soul in the world to come and the purpose of life in this world is to prepare the soul for that eternal life. Man exists in order that he might earn eternal salvation for his immortal soul. That is the overriding task of this world, and by comparison all other human activities pale into insignificance.

Faith is a prerequisite to salvation and the Church is God's chosen instrument of salvation. Because the saving of souls is the chief end of this life it follows that anything which disturbs faith must be proscribed. Similarly, because the Church is the sole instrument of salvation it follows that all other institutions and authorities must subordinate themselves to it. The result was a centuries long dispute between the secular authorities and the Church in which the latter never renounced its claim to full authority in all matters pertaining to "faith and morals" and the sole right to determine whether or not any particular matter touched "faith and morals."

By and large, these were the assumptions which underlay the conservative-nationalist perception of French-Canadian society. This is not to say that the Church alone bears full responsibility for the philosophical foundations or subsequent development of traditional French Canadian society. Nor is it to say that the leading classes of French Canadian society were prepared to follow blindly wherever the Church might choose to lead. It was a coincidence that in the middle of the nineteenth century when, for reasons which lie beyond the scope of this introduction, the leading classes of French Canada were seeking a philosophical justification for a regressive and conservative social policy and an ally to aid in the implementation of that policy the Church, for reasons which had nothing to do with French Canadian affairs, provided just such a philosophy and was prepared to co-operate in its implementation. Some of the more extravagant claims and some of the more extreme positions of the medieval period were abandoned, but the underlying assumptions remained. And if these were often ignored in daily life they were nonetheless accepted as the ideals of French Canadian society.

In practise, these assumptions resulted in a society characterized by what Michel Brunet has called the three dominant themes of French Canadian thought. Agriculturalism: the imputation of a special legitimacy to a bucolic life on the soil and, conversely, the imputation of illegitimacy to cities and to everything that cities represented — modernism, commercialism, industrialism, capitalism, socialism, cosmopolitanism and all other secular "isms" including secularism itself and, in general, the breakdown of the stability of the traditional way of life. Anti-statism: the fear and distrust of the only other institution which had the resources and potential to challenge the primacy claimed by the Church, to absorb its functions in many fields and to compete with it for the primary allegiance of the masses. Messianism: the belief in an eventual collective redemption to be purchased by remaining faithful to the values and beliefs espoused by the accredited leadership. In the case of French Canada redemption would take the form of the establishment in North America of a French and Catholic civilization whose successes, when contrasted with the inevitable failure and disintegration of the godless and mistaken way of life of the rest of the continent, would serve to bring the rest of North America back to the one true path. This was French Canada's apostolic mission.

French-Canadian nationalism, as defined by the conservative nationalists, was a xenophobic retreat from the realities of the world into a blind acceptance of the messianic vision and all that that entailed. Nationalism was defined to include the outlook, values and goals of the traditional conservative leadership. Opposition to that leadership by a French Canadian was regarded as treason against French Canada. Reformers who sought to align French Canada with the contemporary western world were looked upon as saboteurs. Nationalism became the alibi, the justification and the major prop of the status quo.

In practice, the traditional values gave rise to a society headed by an elite of professional men (doctors, lawyers, notaries) and clergy who paid lip service to the traditional ideals, attempted whenever possible to regulate the affairs of their society in accordance with those ideals and expended a great deal of time and energy convincing themselves that they were succeeding. But they were not succeeding.

The small elite was able to achieve a certain degree of detachment from the modern world. Insulated behind the walls of their professions they were able to ignore, to a greater or lesser extent, the world created by modern industry and commerce. This option was not open to the French-Canadian masses. Overpopulation forced massive migrations to the industrial areas of New England while the plentiful supply of labour in Quebec attracted industry to the Province. The traditional French-Canadian leadership taught the masses one set of values while their daily experience taught them another. The ultimate triumph of the latter was inevitable. By refusing to adapt to changed circumstances, the leaders of French Canada forfeited their right to lead.

The authors of the Tremblay Report recognized that the values they were defending enjoyed little credibility among the working classes of French Canada. But they saw other reasons for this development. Speaking of the decline of the traditional values they said:

> Already signs can be seen of such a turn of mind . . . in many circles, particularly working class, when social security is spoken of it is in terms of federal laws. That may be explained . . . thanks to the method of distributing family allowances to all mothers of children and pensions to all persons regardless of means. (Vol. III, Bk. II, p. 129)

And further, in attempting to distinguish between insurance schemes, of which they approved, and state social assistance, of which they did not, the Tremblay Commission noted:

> In certain circles it is claimed that the lower classes, and particularly the working class, do not want, or no longer want, insurance. . . . If such a state of mind exists – and it assuredly does in certain circles – we must see in it . . . the result of the propoganda which in all parts of the world is endeavouring to secure the triumph of state-controlled and socialistic forms of social security. (Vol. III, Bk. II, p. 139)

But it was neither the subversive effects of a federal government acting to meet social needs nor an international communist conspiracy which was undermining the bases of the traditional French Canadian way of life. It was the advent of a different economic system. Industrialization had created new needs and given currency to new ideas. With the passage of time the supporters of the traditional values, the traditional elite, found themselves ever more embattled. The preservation of the credibility of the traditional values and of the legitimacy of their leadership became correspondingly more difficult.

The Tremblay Report is a document of the 1950s, the last decade during which the traditional values and the traditional leadership retained their legitimacy. By the end of the decade a new middle class, also alienated from the status quo, had joined the relatively docile working class. This middle class leapt into the vacuum created by the absence of a credible leadership and during the early years of the following decade did battle with the traditionalists for possession of the concept of nationalism. Their victory won, they re-defined French Canadian nationalism. Formerly a doctrine of conservatism it became a doctrine of change and, in some cases, of revolution.

ORGANIZATION OF THE ABRIDGED EDITION

The Tremblay Report runs to five substantial volumes. The governing principle in the preparation of the present abridged edition was the preservation, whenever possible, of those parts of the Report which are of enduring value. Since this volume is intended primarily to help students of Canadian history or politics to understand traditional French Canadian society, the term "enduring value" was taken to mean those parts of the Report which discuss, exemplify or exhibit trends of thought or interpretation which were of consistent importance in traditional French Canadian life and thought.

The present edition consists of five parts. It begins with the terms of reference of the Commission, which are reprinted in full, and it ends with the recommendations. The latter have been edited to include only the major recommendations in the field of relations between the two levels of government. The remaining three parts make up the body of the present edition.

The first, entitled "Culture" consists of five chapters of which the first four are taken from the first half of Volume II of The Report. The fifth chapter is taken from Chapter 5 of Volume III. The purpose of this part is to present the basic premises upon which the traditional French Canadian way of life was based.

The second part, entitled "Federalism," consists of two chapters taken from the second part of Volume II of The Report. The first of these chapters, entitled "The General Theory of Federalism" is a very condensed discussion of the classical theory of federalism along Dicey-Wheare lines. It is assumed that the student is already familiar with this material and therefore a short discussion, for the purpose of providing continuity, is all that is intended. The second chapter, entitled "Federalism as a System of Social Organization" is an attempt to demonstrate the manner in which political federalism makes possible the existence of a variety of forms of social organization and, in particular, how it corresponds with traditional French Canadian ideas of social organization.

Part three, entitled "Some Aspects of Culture and Federalism in Canada 1867-1955", consists of eleven chapters. They contain an interpretation, based upon the compact theory and the theories of culture and federalism which precede it, of certain aspects of Canadian history. The first eight chapters are condensed from the first part of Volume I of The Report. The remaining chapters are taken from the second part of Volume II.

The Tremblay Report was prepared in French and the English version is a translation from the French. It is apparent upon reading the English version that the translation was not prepared by a person who possessed a knowledge of idiomatic English. Scattered throughout the translation are split infinitives, literal translations of idiomatic French expressions, misplaced verbs and other faults. A number of these have been corrected. All such changes in the official English text were made only after comparison with the original French version and for the sole purpose of rendering the translation more faithful to the meaning of the original.

TERMS OF REFERENCE

Act to Institute a Royal Commission of Inquiry on Constitutional Problems

Assented to, the 12th of February, 1953

Whereas the Canadian confederation, born of an agreement between the four pioneer provinces, is first and above all a pact of honour between the two great races which founded it and each of which makes a most valuable and indispensable contribution to the progress and greatness of the nation;

Whereas the constitution of 1867 grants to the provinces, and to the Province of Quebec in particular, rights, prerogatives and liberties scrupulous respect for which is intimately bound up with national unity and the survival of confederation, and it imposes on them responsibilities and obligations which imply correlatively the necessary corresponding means of action;

Whereas the Province of Quebec intends to exercise and discharge these rights and obligations, to which end it must safeguard the fiscal resources which belong to it and preserve its financial independence as well as its legislative and administrative autonomy.

Whereas, since 1917, the central power has invaded important fields of taxation reserved to the provinces, thereby seriously limiting the ability of the provinces to exercise their fiscal rights in those fields;

Whereas these encroachments deprive the provinces, Quebec in particular, of sources of revenues which belong and are necessary to them, restrict them in the exercise of the legislative and administrative rights and powers recognized as theirs by the constitution, pervert the application of the confederation pact and endanger its existence by the impoverishment of the provinces and a centralization of powers incompatible with the federal and democratic system;

Whereas such centralization can only lead to bureaucracy and the gradual disappearance of responsible government;

Whereas, in a country as vast and diverse as Canada, only a decentralized administration can meet the needs of every region and ensure the harmonious development of the whole;

Whereas respect for the rights of all the component parts of the federation is essential to its survival and to the future of the Canadian nation;

Whereas municipal and educational institutions, which emanated from the provinces and are democratic forms of administrative decentralization, are entitled to their fair share of the national revenue which they can only obtain under a decentralized fiscal regime;

Whereas it is expedient to refer to a royal commission the study of the vitally important problems resulting from this situation and the steps to be taken to solve them;

Therefore, Her Majesty, with the advice and consent of the Legislative Council and of the Legislative Assembly of Quebec, enacts as follows:

1. The Lieutenant-Governor in Council may constitute a royal commission to inquire into constitutional problems, report its findings to him and submit to him its recommendations as to steps to be taken to safeguard the rights of the Province and those of municipalities and school corporations.

2. Without restricting the scope of the preceding section, such commission shall study in particular

a) the problem of the distribution of taxes between the central power, the provinces, municipalities and school corporations;

b) encroachments by the central power in the field of direct taxation, especially, but without restricting the scope of this provision, in matters of income and corporation taxes and succession duties;

c) the repercussions and results of such encroachments in the legislative and administrative regime of the Province and in the collective, domestic and individual life of its people;

d) constitutional problems of a legislative and financial nature in general.

3. The members of such commission shall be appointed by the Lieutenant-Governor in Council who shall designate one of them as chairman and may provide them with any officers,

jurists and other specialists whose services he considers necessary and fix the remuneration of each.

As soon as it is formed, the commission shall proceed with such inquiry, complete it with all possible diligence, report to the Lieutenant-Governor in Council on or before the 1st of March 1954 and at the same time deliver to him all the documentary matter accumulated in the course of its inquiry.

4. For such purpose the commission may sit, in public, at any place in the Province which it deems suitable, hear experts, representatives of public or private bodies and other witnesses, receive reports and procure by such means as it deems suitable any documentary and other information which it considers useful.

5. The expenses incurred by the application of this act, including the remuneration of the members of the commission, officers, jurists and other specialists, shall be paid out of the consolidated revenue fund.

6. This act shall come into force on the day of its sanction.

PART ONE:
CULTURE

1. CULTURE, NATION, SOCIETY: RELIGION AND SOCIETY

If, in fact, the province of Quebec as a territorial and economic unit is a province like the others, it is neither assimilable to any other, by reason of its origins, religion, culture or the history of the great majority of its population, nor, consequently, by most of its juridical and social institutions. To understand its present attitudes on the political and constitutional plane, it is necessary to go back beyond Confederation, and consider it in its human, historic and sociological reality and the general philosophy of life which has at all times animated its daily existence. We are here touching upon the problem of culture and cultures in the Canadian socio-political context: the fundamental problem of Canadian federalism. The problem of federal provincial relations, from whatever aspect it is considered, is intimately connected therewith.

The term "bi-cultural" as applied to Canada designates a reality far more complex than most of those who use it seem to think. The particularism of the groups under consideration is double and re-states the whole Canadian problem from each of its aspects: (a) religious: The French-Canadians are almost all of the Catholic faith, while Anglo-Canadians are, in the great majority, Protestants; (b) cultural: The French-Canadians are of French origin and culture, the Anglo-Canadians of Anglo-Saxon origin and culture. The French-Canadians are the only group whose religious and cultural particularism almost exactly coincide. Only French Canada, as a homogeneous group, presents the double differentiating factor of religion and culture.

RELIGION AND CULTURAL RELATIONS

Religion and culture cannot be confused, for they belong to orders of differing values. The first has for its object the supernatural vocation of man, his eternal salvation; the second, his natural vocation or success in his temporal life. The first is a life, the second a development of life's forces. But neither can these two be completely separated, for both have as their object the same being for whom they must together ensure an ordered existence. To speak of culture is to speak of a sense of human vocation and, therefore, of a sense of Man's relations to God.

Even the atheist cannot help giving metaphysical roots to his culture, by attaching it to a system of ordered values and by tending towards a certain explanation of the universe. Religion and culture thus meet in humanism, with culture receiving from religion, more or less directly and completely, its general inspiration and directive thought; while religion borrows from culture such and such means of integration within the diverse manifestations of daily life, such as morals, customs, traditions, etc. That is why a given cultural milieu always carries the mark of the religious conception by which it is inspired, even when it is more or less remote from the religion itself, or when it only admits the influence of religion in certain diverse sectors of thought and action.

POLITICAL CONSEQUENCES OF THE RELATIONS BETWEEN RELIGION AND CULTURE

Religion and culture comprise, each for its own part, the whole Canadian problem. This problem resides in the duality of cultures and of religions; in their spontaneous opposition, in their natural tendency, by sole reason of their existence, to infuse social and political life as widely as possible. If, as a hypothesis, one or other of the cultures were some day to disappear, the problem would re-present itself from the religious angle. If, conversely and still hypothetically, one of the two religions were to disappear, the problem would subsist in terms of culture.

The fact that culture is in more or less close relation to religion, and that, in meeting on the plane of humanism, they simultaneously inform all life's manifestations, gives each group present in Canada an almost monolithic homogeneity. This is particularly true of the French-Catholic group to whom, for each of its living units, this union is a personal reality. Hence its total reaction, sometimes at the risk of confusing the orders, as soon as one or other of its governing values is called into question. Hence, on the political plane, its aspirations for autonomy, that is to say, for the direction of its own life. Nothing of its psychology, or of its special sensitivity, can be understood if one loses sight of this meeting of the cultural and religious at all levels of its existence.

The religious identity of the groups in Canada does not lend itself to any ambiguity. This is not so with regard to culture. The fact that political or social leaders, university men, jurists, historians and sociologists interchange the terms "bi-cultural country" and "bi-cultural nation" and speak of "Canadian culture," of "'French-speaking' or 'English-speaking' Canadian culture," etc., denotes a general uncertainty of ideas respecting one of the major premises of socio-political thought in Canada. A thorough study of the difficult problem of culture would, therefore, meet a great need. There can be no question of undertaking it here and we shall limit ourselves to a recapitulation of the data most necessary for the general understanding of the subject.

Culture

ITS OBJECT

In its highest aims, which are consequently beyond any utilitarian pre-occupations, culture has Man himself for its object; the systematic, balanced, hierarchic "valorization" of his complex potentialities with a view to his completest fulfilment and the fullest fruition of his existence. Since Man is Man through his spiritual participation, to speak of culture is to speak of improving the spiritual faculties.

ITS CONTENT

Considered in its content, culture may be defined as an organic collection of knowledge, of means of expression and of values. We say "organic" because, if the constituting elements each have their special purpose, they are none the less mutually dependent. Since Man, as an object of culture, is both order and synthesis, culture should also be order and synthesis.

Knowledge

In its principle as in its process of development, culture is primarily knowledge, the acquisition and mastery of learning, and the shaping, for that purpose, of the intelligence and of other faculties of the mind. By knowledge must be understood the infinite diversity of human learning, from elementary rules of practical life and the instrumental notions propounded to the child as an initiation into the life of the mind and as a means of augmenting it, up to the sciences, philosophy and theology, themselves considered as intellectual disciplines and as autonomous branches of learning.

Through knowledge, culture tends to be universal. Whether it be philosophic, scientific or artistic, the data of learning know no frontier. They are in the service of the good, the true and the beautiful and in the service of Man seeking an answer to his highest aspirations. Through them, Man nourishes his thinking, widens his horizons and augments his means of action. But because of the variable tendencies and limitations (as between one individual and another) of his mind, Man must make a choice from the knowledge offered for his mastery. He specializes. But specialized knowledge deserves the name of culture only if the specialist, aware of his limitations, knows how to discern the ties which link his special discipline to connected or neighbouring disciplines and if he can posit it in the ensemble of human knowledge.

Means of Expression

No culture can make progress, or even exist, if it does not express itself. Its means of expression are language and the various techniques whose mastery allows Man to perform personal work. Language (the mother tongue) is not culture, but it is in such intimate relation with culture that one and the other are intermixed. And this obtains to a certain degree in techniques, whether industrial, professional, scientific or artistic. They are not culture, but they are its instruments. Relations between culture and means of expression are all the more intimate by reason of the fact that the latter are also means of acquisition. One cannot arrive at culture without language which grasps the idea, organizes it, precisely determines its shades of meaning and allows comparisons and judgments. Man first of all cultivates himself by his management of the instruments of culture.

Values

Values are the criteria of appreciation, the norms according to which Man judges, not knowledge itself, but the use to be made of knowledge. In terms of values, branches of knowledge are chosen and classified according to their respective purposes and ordered for life. The sense of values is the integrating principle, the very soul of culture.

These values correspond to the most fundamental aspirations of human nature: beauty, truth and good. They are themselves, like the other elements of culture, the object of knowledge. But they exceed learning as a work of art exceeds a picture, as virtue exceeds moral science, as wisdom exceeds the rules of logic. Values are either knowledge which directs life from above, or knowledge susceptible of being transformed into life.

Every culture carries with it, implicitly and adjacently, a concept of Man and of the realities capable of fulfilling him. Every culture is tied up with an explanation of the world, with a metaphysic, that is to say, with an attempt at integral interpretation of total reality – of nature, Man, and of society considered in their reciprocal relations and also in time (history). Man cultivates himself according to his own idea of himself, of his place in the world and of his purpose.

There can be no truly human complete culture if its formation does not refine the sense of values at the same time as it is widening the field of knowledge. By awakening, developing and refining the sense of values and of their hierarchic order, culture lays hold on Man simultaneously in his mind, soul and heart, and even in that irrational part which lies deepest in humanity, whose most synthetic expression is love, and which, subject to the authority of thought, is none the less at the root of all creative effort. Thought illuminates action and multiplies its modes and efficiencies; but in its initial glow, all action is an offertory, a gesture of communion.

There is no culture if there are no fruits. Learning by itself is a fruit but an imperfect one; it is only a rudimentary culture. It only becomes culture if it is put in order, organized by thought. Aptitude to think by oneself, to progress through one's own efforts in the order of thought, is both intellectual culture and the fruit of intellectual culture. Intellectual culture itself completely fulfils its purpose only if it flowers into wisdom and translates itself into vital values. The natural virtues, the conscientious search for the rules of life most fit to ensure the fulfilment of personality are the fruits of human culture.

The drama of modern culture is that it has forgotten the distinctions outlined above. Sprung from the old Christian-humanist culture, which procured the most glorious conquests of the human mind, it has borrowed nothing of its system of values. It has even sought to destroy it. It has developed, in the extreme, natural sciences and their technical applications. And it has accomplished prodigies in this field. But it has ignored Man himself or has thought to have discovered the laws of his fulfilment at the bottom of a test-tube or at the end of an algebraic equation. It has thus resulted in a pragmatic materialism, larval and long-winded, while at the same time creating the propitious spiritual and social climate for the advent of all kinds of totalitarianism – of communism itself. By neglecting to deepen and fortify the sense of values with the same care for reality with which it explored and enlarged the field of knowledge, modern culture has cast off its governor and divested itself of its soul. To realize its objective, to fructify in veritable human values, it must henceforth think itself out again in terms of Man. That is the present-day problem.

CULTURE: AN EXCHANGE PRODUCT

Man cultivates himself by applying his diverse powers to the formation of his intelligence and to his own perfectioning. Culture is the fruit of a personal, conscious, voluntary, methodical and persevering effort. Thus, there is no culture possible save in a climate of freedom. But Man does not cultivate himself alone. He lives in society and needs the help of his fellow-beings for his full flowering. Personal in its object, culture is social in its vital processes, in its modes of operation and transmission. It is simultaneously the product and the fruit of an exchange. But it is precisely on this subject that there is that danger of confusion. Hence the usefulness of new distinctions.

NATIONAL CULTURE AND "GENERAL" CULTURE

As an exchange factor, culture may be envisaged from the point of view of either of the two participants (community and individual).

From the community's point of view, we may distinguish:

1. The culture proper to a given human group, that is to say, the totality of spiritual and rational values which are, at one and the same time, the bond of communication and its differentiating principle. Such values, handed down from one generation to the other throughout history, derive from interpretation according to a particular genius (French, English or German, etc.) and from a general philosophy of life (Christian, materialist or pagan). This is the culture which is lived; national culture.

2. The "general" culture, that is to say, the totality of knowledge and values which, free from all national affinity, are laid before Man, in his quality as a man (sciences, arts, philosophies), and which the national cultures themselves develop by reason of their propensity for universality or by which they enrich themselves through assimilative methods.

From the individual's point of view, these distinctions correspond to:

1. The culture which Man owes entirely to his environment or which he acquires in relations with it – unconsciously, dur-

ing the first phase of his formation; and then, consciously, when, wakening to his quality and responsibilities as a man, he assumes the fulfilment of his own personality with the help of institutions created for that purpose by the environment, such as schools of all levels, and para- and post-school teaching. This is "academic" culture, a direct product of education. It proceeds from the national culture, whose spirit it borrows and of which it is both the expression and the excedent.

2. The culture which Man gives himself through his own initiative and by means such as books, newspapers, radio, television, theatres, museums, etc. These cultural means emanate from the environment itself and continue its influence, or else they come from outside. They are the vehicles and exchange instruments of culture and of cultures.

The ways of culture, therefore, are complex. Education, national culture, general culture, academic culture, intellectual culture, human culture, these are all so many ideas corresponding, for the individual, to so many aspects of a work that he accomplishes both freely and by dependence — his self-fulfilment.

CULTURE OF THE ELITE, POPULAR CULTURE

The idea of culture spontaneously evokes that of degree within the individual himself as between one step and another of his evolution, and as between one individual and another. Hence the idea of an elite. Normally, the progress of culture in a given environment should result in the creation of a certain more or less diversified and "hierarchised" elite of which one generally thinks when speaking of culture. But there also exists a common culture which is that of the mass.

This culture is made up of knowledge, means of expression and values blended in a tradition of life. The more universal it is in its fundamental postulates, the more chance there is that there should be born of it a vigorous elite, itself comprehensive in its thought and in its world view, and, through the latter, a civilization highly representative of humanity's greatest ideals. The level of the common culture tends all the more to elevate itself to the extent that an active elite, through its works, specific action and general influence, incites it to surpass itself. In return, there is all the more chance of the elite increasing in quality and number as the level of the common culture itself becomes more elevated. Between the common culture and the culture of the elite, there is, consequently, such inter-dependence and constant inter-action that the problem of culture remains a single one. Whence, three remarks.

1) The common culture and the national culture are identical. It is that which Man owes to his environment, that which he acquires unconsciously during his very first years in his family and in his small social circle; then, later, and more or less consciously, in the educational institutions which are in communion with the cultural environment and serve it as a centre of "explicitation" and renewal.

2) The mass thus brought up in a certain culture is a living complex, wherein the cultural influences which develop within it by the action of the élite or come from outside, are assimilated to the culture of origin and are translated into ways of life, of thought and of action which tend to maintain the culture and to renew it from one generation to another.

3) If the development and diffusion of culture with a view to raising the common culture and the constitution of an elite is one of society's very first functions, the conservation and renewal of this same culture, according to its inspirational thought, is primarily the nation's doing.

Transmission of Culture

STATE AND NATION

Collective life is made up of a network of infinitely varied relations governed by morals, law and good breeding and all imply the dispositions of mind and character of the policed and educated man. Contemporary sociology distinguishes two forms of it, societal and communal.

Society and community are social groups having Man as their object and responding to a natural need. But "society is rather a work of reason and is more closely connected with Man's intellectual and spiritual aptitudes; the community is rather a work of nature, more closely allied to the biological order."[1]

The state, society's supreme organ, is a political entity. It is born of the need for regulating, according to defined norms, relations of the individuals and of the groups whereof society is formed. It proceeds from the idea of law. Its object is the common good, that is to say, the organized aggregate of the

[1] Jacques Maritain, *Man and the State*, p. 2

needs necessary to Man in the accomplishment of his vocation – from the political angle, that is to say, from the angle where the conservation and promotion of these needs are within his own competence. The state deals with Man as Man, and therefore independently of his particular affinities; it "governs" him, that is it surrounds him, sustains him, assists him, if necessary, and so orders everything that he may, either on his own initiative or through the intermediacy of the communities which arise from the daily practice of life, be able to assure himself of the needs necessary to the realization of his ends.

The nation is a sociological entity, a community of culture, which forms and renews itself down through the years by the common practice of a same general concept of life. It may not be conscious of itself if the individuals who compose it do not take note of the fact that they form a community. But beginning with the day when it becomes aware of its own identity and when there is awakened in it the collective will-to-live, a will common to the individuals composing it to preserve it, it exists as a living sociological unit and sets itself up as such in the face of the state. Its object is not to "govern" Man but to supply him with a culture, a style of life, a manner for self-realization and for attaining the plenitude of his being.

NATION AND CULTURE

Even before Man has become aware of himself, of his presence in the world, of his destinies and of his responsibilities, there intervenes the influence of the environment, both of family and of society, which presides over the first awakening of his personality, the putting into motion of his development; which supplies him with his first instruments of culture, the foundation on which he will later build his personal formation and the spirit in which he will pursue it. This culture, special to a given environment, is by definition the nation's informing principle. It is the national culture: the totality of the rational and spiritual values forming the collective patrimony of a determined human group; modes of life, morals, customs, traditions, language, laws, etc. The national density of a given group is relatively higher as the values it possesses in common are more numerous, varied and comprehensive.

These values proceed from a certain general philosophy of life. In fact, every national culture is a more or less conscious particular interpretation of a philosophy either universal or tending towards universality. What there is of *national,* and consequently of difference in it, is not the thought but its form; on one side the expression and, primarily, the language; on the other side, the diverse modes of integration in daily life, such as usages, customs, traditions, etc. This "particularization" of culture is the fact of the national genius acting within time, and therefore undergoing, from generation to generation, influences of the environment and of the moment.

THE NATIONAL GENIUS

The national genius, like personal genius, is the product of native qualities of temperament and of the group spirit which make up the nation, worked over from one generation to the next, refined and carried to their highest value by culture. It is a complex reality, subtle and one might almost say incommunicable otherwise than by a slow maturing to whoever is not of the nation.

Peoples do not choose the data of culture; they accept those which environment and modern life offer them. But, acting upon them according to their native qualities of temperament and of mind they assimilate such data, each interpreting and expressing it in his own way, and they make out of it a special culture which, in turn, acting on minds, helps to fortify and fecundate diverse abilities and the group's assimilative power.

National values, the common heritage of the nation which owes to them its character, exist primarily in Man. Man makes the nation in the sense that he is the point of reference, the retail incarnation of the values of which the nation is the wholesale depository. In return, the nation creates the national type. It constitutes, as a collectivity, an environment in which, from one generation to another, Man receives in his inmost personality the deposit of cultural riches which identify him and place him in a position to participate, through the sole fact that he lives, thinks and acts, in the unending reconstitution of the nation. In other words, there is no nation unless there is a national type and there is no national type unless a nation – and hence a cultural environment – exists to give it form.

National culture is a culture in the word's exact meaning; it has the same object, Man; the same components, namely, learning, means of expression and values. The level and tendencies of this culture depend on the genius of the nation – and thus of its own reaction to cultural influences – and on its degree of evolution at a certain moment of history, then on the presence of a more or less numerous, more or less diversified, and more or less active élite. When he awakens to the requirements of his own life, the individual has already received from his environment a deposit of cultural riches which will serve as a support, a framework and a guide in his personal formation.

NATIONAL CULTURE AND HUMAN CULTURE

This intellectual and moral acquisition is a state of mind and soul rather than reasoning or organized learning. But precisely because it is identified with the individual to the extent that it constitutes a second nature, and that it precedes or prepares voluntary decisions and that it spontaneously decides attitudes, sometimes with the blind force of instinct, its value as a means of access to personal culture is irreplaceable. The data of culture are all the better received and all the more easily assimilated to the degree that they go along with the trainee's innate disposition of mind, heart and soul and to the extent that they mate more intimately with the diverse possibilities lodged in him by the cultural tradition of successive generations.

For example, the mother-tongue, the most national datum of all particular cultures, is of a piece with the mind which, through the ages, has wrought it out. It bears within its own texture the qualities of the genius whose expression it is and of the culture by which this genius is itself nourished. Because it is so, the mother-tongue is the most effective instrument for regenerating the same genius and the same culture from one generation to another.

So it is with tradition or with traditions: whether they be popular traditions or great social or intellectual traditions, transposed into living habits by a certain concept of order and of human progress. They are the products of temperament and of a given people's turn of mind. Everything which corresponds to them is accepted more or less as "going without saying" – everything which contradicts them is confusing and requires a special effort at adaptation.

The mother-tongue and national traditions cannot be transmitted from one generation to another with their full, intrinsic cultural value and with their full efficacy for regenerating both genius and culture unless, in the environment where they are practised, both are in current use.

As a particular interpretation of a general philosophy of life, the national culture is, therefore, a form of humanism – not organized or formulated into a doctrine but lived spontaneously from day to day and therefore extremely effective. The more universal it is in its profound implications, and the closer it is, by reason of its internal exigencies, to the ideal manner of living human life, the more it permeates individual personalities and favours their expansion.

NATIONAL CULTURE AND CIVILIZATION

In their relations with Man, culture and civilization may be considered synonymous. The civilized man is, first, a cultured man, that is to say, a man who, having become aware of his human quality and of the laws of his fulfilment, has put creative forces to work to achieve self-realization and to give himself a suitable environment. This liberation of Man – physical liberation (state of techniques and tools) and spiritual (state of morals and thought) liberation – this awareness of the universal identity, the universal solidarity and the universal brotherhood of men is the fruit of culture.

Considered in their social manifestations, culture and civilization are like two aspects of a single reality – one being to the other as work is to thought – an incarnation. Culture expresses itself in various works; it inspires a social order, that is to say, an order aggregation of economic, social and political institutions; it animates the rites, usages and customs which, handed down from one generation to another, establish themselves as traditions: in short, it incarnates itself in a civilization which, in turn, becomes a centre of cultural fertilization and enrichment. Civilization reproduces the features of the culture from which it proceeds. The same differentiating forces which make from *the* human culture *these* or *those* particular cultures also make from *the* civilization *these* or *those* particular civilizations. And so long as these forces continue to operate, the progress of mind in the world will continue to be brought about through particular modes of culture and civilization, with one fertilizing and influencing the other. Moreover, neither the existence nor the character of these particularisms nor yet their more or less accentuated character are to be deplored. On the contrary, through their very diversity and their incessant interaction, they are a source of cultural wealth, like the diversity and interaction of individual minds and cultures.

All national culture starts from Man and from the particular to emerge into the human and the general, leading from one to the other as to a conclusion. If, through a false concept of itself or for motives foreign to its purposes, it denies itself this opening to the human, this development into the general, it consigns itself to decay and deprives itself of its highest justification, even if, as a hypothesis, the nation which produces it were, moreover to be (as a society) the epoch's leading economic and political power.

CULTURE AND EDUCATION

Considered in Man, who is its object, culture is a more or less advanced, more or less progressive stage of development, and therefore a result. Education, whose object is to improve Man, may thus be defined as a process of cultural access.

Regarding the means used to encourage the culture either of the individual or of the population, it is well to distinguish between (1) formal education; and (2) the more or less rich and diversified cultural influence of the milieu. For Man proceeds along the ways of culture through the help of this complex aggregate of means. In any given cultural milieu, these works and institutions are, to some extent, part and parcel of the common culture, of which they are at once the product, the centres of explication and the organisms of renewal and enrichment.

The diverse influences brought into play with a view to culture should conform to that culture's purposes. These include the setting free and valorization of the individual's talents, in their hierarchic order. The better to succeed therein, the subjects under formation should be matched with their individual traditions of life and of milieu and should thus be incited to make an effort towards transcendence and complete humanization. Nothing in this concept of education and of culture implies a retreat upon oneself nor a refusal of what is not *sui generis*. On the contrary, everything implies an opening on all the horizons of the mind, a sympathetic welcoming according to its own innate ideas, of everything which has a humanizing value.

From the standpoint of the individual, culture in the full sense here used, is a work which each performs both in subordination and in freedom according to his own evolution. At first entirely dependent on his family and social environment, everyone raises himself from it, as his education progresses and as he becomes more aware of his individuality and his freedom. Little by little, there is substituted for the original dependency a process of exchange. Education and culture (both terms being used in their full sense) are thus separate ideas but they are so intimately connected that they are like two aspects of the same thing.

If it is a question of the individual, the relations between education and culture present no problem. But if it is question of a cultural community, of a particular culture to be preserved and developed, it is a different matter. Here, the relations between education and culture present a practical problem. Education and culture should proceed from the same norms and tend towards the same objectives. In the event that there is a divergency, individuals and communities enter a conflict whose prejudicial effects on education and on culture depend upon the seriousness of the clash. This is the case in our day and in our milieu; children and adolescents are brought up in families and institutions according to Christian principles; then they enter a professional or social milieu, a system of institutions foreign to the Christian idea, with resulting conflict and hybridization of minds.

THE ETHNIC MILIEU

As a cultural reality and as a means of access to culture, the nation, like all living organisms, possesses its renewal organism – the ethnic environment. The nation, being a collectivity, constitutes by that very fact a complex of social relationships, a centre of exchanges, where the data of the common culture, such as customs, morals, traditions and language are, of necessity, at least of high social convenience. To this centre, by the very fact that he has grown up within it and undergoes its influence from day to day, the child is attuned, from one generation to another. From this community of culture and from the advantages which flow from it in the daily routine of life proceeds the will to preserve them; this is the collective will-to-live, the primary condition of national survival.

To be efficacious, the ethnic environment should be homogeonous; this homogeneity consisting of cultural and lingual unity, organization in the spirit of the national culture of the main functions, whether economic, social or political, of collective life. If the data of an outside culture become of current utility or if one of the functions of collective life proceeds from an inspiration foreign to the culture or is dominated by foreign elements, the relations of cultural exchange between Man and his social environment are mixed up; the homogeneity of the ethnic environment is weakened and the nation's renewal organism and then, sooner or later, its survival are threatened. Hence the spontaneous propensity of national groups, which are conscious of themselves and of their living conditions, for an autonomy which puts them in a position to organize the most general framework of their common life according to their ideas. A nation is only sure of its destiny if it has thus succeeded in infusing its spirit into the main functions of collective life, and has succeeded in establishing harmony between its human members and their social environment. That is why, without being by its nature either an economic or a political fact, a nation is led by the very requirements of its maintenance and progress to undertake both economic and political action, and thus to set itself up in presence of the state and to require of it certain attitudes.

The Nation and the State

The state and the nation, though entities of differing nature, have Man himself for their common object. Hence the problem of their reciprocal relations.

The state is the guardian of the common good from the political angle. It does not substitute itself for either individuals or natural communities but helps them to realize their respective ends. The nation, as a community of culture, is an object of the common good and thus subject to the state's authority. But, like all other natural groups, it has its special purpose, its particular common good – and the co-relative right to the state's assistance. Since Man, *per se,* stripped of all cultural or national particularism is nowhere to be found, the state should favour the conservation and fruition of the cultural values, whose benefit the nation brings to Man.

RELATIONS BETWEEN NATION AND STATE

In practice, nation-state relations may be settled according to infinitely varied modalities. It may happen that the state and the nation coincide, where the nation and the political society form one and the same human entity. This is the nation-state, within whose ranks the ends of the nation are exactly in accord with those of society. In such event, there is no problem, with the state espousing the nation's ends in the name of the common good. But it also happens that state and nation are not concordant terms – the political society being itself formed of heterogeneous national elements. In such cases, tensions of all kinds may develop if the state on the one hand and the national groups on the other do not, in pursuit of their respective ends, inspire themselves with a just concept of their rights and duties.

THE HETEROGENEOUS STATE

Man inserts himself into society with his entire personality. As a citizen bound to a political entity whose help is indispensable to him, he should, in fairness, devote himself to its stability and progress. To the extent that the cultural values integrated in his personality are useful or necessary to the full realization of himself and his life, society should facilitate their conservation and fruition. He may then claim from the state certain liberties such as civic liberties to be exercised within the limits of the common good; right to life and security, individual liberties, civil equality, etc., as well as such cultural liberties as religion, national spirit, mother-tongue, etc. These two categories of liberties concern the nation, the second directly through the definition in political rights of the citizen's cultural preroga-tives, the first indirectly through the faculty accorded Man to organize his life and that of the community in conformity with his own concept of order. This faculty is as important for the nation's progress and survival, and consequently for the con-servation and fruition of its cultural values, as are the cultural liberties themselves.

The nation, as a nation, does not confer juridical existence upon the institutions of common life. This prerogative belongs to the state acting in the name of the political body. In return, the state does not confer upon institutions their cultural char-acter, but it is the nation which, by its presence at the very heart of the institutional system, communicates a certain spirit to it. It is, therefore, not enough for the state to guarantee cultural liberties. It has a positive duty towards national groups to co-operate in the conservation and fruition of their cultural values, and, consequently, it has a duty to have its policies, con-form to the profound requirements of this culture; its economic policy, its social policy with modalities variable according to circumstances but with constant intent.

Such collaboration is at the same time both particularly necessary and particularly difficult in our era of intense social integration and of more and more extensive and varied inter-vention by the state in the operations of common life. The temptation is strong for the state, while externally respecting the cultural liberties of its subjects, to practise, in the name of simplicity and administrative efficiency, policies which meet certain requirements of modern life but which ignore the permanent exigencies of the culture and even contradict them. Such a policy falsifies operation of the ethnic environment. It faces Man with the alternative of either abandoning his own culture or else accepting the inferior condition of a foreigner in his own country. Since it is a matter of a collective phenomenon, involving high considerations which Man, without having any clear conception of them, often holds as dear as life itself, the personal alternative cited above cannot, in fact, be suggested to each individual as a personal option and as a possible object of a deliberate choice. Were it so, moreover, the problem would, so to speak, still exist. For, no matter how hard he may try, Man cannot easily rid himself of his origins or remove the imprints of his earliest culture. Thus it is the second alternative which operates. Man pays for his spontaneous fidelity – not always conscious but rooted in him like an instinct – to his original culture with a diminution of his social condition, and of his normal chances of progress and expansion. Hence arises unease, and tensions that may end in disorder.

It is because of its deep and multiple implications that national life raises in heterogeneous states such delicate and diverse political problems. Hence the decentralizing attitude of national groups integrated into such states, their tendency to constitute themselves into distinct political societies enjoying legislative autonomy as it affects the data of collective life most immediately concerned with culture.

POLITICAL NATIONALISM

States whose members are of different national cultures should define their policies according to the requirements of the common good, with a very clear awareness of the reciprocal relations between the political society and the nation. It does not appertain to them to fashion at their whim the national culture or cultures which history has made to arise and spread within their ranks; no more does it appertain to them to raise up a new national culture, for that purpose forcing existing cultures to abandon all or some of their particularism. Nor should they adopt the spirit and cultural aspirations of one of the groups, to the detriment of the other group or groups. On the contrary, they have a duty to favour equally the progress of particular cultures and to see that, in the competition of these cultures among themselves, the common good should be safeguarded so that, finally, the aggregate of the population may benefit from the efforts undertaken by the national groups to realize most completely their respective cultural values.

BI-CULTURAL NATION?

Finally, a last point in an already long series: Can a bi-cultural or multi-cultural political society ultimately become a "nation" in the real sense of the word, and thereby possess a common culture which each of the other groups may consider a flowering of its own particularism? Yes, but only in a certain way and on certain condtions. Its renewal organism necessarily exposes every national group to external influences, of which, moreover, it has need for the enrichment of its own culture. The influences which form within a shared political framework and from daily contact are, naturally, those which act with the greatest immediacy and power. Exercise of the same rights and the sharing of the same political responsibilities; the participation, beginning with a given era, in the same history and the correlative accumulation of common experiences and memories; habitual exchanges of view on subjects which, though sometimes exceeding particularisms, nevertheless imply them – all that cannot fail in the long run to arouse between the groups mutual comprehension and friendship, an innate disposition to help each other, to determine the formation of a common heritage of values and a collective soul.

Such a phenomenon does not imply fusion of the cultural groups involved, for fusion necessarily brings about the destruction of certain values and is, consequently, an impoverishment. The type of nation we have here sought to define, can only be the product of an enrichment, and consequently of the completest expansion of the particularisms from which it proceeds. Such a community, a superior form of the nation, issuing at once from politics and from diverse traditions going back into history, far from destroying the original particularisms, rather incites them to transcendence and to the full realization of themselves. It is the fruit of mutual comprehension and confidence and is only possible in a climate of justice and of liberty and then only by the express, intelligent and ceaselessly vigilant action of the state.

In the light of these theoretical indications, let us examine the Canadian case.

2. THE CANADIAN CULTURES

To grasp fully the political import of Canadian bi-culturalism would require a profound study of the cultural types which co-exist within Canadian society. But a study of that kind, even if only lightly pursued, would soon take us beyond our assigned limits. No matter how definite a cultural type may seem, particularly if, as in the present case, it has to do with communities, it always has many more shades of difference than can be discerned at first sight. A lived and living culture should, in fact, ceaselessly re-invent itself in new expressions so that, observed in its successive modalities, it gives an impression of incessant mutation.

Nevertheless, new forms and expressions do not imply a differing inspiration. If the underlying thought itself changed, there would be substitution of one culture for another. This is the case of scientific-technical culture which, originating in the midst of the old Christian humanist culture and out of the fecundity of its genius, has retained nothing of its fundamental postulates. The problem which dominates our era lies precisely in the choice which individuals and peoples must make between the old and the new culture – or, rather, in the integration which they must effect between one and the other in a new humanism. If they are to be understood, it is in their deep inspiration that one must try to comprehend the two cultures which live side by side in the Canadian society.

THE FRENCH-CANADIAN CULTURE

The territory which was to become the province of Quebec had, at the time of the British conquest, a population of approximately 65,000 souls and constituted, despite its small numbers, a homogeneous national community clearly characterized by its culture. Its way of life, its various traditions, laws, and institutions all proceeded from a same general idea of life which owed its highest inspiration to religious faith, from which came this philosophy, this sort of common wisdom, lived daily and in terms of which the data of everyday life were spontaneously interpreted and integrated in ways of being and of doing.

France at the time of the Canadian immigration (approximately 1632-1740) was:

1) A Catholic nation which had just gone through the wars

of religion. There, religious questions, both then and for a long time to come, were to be a cause of social and political tension. Moreover, during the first twenty-five years of Canadian immigration the country was caught up in a strong spiritual current which profoundly influenced the progress of the Canadian colony, and for a long time afterwards fashioned the spiritual climate.

2) An absolute monarchy which believed itself as being by divine right. Collective life therein was ruled by authority, without the citizen's participation.

3) An agrarian domain of the feudal type. As a political structure, feudalism continued to subsist but only as a juridical form, a survival of an outlived era. Yet property was still everywhere held in seigneuries, both in law and in fact, and would so continue until 1789.

With the mercantile age and with the growth of the bourgeoisie, the French economy evolved towards capitalist forms. Immigration to Canada was continuing at the time when the mother country's economy was undergoing this transformation. Drawn from the popular classes, with their old peasant and craft traditions, this immigration had, at least partially, known other forms of organization and economic life.

4) The intellectual centre of the world. From a cultural point of view, France was then at a peak. In full possession of its own culture, it passed on its message to the world, and it was a humanist message *of Christian inspiration*.

But before it expressed itself in works of universal compass, the culture had inscribed itself in the soil; it had permeated the deep strata of society, animating the life of individuals and of social bodies; it had given birth to usages, customs, traditions, modes of feeling and of doing: in short, it had fashioned the nation's soul. And, because it had, like an animating principle, thus permeated the very substance of the national community, it was able to develop an élite, through whom it could express itself in works stamped with the mark of personal genius, and therefore widely differentiated yet all related, not only by language but also by the underlying philosphy which was their animating influence and general inspiration.

But this peak was also a turning-point. The sciences had made their first conquests and were developing. The century of Racine and Bossuet was also that of Descartes, of Mariotte and of Pascal. Scientific thought and the forming currents of philosophy had not yet, however, reached the popular classes nor had they altered the culture which was in the life of the masses.

Obviously, the peasants, artisans and soldiers who, at this period, set sail for Canada were neither artists, philosophers nor scholars. What, then, did they bring with them which might have an historic influence? What they did bring was a religious faith, a language, an aggregate of usages and traditions, laws, an historical conscience, in a word, the culture and the way of life followed by French popular society of the period. Thereafter, with advancing intellectual progress, would come the ability to produce, in their turn, an élite through whom would come works which, while original, still shared the same general inspiration.

While conserving the essence of what they owed to their origins, the French of the New World would nevertheless evolve in a certain way; they would acquire a tone of life which would make them a distinct group in the community of peoples of French culture. The salient points of this history can only be indicated here:

1. The first generations of Canadians lived in a sort of isolation. They thus escaped the influences which, during the same period in Europe, and especially in France, directed the evolution of culture and of civilization, gave birth to modern thought and provoked the more or less rapid and radical transformation of the social and political economy of countries and of peoples – philosophy, sciences, techniques, etc.

2. To compensate, they underwent influences which their contemporaries in Europe never knew:

a) The influence of a completely new physical environment that had to be penetrated, explored, and cleared while contact with this environment naturally forced men to adapt themselves, their usages and their traditions to it.

b) The homogenizing influence of the Canadian environment itself which, through their daily practice, in isolated surroundings, of the same religion, the same language, the same law (the Custom of Paris), the same methods of settlement, the same work regime, etc., brought about the fusion of the various provincial types which had come from France.

c) Finally, the preponderant influence of the Catholic Church at a time when religious influence elsewhere was waning. The Church supplied French Canada with its thought, its way of life, and the majority of its social institutions.

Two principal features thus identify the culture in which this human community at that time lived and continued to live.

These are its Christian inspiration and its French genius. French-Canadian culture is a particular form of the universal Christian concept of Man and of order.

These two realities – the Christian concept of life and the French genius – the latter interpreting the former and the former illuminating and nourishing the latter – express themselves in three ways. The first of these is by a language, the French language, which carries in its vocabulary and structure the same requirements for precision and order as the genius and culture which created it. The second is in its modes of being and doing which, because they proceed from it, tend to reconstitute themselves from one generation to another. The third is in the work of an élite which renewed it in its sources and manifested to the world whatever it contained of universality. French-Canadian culture, an American variant of the original type, bears the marks of its double heritage.

1) Like all cultures, it is *qualitative*, that is to say, it conceives Man, its object, as being ordained to fully realize himself over and beyond the utilitarian purposes of daily life,

2) As a Christian culture it is

a) *spiritual*, that is, it accords supremacy to values of the spirit and conceives human values as being ranged and ordered for Man's natural and supernatural vocation. Hence its repugnance for any kind of doctrinal or pragmatic materialism.

b) *personal*, that is, it conceives Man, endowed with intelligence and free will, as being called to a personal vocation of which he is the master-artisan and for which he is alone responsible before time and before eternity. So, by that very fact, Man possesses rights against which no human power can prevail. Hence his concept of liberty and authority and his desire for order; and hence also his refusal of all forms of collectivism and totalitarianism.

3) Like all Catholic Christian cultures, it is *communal,* that is, it conceives society not as a multitude ruled only by the constraint of public order but as an organic entity, ordained for the common good and specifically for the development of the person; with Man inserted in society through the intermediacy of groups and communities which he himself creates through his natural need.

Long before it implanted itself in Canada this culture, as we have pointed out, had in France itself informed a civilization, that is, an organic aggregate of diverse works which, by the sole fact of its existence, acted as a centre to fertilize, renew and enrich the culture itself. And it had accomplished this through men in whom it had inspired a creative initiative. It had also fashioned a human type with a particular psychology which motivated his attitudes on all levels of activity. From this type, re-made, and re-touched by the American environment, there issued the Canadian variant or French-Canadian type.

What are the keynotes of his personality and the fashions of thinking which, without being formulated, are lived spontaneously and determine his attitudes, which in all cases precede voluntary decisions on every plane where action can be taken? We believe it necessary for present purposes to consider, for a moment, the dispositions of mind which condition the socio-political behaviour of French-Canadians with respect to Anglo-Canadians. If through culture and religion the two groups are clearly distinguishable one from the other, this is not so with their respective concepts of society and of politics. Linked together by the force of circumstances in the same state, they meet each other on the plane of action without being able to explain their differing attitudes to each other.

If the French-Canadians succeeded, shortly after the conquest, in ensuring for themselves the free exercise of their religion and the use of their mother-tongue, they nevertheless had to accept the political structure and the social organizational forms of the country's new masters. They had, consequently, to submit themselves to an institutional regime bearing the stamp of a genius different from their own and whose spirit they neither possessed nor shared. And it is through this subjection that the conquest of 1760 has produced its most lasting effects, to the extent that after almost two centuries and despite the immense progress realized elsewhere, the French-Canadians have not yet succeeded in overcoming these effects.

Three concepts, not expressed as a thought but lived spontaneously as a tradition are, it would seem, the keys to the French-Canadians' socio-political behaviour, and all three derive from their religious conception of life, though they are interpreted according to the particular genius of their ethnic group.

1. *The sense of order*. Like all Catholics, the French-Canadians make a distinction between the natural and the supernatural, each of them having its own object and exigencies. But they conceive the former to be subordinated to the latter. Temporal, personal or collective life, either public or private, should be organized according to the rules of the natural law, that is,

according to the laws of Man's fulfilment which are themselves illuminated by religious faith. Thus the order of life
proceeds from transcendent, permanent and universal norms
which are therefore valid for men at all times and in every
environment. Whether it be private, personal, family or professional life, or collective, social or political life, the methods
of organization, valid from one setting and from one era to
another, should nevertheless at all times and in all places contribute to the integral realization of Man himself and to the
accomplishment of his eternal salvation. This is the very
essence of what is called today *the social doctrine of the
Catholic Church.*

2. *The sense of liberty.* For every Catholic, liberty is defined
not as a simple equilibrium of individual freedoms, but as the
faculty to choose the best from among various lawful means of
attaining a legitimate end, and, in the final analysis, of realizing
their natural and supernatural human vocation. Such a conception of liberty implies a corresponding sense of responsibility.
Liberty and responsibility are the two facets of a single personal attribute. To live freely does not mean to live as one
pleases, but it means living according to the requirements of
order as established by the natural law, which is itself illuminated by Revelation. Whether on the private or public level, Man
is free to choose his own ways of life but he is responsible, both
to his own vocation and to the good of the whole society, for
the ordering of his actions.

3. *The sense of progress.* Like all Catholics, they conceive it,
first of all, as being the act of perfecting the human individual,
according to a hierarchic order of values of which every
human being is the synthesis. There is no real progress unless
the workings of common life, either social or political, definitely
translate themselves into an improvement of the man himself
by a constant raising of his intellectual and moral level. Economic progress, naturally, also has a place therein, but in such
a way that, while meeting specific needs, it contributes to the
intellectual and moral progress of the population. Social ascent
is itself conceived as being primarily bound up with the intellectual and moral value of the man and of his function.

The first Canadian society, that of New France, was organized according to a fashion which was a projection of the concept of order common to all elements in the population. Of
necessity, this society was rural, since it was established in the
heart of a wilderness lacking easy communication with the

civilized world, and it had, first of all, to ensure its daily subsistence. In the very warp and woof of its organization, it bears the main characteristics of the general concept of life from which it issued.

1) *It is personalist.* It is primarily ordained to the accomplishment of Man himself. And so that this personalism may not be a vain word but a living prerogative for each person, it gives it as a basis, a *system of work* and a *system of property* conceived in such fashion as will ensure Man's autonomy on that plane where personal initiative and responsibility have their full significance and real value – the plane of private life and daily activity. On one hand, landed property, the source of work and subsistence, leads to agricultural establishment; on the other hand, the loom and workshop lead to the establishment of crafts. In one case as in the other, Man as a master of his work instruments possesses the initiative of his own life and bears the responsibility for it – these being first requirements of a work system with a humanizing value. In fact, it may be said that the social order of the French-Canadian rural environment rests first and foremost on the individual's personal responsibility to himself, to his dependents and to society.

2) *It is communal.* At the first level are *family* and *profession.* By realizing, under the responsibility of a head, the association of family, work and property, the autonomous agricultural or craft establishment supplies society with its basic unit.

At the second level, to unite families among themselves and to fill or regulate the functions which they cannot themselves perform, there are two institutions of which the second has finally assumed the functions of the first. These are the *seigneurial régime* and the *parish.* The seigneurial régime consisted essentially in an economic system for improving territory. Under this régime, the *censitaire* had no ownership in the land but its possession was ensured to him in perpetuity, in return for certain conditions which, in the aggregate, were far from onerous. Through its system of recriprocal obligations the seigneury effected a certain social integration of the families established in its ranks and ensured the whole a minimum of security.

The role of the parish is all the more important in French Canada since the seigneurial régime did not completely fulfil its special purpose. The parish meets specific purposes of a religious nature; it also meets social needs which, in whole or in part come under the aegis of the Church, such as relief and education. The shortcomings and deterioration of the seigneurial régime led it to assume economic and administrative functions which its particular purpose did not imply. The parish thus became the veritable centre of social life, the mother-institution of public institutions in the province. Even today it still precedes the municipality and the school commission which, in rural centres, are erected and operate within its framework.

Finally, at the superior level, are found the religious and civil authorities. The first instils its spirit, while the second co-ordinates the various branches of activity.

This was a rural society but not an exclusively agricultural society. The economy aimed at complete utilization of the territory's diverse resources, including land, minerals, furs and fisheries. Commerce and industries consequently had their place in it, as a complement to agriculture and the crafts which were themselves considered as having to meet the needs of each family as fully as possible. But there were also functions of the general economy such as furs, fishing, ship-building, manufacturing, industry, metallurgy, textiles, milling, brewing, etc. In short, it was a diversified economy which was, above all, founded on personal initiative and personal responsibility, backed by the state.

In 1760, the little community underwent defeat. What was its situation on the morrow of this painful event? It was 1) ruined financially through many years of war, the malversations of certain of its administrators, and the state's monetary bankruptcy; 2) cut off from its original mother country of which, for many years to come, it would still have been in great need from the triple viewpoints of economy, culture and religion; and 3) deprived of its higher education; the colleges of the Jesuits and the Recollets, which had provided secondary education, were closed and the two directing congregations interdicted, the sole survivor was the Séminaire de Québec. Its clergy alone remained to direct its religious, cultural, social and even its political life. It retained also its faculty for work and for recuperation which, conceived as it was for stability and security, was scarcely appropriate for an economy of competition. For long years to come, the French-Canadian community would have to content itself with a diminished form of colonization and rural expansion.

THE ANGLO-PROTESTANT CULTURE

Then new masters took over the country. Quite naturally, they wanted to organize it according to their own concepts of life and of social and political order. What, then, was their mentality and from what general philosophy of life would their actions in Canada normally proceed? They came, either directly or by way of the American colonies from a country which, during the preceding centuries, had carried out and assimilated three great revolutions: A political revolution which had caused it to pass from an absolute monarchy to a constitutional monarchy with parliament supreme. Political traditions of participation by the citizens in the communal life were already firmly established; An economic revolution which had transformed it from an agrarian economy of the feudal type to an exchange economy directed towards profits and the conquest of power, and which prepared it technically and financially for the industrial revolution; A spiritual revolution, the Reformation, which through private judgment made religion a strictly personal affair and emancipated its social morality from all ecclesiastic dependence.

Canada's new masters were of Anglo-Protestant culture. Thus, they were of a culture a) of Saxon genius re-shaped by the centuries of British history; b) of Christian inspiration, but Christianity according to the Protestant interpretation. From these two sources, differing in genius and in interpretation — which, moreover, is itself still evolving — of a single profound concept of life, arise the differences of mentality which separate and even frequently bring into opposition the two human groups in Canada.

The French genius, as we have said, is logical, inclined to reason from principles as a base. The Anglo-Saxon genius is pragmatic, little inclined to build theories or to embarrass itself with them. It prefers the logic of facts to that of principles. In a word, those of French origin and those of English origin represent two distinct temperaments, two casts of mind, two distinct geniuses which differ as profoundly in their ways of understanding life and of practising it as they differ in their ways of expressing themselves. The Anglo-Protestant culture, since it is of Christian inspiration, is, like the French-Catholic culture, spiritual, personal and qualitative. But, because it is Protestant, it does not conceive the order of temporal life and Man's relations to society in the same manner. It is not communal, but individualist and liberal.

From the viewpoint of religion and language, the identities of the two groups brought face to face by the conquest are clear-cut, and the highest political privilege which one or the other can claim is the freedom to practise and teach, with their corresponding prerogatives. But this is not the case from the socio-political viewpoint. Here there intervene the concepts of order, liberty and progress which the two groups interpret differently. Masters of the country, the Anglo-Protestants insist on their own interpretation and thus put into effect, according to their own methods, a social and economic policy to which the French-Canadians must accommodate themselves at the price, on certain occasions, of heavy sacrifices. Wherein does this interpretation differ from that of French-Canadian Catholics?

The difference arises mainly from the fact that, by making of religion, through private judgment, a strictly personal affair, Protestantism withdrew its social morality from all eccesiastical discipline and liberated socio-political thought from any reference to a transcendent order. For a Catholic – as we have said of the French-Canadians – the social order is the arrangement of society according to an organic principle founded on the dignity of the person and tending towards the common good, that is, the accomplishment according to their hierarchic order of all the goods necessary to the fulfilment of the human, natural and supernatural vocation. Liberty defines itself with respect to this order. For the Protestant, who establishes no reference to a transcendent order, liberty is pre-eminent and the best order is that which arises spontaneously according to the circumstances under which liberty is exercised. This is, in short, the social peace necessary for the common prosperity and which should be ensured through a minimum of restrictions on personal liberty. This liberty is defined with respect to the individual and realizes itself in practice by an equilibrium of particular liberties under the aegis of the law – obedience to the law being itself considered as a requirement of personal liberty.

But Protestantism is not a homogeneous fact; it is a complex of differentiated denominations becoming more and more numerous and for whom devotion to personal liberty is the common denominator. On historic occasions, the particular genius and temperament of peoples have been powerful factors in this phenomenon of continuous differentiation on the religious plane and of group re-unification within the framework of the state on the political plane. The case of the Anglo-Saxons is revealing from this viewpoint. To conciliate the divergent requirements of personal liberty, considered as pre-eminent, of integral respect for the law considered as a safe-guarding condition of liberty, of service to the nation considered as synthetic expression of individual aspirations, their eminently practical genius had, long before the Reformation, invented parliamentarianism and had started the simultaneous process of political devalorization and patriotic exaltation of the monarchy which was to lead to the system, unique in the world, of a king who reigns but does not govern. The same attitudes, proceeding from the same deep impulses, may be noted at the time of the Reformation. The exigencies of personal liberty, of respect for the law and of assiduous service to the nation, find their religious expression in Protestantism and are fused in a tradition of life with which only the people who conceived it according to their genius can truly commune. It is these complex perspectives of liberty, of individualism, of patriotism and of mysticism that the concepts of order and liberty which we recently referred to must be placed, if we desire to live and understand them as do the Anglo-Protestants. For a French-Catholic this is not easy, if, indeed, it is possible at all.

Anglo-Protestants and Franco-Catholics also differ in their respective interpretations of progress and of the significance of material success in human life. The two groups do not attach the same importance to the same values. It is not for us to take part in the discussion that has long ensued on the historic and philosophic relations of Protestantism with the modern economy, nor on the influence of a certain Reformer on the formation of what the historian Lower calls "the acquisitive way of life" of the Anglo-Saxon centres. As the same author has established, the difference in the mentality of the two groups from this viewpoint appeared immediately after the conquest, and it still remains one of the most fundamental features of what we have called the major premise of the Canadian political problem.

Such, then, reduced to very general indications, are the historic and ideological origins of the two cultural types which, since 1760, have lived in competition in Canada; one desiring to preserve its particularism and, with that end in view, seeking to take back into its own hands, and as extensively as possible, the conduct of its own life; the other, resolved to install its institutions and to organize the country according to its ideas and its interests.

Let us, moreover, note this: it is not on the purely intellectual and artistic plane, nor on the plane of disinterested activities, that the duality of cultures within a given country presents a political problem. On that level, cultural activity tends to unite rather than to divide. But it is on the plane of everyday activity, on the plane of economic, social, juridical and social action where, the interests of two groups being engaged, their respective concepts of life and of order oppose each other and clash. Of that, the province of Quebec, as the national home of French Canada and as the initial geographical centre of cultural duality in Canada, has had and continues to have, experience.

3. THE SOCIAL CONSEQUENCES OF THE OPPOSITION OF CULTURES

For a people, the tragic drama of conquest is to be subjected to institutions of which they have neither knowledge nor usage, and to be thus set at variance with their design of everyday living: Expressive as they are of a certain sense of order and, consequently, of a culture, juridical, political, economic and social institutions set up rules and constitute the framework of communal, individual and collective life; and they tend to perpetuate the thinking from which they proceed. They thus effect the harmony between Man and his milieu and create conditions such that a man feels himself and knows himself to be at home in his country.

The French Canadians lived this drama. On the morrow of the British conquest, they were faced with the alternative of either yielding to the conquerors' will and presence and disappearing as an ethnic group, or else attempting the obstacle-studded adventure of national survival. With the help of external and internal circumstances, they made their option for resistance. Thereupon, two great tasks lay before them: 1) on the political plane, the earliest reconquest of their essetial liberties of religion, language, laws and, if possible as a long-term objective, the return to their own hands of the direction of their lives; 2) on the social plane, a continuation of living according to their own conception of order and in accordance with the spirit of their original culture.

Two main tendencies of opposite direction thereupon appeared which have dominated their history up to the present day. The one was political tending towards autonomy, of which the 1867 federal regime marks the high-water mark; the other was sociological and tended towards the breakup of their traditional communal life with reintegration of their human effectives in the great Canadian and even continental entity then in process of formation. The first corresponds to the persistent desire of the French-Canadians to preserve their cultural particularism and to live their own national life within the political framework of Canada; the second corresponds to the conqueror's will to impose everywhere his culture and his institutions and to organize the country according to his own ideas and purposes.

SOCIOLOGICAL EVOLUTION

If, within the political and constitutional framework instituted by the mother country the French-Canadians benefitted by an increasing measure of religious, cultural and even political freedom, the initiative of creating their own political and economic system according to their own concepts of order, liberty and progress was never entirely left in their own hands. Even since the advent of federalism, they have had to use political institutions of British origin and content themselves, on the economic plane, with the limited economic prerogatives that the constitution confers upon the provinces. That, let it be remembered, is essentially the drama of the conquest.

However, and despite everything, they were fortunate that conquest overtook them at a moment of history when economic and social life was still everywhere within the immediate resort of personal and communal initiative and historic circumstances soon allowed re-establishment of their civil laws, that is, of laws which most closely govern the person in his relations to things and people and which have the most direct incidence on culture and its conditions of preservation and development. It was thus possible for them to preserve the profound ideological inspiration of their communal institutions and to make of them a sort of refuge from the conqueror's direct influence. From that circumstance stems their national survival.

Considering, on the one side, their tradition of life and social institutions and, on the other, the situation in which war and conquest had placed them, the only economic and social policy that could allow the French-Canadians to live and develop in rhythm with their natural increase and to evolve without grave social consequences would have been 1) on the economic level, a policy of colonizing expansion tending towards the mastery and rational utilization of the territory's diverse resources, such as soil, forests, fisheries, etc.; 2) on the social plane, a policy of widespread education which, while respecting its culture and religious convictions, would have prepared youth for the tasks awaiting it in a country being built up. It was especially required that free space and natural resources should at all times remain available for work and exploitation according to definite rules, known and understood by everyone, and that youth should be prepared to play its part fully from one generation to another.

It was precisely the opposite which took place. Natural resources were not made available according to the population's needs; they were arranged according to the new masters' ideas and with a view to the expansion of commerce for the immediate profit of the British population in process of establishing itself, and in the general interests of the mother country. As for education, decades passed before it was re-established, with all the consequences which such a deficiency entails.

The chronic inadequacy of the economic and social policy for the needs of a disorganized and impoverished population would largely determine the sociological evolution of the succeeding century – an evolution which ceaselessly tends to weaken if not actually to ruin, on the social-economic plane, the gains realized elsewhere on the political level. This evolution may be divided into three main periods, all nevertheless characterized by the same major factor – the inadequacy of the social and economic policy for the population's mentality and for the needs of its rapidly increasing numbers.

FIRST PERIOD: EXPANSION

The first period extends from 1763 to around 1820. The socio-economic system erected during the life of New France, which was of a peasant and craft type set in seigneury and parish, continued to suffice both for the people's subsistence and for its natural increase. Possessing their work instruments and largely withdrawn from commercial dependence, masters of their communal institutions and in a position to direct these themselves, the French Canadians, although subjected to a foreign political regime, could live from day to day in the illusion that nothing of real importance had taken place in their country's history and that, with time, they would be able to repair the ravages of war and lead their lives as before. The national environment still preserved its homogeneity, with language, traditions and ways of life having become social necessities to the degree that whoever might come in from outside would have to adapt himself to these.

The events of 1760 had not produced all their effects. Not only had the French-Canadians lost the political direction of their country but they had also lost the control of its economy. They were driven back towards exploitation of the soil as their sole source of subsistence and towards agricultural settlement as their only method of establishing new generations, and reduced to the margin of limited savings from subsistence farming towards the reconstitution or increase of their possessions. For them there could be no question of counting on either the state's collaboration or upon foreign capital to re-make, develop and diversify their economy.

SECOND PERIOD: MIGRATION, EMIGRATION

The period from approximately 1820 to about 1880 was characterized by the double paradox of over-population in a vast and empty country and of emigration in a country whose principal weakness was lack of population.

The old economic system still sufficed for subsistence of the established population and the national milieu always conserved its homogeneity and traditional structures. French Canadians remained masters in that part of the country they had cleared and developed from the colony's beginnings and in that sector of activity accessible to their personal and communal initiative – the peasant and artisan crafts. But from lack of an appropriate policy for developing the territory's wealth, their expansion was hindered. The birth rate remained high and the population grew at a rapid rate. From 1832 to 1881, it increased from 327,000 to 1,075,130. Two great population movements marked this period: 1) expansion within the interior of the province; 2) emigration a) to the United States and b) towards the other Canadian provinces in process of organization.

Certain measures aimed at outfitting the country, promoting commerce or correcting particular conditions, provided employment and opened the ways for establishment. Failing action by the state, the initiative came from the people themselves, aided by their clergy and colonization societies. Along the roads and along the railways, following the forest industry step by step, groups established themselves and formed themselves into parishes. The movement was rapid and spread out in all directions. It was not until nearly the end of the last century that a somewhat more methodical policy of settling new districts was inaugurated.

This sort of conquering humanization of the Quebec soil, however important present-day results show it to have been, was not accomplished without French Canada in other respects suffering serious and steady losses of manpower. Hardship of settlement conditions in the new districts as well as the insufficiency of employment opportunities made the phenomenon of over-population a chronic condition in the older centres. This phenomenon, in turn, called into being another – emigration, the social drain which, for more than a century, was to offer itself as a cure for the inadequate economic policy.

It developed, indeed, in two directions, first and especially towards the United States. The American census of 1900 enumerated 395,000 Canadians born in Canada and 804,000 American citizens born of Canadian parents. Then the movement went towards Ontario and the prairie provinces where today's French-Canadian minorities were then in process of formation.

But emigration was only one aspect of the problem. A pioneer population, settled in the wilderness without the slightest state assistance, could only provide itself very slowly with the resources needed to organize its social services and notably its schools. It was not until 1826 that the first public schools were set up, so that many generations were thus completely deprived of education. The social and human consequences of such a lack can never be measured. The phenomena subsequently observed, the rigid lines in which its agricultural techniques had bogged down with a corresponding exhaustion of the soil, the slowness with which it adapted itself to the economic requirements of the later period, are attributable, on the one hand, to the hardship of its conditions of settlement and to the poverty in which it was kept all through the previous century, and, on the other hand, to the prolonged pitiable condition of its schools. Here again the remedy did not come from the state. It came from the people themselves and from their clergy. So it was with other social works, such as health, charities, mutual aid, etc.

If the French Canadians of Quebec had difficulty finding their place in the economy of the period, that does not mean to say that the economy itself made no progress, but it does mean that it was neither conceived for, nor organized by, them. Thus the first conclusion to be drawn from a story which is now remote, but whose consequences are still far from being extinguished, is that it is not sufficient to give a people certain general, religious and cultural liberties; the economic and social policy must be adapted to their mentality and situation; and help must be given them in order that the people may assure themselves of the living conditions necessary for the full exercise of their higher liberties and for their full fruition. Lacking these elements, the people suffer thereby in their daily existence and in their material and cultural development.

THIRD PERIOD: URBANIZATION

The third period of the Province's evolution took the form of industrialization and urbanization. It extended from 1880 to our day and can be divided into two phases, with the first ending at the opening of the present century or, to set a date, let us say with the war of 1914.

Industrialization ought to have been provided for in a province whose principal resources were industrial. It offered a remedy to the social sore of emigration which had attained the chronic stage. But, at the same time, it set off the sociological evolution of the French-Canadian community itself. Thenceforward, the old economic regime not only would fail to ensure the establishment of the young generation, but it would have to evolve, if not towards other forms, at least towards other methods of production and exchange. The agricultural establishment, without ceasing to be based on the family would, in effect, be transformed from a peasant to a commercial type.

The first phase of the Province's industrialization corresponds with the last of liberal capitalism. It was characterized by individual or family enterprise which, in its techniques, juridical forms and financial structure, still closely resembled the craft establishment. This kind of enterprise was, therefore, well within the reach of the French-Canadian entrepreneur, generally lacking in capital and industrial tradition, but heir to an artisan tradition of very great fertility.

The French-Canadian national environment still generally retained its homogeneity at this time. The towns were growing rapidly, especially Montreal, but the old social institutions had not yet undergone the profound shaking-up which would later compel them to make a completely new self-appraisal. New institutions which rounded out the old ones and met the needs of a growing population came into being. Urbanization was carried on normally and, if it had maintained the tempo of its first phase, it seems that French-Canadian adaptation could have been effected without serious mishap.

But with the appearance, at the beginning of the century, of big business and, especially with the war of 1914 and the drive towards industrialization which resulted from it, the tempo changed. Now the second phase began, the phase of authoritarian capitalism and of organization capitalism.

Big share-company capitalism, which borrowed, so to speak, nothing from the juridical, administrative and technical tradition of the previous period, substituted itself for the individual and family enterprise. Its advent provoked or accelerated two major phenomena, intimately related one with the other and of extreme importance for the whole of Canada and especially for French Canada.

1) The displacement of the majority of the population into the towns and at a correspondingly faster rate as the accent on industry was thenceforward stressed.

Rural in spirit by tradition and formed within the framework of a rural society, French Canada thus became in great part urban. Such a transformation could not fail to engender numerous consequences. Henceforward it would affect every aspect of collective life and would bring into question all data of the social order, even the most fundamental, such as family, work, property, charities, education, etc. And in every case, these problems presented themselves in terms all the more complex since the old juridical framework was no longer adjusted to a situation which was itself created and imposed under the inspiration of thinking which was "foreign" and even hostile to that from which French Canada itself had issued.

2) The transformation of the work system and, consequently, of the general sociological complex including the system of property, family, education, social welfare, etc.

The preservation and development of a particular culture depends not only on personal decision but also on daily relations and exchanges between men and their milieu. The French-Canadian civilization as an institutional expression of culture was moulded in a rural setting and autonomous establishment was one of its distinguishing sociological modalities. Industrialization, with its large masses of wage workers, brought about a radical transformation of this system. If the conquest put the French Canadians out of tune with the political institutions, the industrial revolution put them out of harmony with the social institutions. Loss in 1760 of political autonomy was balanced in the succeeding century by the slow-down of their socio-economic expansion, by emigration and by the dispersion of a large part of their natural increase; today it compels them to re-think their life within the limits of new sociological frameworks of "foreign" inspiration.

Constituted in 1867, the Province of Quebec, as an autonomous political entity, inherited the social situation created during the preceding period. Neither its financial resources nor its limited jurisdiction in economic matters, nor the state of mind existing in an era of economic liberalism and of social conservation permitted it to undertake the vast initiatives set before it. In default of being able to count on its own nationals to set up industries in sufficient number, the Province had and still has to show itself accessible to outside enterprises, even at the risk of seeing built up in its very midst centres of influence whose inspiration is clearly foreign to the population's cultural tradition. Moreover, its socio-economic policy had and still has to be developed a) within a federation and, consequently, in such manner as not to create too great disparity with the rest of the country as regards systems of labour, industry, taxes, etc.; and b) under the authority of the central government which, by virtue of the constitution, commands the most powerful means of controlling the economy, such as customs, currency, banks, etc. All this, it goes without saying, largely conditions exercise of provincial autonomy.

Thanks to this autonomy, the French Canadians have, however, as a majority group, the political initiative of their cultural and social life and partly of their economic life. They can endow themselves and, in fact, have already endowed themselves, with educational institutions, a system of charities, labour laws, etc., in conformity with their thinking and adapted to their needs. The advent of large-scale capitalism and the rapid expansion of industry brought them into the embrace of an economy whose control does not belong to them and which, to a large extent, escapes the jurisdiction and possibilities of action of their province and even of their country. If they want to preserve their original culture and make it an instrument of progress for themselves and for the whole of Canada, present circumstances oblige them to make a very conscious effort, increasingly enlightened and attentive.

This is far from being the time for them to abandon the slightest iota of political initiative in any of the sectors of activity where they can still effectively exercise it, as for example in education, health, charities and social security, property, civil rights, etc., all of which precisely correspond to the modes of activity where their general concept of life and the most important data of their culture are most widely implicated. If, under pretext of financial accommodation with the federal government and with the rest of the country, they abandon the initiative in the various domains where they have succeeded in regaining it, or if they deprive themselves of the means of exercising this initiative to the full, it would be as well for them to renounce, immediately and as a group, all cultural future. A culture has a chance to live only when it expresses itself, when it flourishes and when it gives of itself.

To preserve its culture, to enrich it from generation to generation, to have it fructify in vital values for itself and for others, a national community must have the faculty of freely expressing itself and, therefore, in the very first place, of creating its own institutions and of organizing its economic and social life by itself and according to its own spirit. If it lacks that, then whatever may be the constitutional guarantees, it is stricken in its everyday life, fettered in its material expansion and cultural progress and reduced to the alternative of either allowing its culture to perish, or of accepting, in its own country, the inferior status of a stranger.

4. THE PROVINCE OF QUEBEC IN CONFEDERATION

Because of the religion, culture and history of the majority of its population, the Province of Quebec is not a province like the others. All the constitutional systems since 1774 have, both in fact and in law, recognized this special situation.

By attributing to the provinces legislative and administrative authority over everything which, generally speaking, touches the citizen's life and private business, and particularly property and civil rights, instruction and education, the legislators of 1867 gave juridical form to a rule of political wisdom long confirmed by history, namely, that in such matters governments better fulfill their purposes the more closely they come into contact with the people.

From the viewpoint which concerns us, this general provision of the Constitution is of capital importance since it confers upon the Province of Quebec, as indeed it does on all the provinces, authority on all matters arising from its historical, cultural and religious character. The 1867 Constitution made the Province of Quebec, which was already historically its national focus, the French-Canadian centre *par excellence,* and the accredited guardian of French-Canadian civilization. Insofar as its own population was concerned, that was a direct responsibility. It also applied indirectly, insofar as it constituted the cultural focus of the French minorities of the other provinces and to the extent that its influence was exerted on over-all Canadian policy

CULTURE AND POLITICS

It is through the general inspiration of their policies and through their day-to-day attitudes that the public authorities respect the cultural particuliarism of their constituents. To conceive and put into practice the most suitable policy for stimulating the progress of cultural groups dependent on their authority, they must bear in mind the multiple aspects of the general problem of culture, as it presents itself both from the viewpoint of the individual and of the community.

When we speak of culture, we speak of Man himself and of the conditions that have to be created to enable him, freely and on his own responsibility, to ensure full realization of his personality and maximum fecundity for his existence. Over and above all intermediate ends, this is the ultimate object of policies. And when we speak of the attachment of a national community to its special culture, it is to the common culture and to the spirit which gave it birth that we refer. And when, finally, we speak of the cultural action of the state, we envisage an action whose object is, on the one hand, the preservation, renewal and fructification of the common culture acording to the thinking which inspires it, and, on the other hand, the creation of a more and more numerous, varied and influential élite, whose efforts, by very reason of their intellectual worth, will be the source of the common culture's fertilization and enrichment.

The basic situation in Canada has not essentially changed since 1867. Neither of the two national groups has renounced its own existence. But the conditions under which the two confronting cultures can realize themselves are very different. The Anglo-Canadian culture, which is now spread over nine out of the ten provinces, inspires every form and manifestation of life therein. It has at its command the complete institutional system of these nine provinces as well as those of the federal government itself.

However, the Anglo-Canadian majority is far from possessing the cultural homogeneity which, at first sight, might be attributed to it. From the opening of this century, a large proportion of neo-Canadians, drawn from the four corners of Europe, have united with it, but they cannot be said to have become assimilated. These newcomers have learned the English language and have adopted the institutional system set afoot by Canadians of British origin. However, they have none of the social, legal or political traditions of the group to which they have adhered. It must be recognized that their presence, especially in the West, exercises a profound influence on the old Anglo-Canadian culture.

In addition, since 1867, means of transport and of communication, including the railways, roads, aviation, press, cinema, radio and television have developed to a point where the future of Anglo-Canadian culture may well be determined, not only by French-Canadian culture and the internal influence of the neo-Canadians, but also, and especially, by the American culture.

If Canada is to preserve its own cultural identity Canadians of the two groups and the federal and provincial public authorities should become aware of the influence against which they must be on their guard, and of the internal and external conditions in which they will henceforward have to operate. The time is long since past in which we could trust ourselves to the spontaneity of instinctive reflexes for the preservation and renewal of a particular culture. This is especially true of heterogeneous states. Every government must, from now on, have a cultural policy, in the full sense of that word.

On this matter there is much mental confusion, as is shown by the vocabulary of those who discuss it. This vacillating thinking apparently stems from three principal causes:

1) Failure to remember the distinction that has to be made between intellectual culture and human culture, and between national culture and "general" culture,

2) A too narrow intellectual concept of the culture of the élite, without sufficient reference to the philosophy from which every culture necessarily proceeds and to the common culture of which every élite is the highest expression. One speaks of culture as if knowledge were the end-all and be-all of human existence and as if all individuals should or could attain the same level. That is, in some sort, a persistence of the Enlightenment's faith in the humanising value of knowledge, *per se*. Yet recent history has shown how illusory such optimism really is.

French-Canadian culture differs from American culture in its religious inspiration, its language and its great social and legal traditions. Therefore, it is easy to conceive that, even without any special effort at strengthening itself, it might be able, at least for a certain period, to preserve a certain originality within the American milieu. This is not the case with the Anglo-Canadian culture which is identified by no special mark. Without constant reference to a fundamental humanism, one fails to see how, sooner or later, it can resist full Americanization.

3) Failure to remember the conditions under which every particular culture is preserved and renewed. One speaks of "Canadian civilization" as the present and eventual product of two cultures. Civilization being the social manifestation of a given culture, the least that can be said about Canadian civilization is that, even if it constitutes an entity in the structures of political society, it is none the less differentiated in its components to the same degree as the cultures from which it proceeds. The educational institutions of English Canada and of French Canada are both phenomena of civilization, yet they are neither the same in form nor in inspiration. The same is true of the

public charities system, of labour laws, of rural organization, etc. And it is only on condition that it can thus manifest itself socially, and is able to create a civilization which is both an expression of its special genius and of its renewal centre, that a culture has a chance to live and progress. The "singleness" of Canadian civilization is badly adapted to meet this requirement.

With cultures, as with all other realities, to make a distinction between them means putting them into opposition to each other. Consequently, in a heterogeneous state such as Canada, a double political problem arises: a) to ensure for each culture conditions of life and progress such that each of them may be able to make its maximum contribution; b) to arrange everything in such a way that the natural opposition of cultures results in co-operation and not in conflict.

Every particular culture, in order to maintain and develop itself, requires a focus somewhere, an environment within which it is not only taught but lived, a centre where it is of current usage in all spheres and is thus the condition for personal progress for every individual of every social class and of whatever environment. This is the principle of the ethnic milieu. Without such a focus, a particular culture is doomed, sooner or later, to experience decline and sterilization – like a plant without roots.

If the Anglo-Canadian culture – leaving aside the neo-Canadian influence – can count on the organized life of nine out of the ten provinces to live and develop itself, the French Canadian culture can count only on the organized life of the Province of Quebec, the sole centre where, by present necessity, it can freely express, renew and enrich itself. The French-Canadian minorities in the other provinces will not soon be in a position to build themselves a milieu sufficiently ample and consistent as to veritably regenerate a culture distinct from the common culture of their respective provinces. To organize their own education and to prepare an élite, they must depend upon their former province of origin. And that province, whatever contrary claims may be made, remains the veritable cultural focus, not only of its own citizens, but of all French-Canada wherever the vicissitudes of history may have scattered it across the country.

French-Canadian Culture and Autonomy

PROVINCIAL POLICY AND CULTURE

To fulfil the particular mission with which the Province of

Quebec is charged, two conditions are required – liberty and security.

By liberty, we mean the faculty for the province effectively to exercise all the jurisdictions which the Constitution confers upon it. We do not mean merely the theoretical faculty, as defined in legal texts, but the practical faculty, which puts at its disposal the necessary means for its full exercise.

In practice, the problem presents itself in two main forms:

1) One, properly *cultural*, which consists in the sum total of initiatives whose aim is to provide the Province with educational and cultural institutions suited to the modern requirements of a living civilization, and ranging from elementary schools up to research centres and extra-scholastic cultural institutions, both scientific and artistic. It is obviously in and through these institutions, whose object is to form, nourish and elevate the mind of Man, that culture will attain its highest manifestations and its fullest expansion both on the mass level and on the level of the élite;

2) The other form is *general,* and is made up of the aggregate of those initiatives which, without being cultural in their specific object, nevertheless act upon culture because they proceed from the spirit which animates the culture and which, by creating the milieu, tend to maintain and raise the community in the same spirit. These include economic projects for developing territory and the industrial utilization of resources; social works regarding family, work, mutual aid, charities; various laws which inspire these works and insert them into the social reality.

The French Canadians, to the extent that they have been able to shape their own collective, communal and political life, have made progress. On the other hand, when the initiative was taken from them or when they had to conform to a policy of outside inspiration and comply with an institutional set-up of which they possessed neither the spirit nor the usages, they were hampered in their expansion, retarded in their social and cultural development and forced into situations which took a heavy toll in human values.

If the industrial revolution, in progress for half a century, has corrected certain consequences of the preceding century's economic and social policy – as, for example, emigration – it has, on the other hand, generalized the disharmony which that policy had already created between the French Canadian and his social structures. The rift no longer affects merely the annual surplus population, it now takes place at the level of individual and communal life and thus affects the entire population. The whole institutional system which, up to now, has been the broadest and most synthetic expression of French Canada's special culture, must be completely re-made along new lines. It was not a current of ideas born without it nor drawn from abroad which modified the milieu of French-Canadian culture; neither rationalism nor European secularism, neither scientific positivism nor religious or political liberalism, nor even socialist or totalitarian ideologies. Primarily it was the practice of economic and political institutions of British origin which resulted in the creation of an individualistic and liberal mentality among a people whose religious, intellectual and social traditions had within them nothing either individualistic or liberal.

Economic factors, by overturning the old social order, were responsible for having taken its practical value away from traditional thinking as an informing principle of daily life. Men think along certain lines, but they are induced to live along certain other lines, and they end up thinking as they live. It is not otherwise that assimilation proceeds. At such a juncture, a social policy whose object is to revise and, where necessary, to adjust the organic means of Man's relations with society is, by itself and in its relations to culture, of capital importance.

The French-Canadian culture is communal. Three great traditions – family, autonomous work and the parish – have been the lines of force in the social history of French Canada. They retain their full value, for they correspond to the permanent requirements of human life. But, in order to meet new economic and social conditions, they must be simultaneously adapted and surpassed. Every effort at social restoration which wants to remain within the inspirational line of French-Canadian culture must start from there, not in order to maintain outdated modalities but, in order to devise those which are in accord with the old spirit which the new times demand.

This effort is imperative for the present generation and it will be imperative for immediately succeeding generations in a parallel double form: 1) broadening and clarifying the old traditional culture; 2) a judicious selection and assumption of the values of all kinds which the sciences and technology contribute to the current of modern life and of which no contemporary peoples can think of depriving itself once they have practised them.

Such an effort to re-assess itself and the outside world and to re-interpret the one in terms of the other is only possible if full latitude is given French Canada to live, to act and to create according to its spirit. And where can this latitude be fully given, if not first of all within the old province which has been the centre of its existence? At no time in history has that liberty of life and action, which the autonomy of Quebec means to it as a political unit, been so urgently dictated by circumstances.

For the preservation of this political formation, use must be made of it. If, under pretext of economic stability, social security, uniformity of material living conditions from one end of the country to the other or of administrative simplification, French Canadians install in their midst any organizational forms whatever, without first making sure these are in harmony with their general concept of life, they condemn themselves, sooner or later, to anemia and cultural sterility. Then, they will have no one to blame but themselves.

FEDERAL POLICY AND CULTURE

However, if they do not accept them, these organizational forms should not be imposed on them, either directly or by devious means. That is what we had in mind when we mentioned *security* as one of the conditions for full accomplishment of the Province of Quebec's special mission in the Canadian federation.

This security must, first of all, be internal, that is to say, an assured possession of the means necessary to fully exercise its jurisdiction. These means are legal and financial. The first are co-terminus with authority and are defined by the Constitution. The second are the very gist of the debate which has dominated federal-provincial relations in recent years. For the Province of Quebec, this debate has a significance it cannot have for the other provinces.

A re-arrangement of the fiscal system to the advantage of the federal government would, sooner or later, inevitably bring about a new distribution of powers. For the system of subsidies is incompatible both with federalism and with responsible government. For Anglo-Canadians in general, a redistribution of powers would, in short, be of only secondary importance. They belong to the same spiritual and cultural family. If social security, public health, civil laws and the schools should be brought under the jurisdiction of the federal capital it might cause them technical and administrative inconveniences, but there would ensue no serious consequences in matters of thought or culture.

It is not so with the French-Canadians, for whom every federal intervention in the above-enumerated fields and, in a general way, in provincial jurisdictions, would be likely to ignore or run counter to their traditional ways of thinking and acting. That is why the Province of Quebec, more than any other province, must preserve the financial means for self-administration, and that is why it must have the certitude that its prerogatives in this domain do not risk being called into question at any time.

Security is also needed in the Province's relations with the rest of the country. From the viewpoint which presently interests us, a problem of very great importance necessarily attracts our attention – the cultural action of the federal government and the spirit in which, from the viewpoint of Quebec and of French Canada, it should be exercised.

In matters of education, using that word in its broadest sense, jurisdiction rests and should rest with the provinces. For reasons which emerge rather clearly from the preceding pages, the Province of Quebec, particularly in view of the climate in which French Canadians must live, cannot make the smallest concession on this point. But the provinces administer only a part of the common good – the other part is within the resort of the federal authority, so that a special method of preparing and exercising political action is required. The common good is a synthesis, so that the government which administers a part of it inevitably influences the aggregate and even, more or less directly, those things which are specifically within the resort of the government which administers the other part. This is particularly true of culture.

Starting from the principle that culture, like its object, Man, is a synthesis; that its development is bound up, not only with organised education but with the entire social reality and that, as a consequence, it cannot be cut up into neat separate slices, cultural pluralism asserts the priority, in certain respects, of culture over politics. The federal government's first duty with respect to culture is to leave with the provinces, upon whom the primary responsibility rests, the corresponding initiative and the necessary financial resources and not, under pretext of financial stability, and by having recourse to more or less subtle distinctions, to seek to substitute itself for them.

But the federal government also has a duty of a more general order. Certain of the activities it now exercises, although their constitutionality might be disputed, are clearly cultural, and these include the education of military personnel, radio, television and cinema; scientific research with relation to agriculture, industry, defence, etc. Moreover, as an administrator of part of the common good, all its activities have, directly or indirectly, a cultural bearing by the very fact that they help to construct the milieu, to fashion its spirit and create its climate.

Save in certain clear and restricted cases, it does not rest with the federal government to take the initiative, but, in the exercise of its own jurisdictions, and to the extent that these have a direct or indirect cultural influence, it has a duty to fully respect the cultural particularism of those under its administration.

Every institution created by the federal government, whatever its object may be, should take into account the population's cultural duality, and it should strive to correspond as closely as possible to the requirements of the two cultures. All French Canadians in all parts of the country have, in such matters, the right to require the federal government to fully respect their cultural particularism.

So it is with interventions in such social matters as health, security, assistance, etc. From this viewpoint, the Province of Quebec, which is vested with the political authority, has the right to expect that the federal government: 1) will take no initiative without its consent; 2) will not put into force any law which runs counter to the particular traditions of its people or ignores the character of their institutions. Few and far between have been the federal government's social laws which have not, on some point or another, been at variance with the most important and soundest social traditions of French Canada.

Today, some would go even further and insist on the federal government's *right* to give its assistance to culture on the grounds that it is a "national" government. The federal government in no way has to go beyond its jurisdiction to serve culture – especially if that word is understood in the broad sense which the very idea of it conveys. If it is a matter of financial assistance, the federal government only has to leave the provinces with the resources they need. It will not cost it a cent more and its financial policy will not be in any way disturbed. If it is a question of influence and of generally providing an impetus, the simple exercise of its own jurisdictions in the spirit of the two cultures would be of great assistance: libraries and museums, radio, television, cinema, research and legislation, since all of these have an immense cultural scope. In each and every case, very fruitful co-operation with the provinces would ensue, in the spirit both of the constitutional law and of the two Canadian cultures.

For example, from the French-Canadian viewpoint, if the federal government, accepting the spirit of the Constitution, once and for all decided that it would put the French language on the same footing as the English language and use the French language in its dealings with all French-speaking citizens, in whatever province they might reside; if it decided to publish nothing that did not appear in both languages and to admit into its service a greater number of competent French Canadians, without first requiring of them a prior knowledge of English, etc., what might not be the cultural effect of such a decision! What a revaluation of their own language would take place in the minds of French Canadians themselves, and what an impetus would be given the study of French in all quarters!

Such, in a general way, could be the federal government's efforts to mesh its various initiatives with the great social and juridical traditions of the two cultural groups – even if in certain cases, as happens in Switzerland, options had to be offered, with each group choosing the system which best suited its mentality. In social matters, for example, such an attitude would, by giving it full meaning, result in the revival of the Christian-humanist spirit from which the sturdiest traditions of the two groups have issued.

Without doubt, it would have to be supported by a majority of the citizens. But, to a certain extent, it would be the federal government's duty to educate them to that view. A frankly and intelligently bi-cultural policy would finally give rise to a mutual pride among the two groups in their respective works and creations. However, any such sentiment of mutual pride is only possible in a general climate of security and confidence, which can spread itself only if both groups know themselves to be equally accepted and protected.

The constitutional system erected in 1867 clearly foresaw the political conditions necessary for the progress of the two cultures. It is all the more important that the spirit of that system should be respected because, for half a century, political functions have had their fields of activity considerably enlarged. For a province placed by history and by law in the position of Quebec, the need for liberty and security is, therefore, more imperative than ever. Liberal automatism having been left behind, governments faced with more and more numerous problems may choose either one or the other of two types of solution, depending on what their ideas are about Man and his relations with society. Unfortunately, it must be admitted that the "directed" technical solution, strongly tinged with socialism, is the one which, because of its apparent simplicity and facility, fascinates most minds. And that is precisely because, through its scientific pretentions, it puts itself in the line of modern economic development, which is the mathematical-positivist line. By that very fact it ignores the Christian solution which, by its attachment to liberty, responsibility and human dignity, lies at the heart of every truly humanist political and social economy.

This last is what the Province of Quebec, if it wants to stay faithful to its culture, must exert itself to make triumph, even if it is harder to interpret and requires a more complex organization and more difficult handling. For Man is of greater worth than the food wherewith he feeds himself and the comfort with which he surrounds himself.

PROVINCIAL AUTONOMY AND THE CANADIAN "NATION"
Must it then be concluded that, because of its need for autonomy, the Province of Quebec will never make any contribution towards formation of a Canadian "Nation"? If the word "nation" is understood in its political sense – which is the least appropriate but, unfortunately, the most widely accepted – we can assert that the Province of Quebec, as the national home of French Canada, has, on many occasions, shown its desire to see built up a strong Canada which will be master of its own destinies, peaceful and orderly within, and co-operating generously with other states to promote universal peace and prosperity. If, on the other hand, the word "nation" is understood in its true sense, as designating a sociological unit formed through practice in common of a single culture, the Province of Quebec, in view of its historical experience, may well ask exactly what is meant. With what are we concerned? With the nation which would result from the gradual weakening and sterilization of the French-Canadian cultural particularism, owing to the fact that all its means of expressing, renewing and enriching itself had been withdrawn from it, little by little? Or, do we rather have in mind the superior kind of nation which, formed by history at the meeting point of sociology and politics and through the voluntary, concerted action of the two groups, would have

mutual understanding and confidence as well as friendship as its principal bond of union? That is the only hypothesis which meets the profound requirements of democracy and of federalism and the only valid one in a country like Canada.

Since it has to do with a transcendence of the particularisms and their full expansion into a creation which would be the common product of their respective geniuses, such a hypothesis requires that these very patricularisms should have full faculty to develop themselves to the very limits of their possibilities. It is here that the requirements of liberty and security which we have insisted upon for the Province of Quebec take on their full significance. It is not only a question of maintaining a more or less stable peace between the two groups and ensuring a degree of cordiality in their mutual relations; it is a question of mobilizing what each of them possesses, with a view to obtaining a highly civilized product. It need scarcely be said that this would only be possible in a climate of perfect liberty and perfect security for each of the two groups and, consequently, in a climate of full justice to each of these groups on the part of the public authorities. The Province of Quebec, by the manner in which it has conducted itself towards the rest of the country, and by the treatment it has always given its Anglo-Canadian minority, has clearly demonstrated its ability to devise a project of this political scope and its willingness to work thereto. All that it asks is that it shall neither have its intentions suspected nor have violence done to the organization and direction of its own life.

THE PROVINCE OF QUEBEC AND THE MINORITIES

It must, however, be admitted that the Province of Quebec's attachment to its autonomy risks putting it into contradiction, if not with itself, at least with that part of French-Canada which historical hazards have dispersed throughout the country. These minorities depend less on the help of their respective provinces than on that of the federal government.

Hence the minorities' more or less openly expressed desire to see extended the influence of the federal government rather than that of the provinces, and of seeing the federal government intervene in fields hitherto considered as being reserved to the provinces – education, for example. Hence arises, also, their fear of seeing the Province of Quebec, through it attitudes, contributing to the general strengthening of the provinces' autonomy. Certainly, the problem is a very serious one.

On the one hand, the Province of Quebec cannot, as such, go to the assistance of minorities. In all its resources it does not have a surplus out of which to meet the needs of its own population. Subsidies to certain French institutions in other provinces have been paid by way of exception and they cannot be repeated without compromising the legal bases of provincial autonomy. For, if the government of the Province of Quebec denies the federal government's right to subsidize institutions within the jurisdiction of the provinces, it cannot, without contradicting itself, claim for itself the right to grant subsidies on a permanent basis to institutions dependent on the authority of other provinces.

Finally, so long as the country's political climate remains as it has been since 1867, it is idle to hope that the federal government will make use, for the protection of minorities, of the prerogatives conferred on it by Article 93. That, moreover, is not in itself desirable — if the autonomy of the provinces is to remain the very seat of Canadian federalism.

Thus, only one attitude is possible:

1) pressure should continue to be applied to the Anglo-Canadian provinces to induce them to respect the constitutional prerogatives of the French-Canadian minorities and to grant them treatment equivalent to that given the Anglo-Protestant minority in the Province of Quebec.

2) in the meantime, help for the minorities should be assured by the people of the Province of Quebec, acting on their own initiative, but without the official support of the government of the Province.

3) the federal government, as administrator of one part of the common good and in the exercise of its own jurisdictions, should not only respect the cultural values of French Canada wherever encountered, but should do everything in its power, within its jurisdictional limits, to stimulate their expansion, in respect of language, juridical traditions, social traditions, etc. Such an attitude by the federal government would do more to change the political climate of the country, and consequently the attitude of the provinces with respect to their minorities, than any direct intervention on its part and more, even, than any campaign originating from French Canada.

THE FRENCH-CANADIAN CASE AND UNIVERSAL TRENDS

We are at a cross-roads of the human adventure, and at one of those moments of generally confused ideas and of extreme tension of souls through which the great renewals of history are forecast. The question is to know 1) whether in ten, twenty or one hundred years there will still be room on the earth's surface for a humanist and Christian civilization, and 2) whether it will be through endless concessions to the invading materialism, either pragmatic or philosophical, that the nations which are the heirs and guardians of the old humanist culture will be able to save it.

The sociological evolution of which we have previously out-lined the main stages is a consequence of the industrial revolu-tion, of the abrupt advent of an economy born of the application of scientific inventions to production, transportation, com-munications, etc. This economy itself arises from a certain concept of economic and human relations, from a general philosophy of life which is seldom formulated but which is spontaneously and generally lived. If we look at it more closely, we observe that this philosophy is in complete disaccord with the Catholic French-Canadian culture and, on three essential points, with the Protestant Anglo-Canadian culture as well.

In the foregoing pages we have defined the principal char-acteristics of the French-Canadian culture: Christian in its inspiration and of French genius – spiritual, personalist, com-munal, qualitative, centred on Man, ordered for his perfection-ing and for the full realization of his natural and supernatural vocation. We have also recalled that the Anglo-Protestant cul-ture, of the same general inspiration although of differing interpretation and genius, possesses the same essential features, except in regard to Man's relations with society. These two cultures are spiritual; the new economy is materialistic in its inspiration and in its objective. The two cultures are personalist, the new economy is scientific and technical, straining after production. The two cultures are qualitative; the new economy's only concern with this order of ideas is insofar as quality is a condition of technical efficiency. The French-Canadian culture is communal; the new economy is individualistic in principle. On this point, it meets one of the dominant features of the Anglo-Protestant culture. But it is collectivist in its ultimate results and thus tends to disassociate itself from one of the fundamental requirements of the Anglo-Protestant culture, which is personal autonomy and responsibility.

This economy should, therefore, have been assimilated, that is to say, from its very inception and at every stage of its expan-sion it should have been thought out again and modified in its characteristics, because failure to do so would upset the social order. However, it has been presented as being non-assimilable to any other philosophy than that from which it issues. Then, too, it has taken many years to realize its impact on the social order and on Man himself. Thus, it could not be assimilated, so that the second eventuality has occurred and the social order has been upset.

For those who have adopted it, the new economy has meant an extraordinary rise in living standards and in collective wealth. It has accomplished wonders. But, in order to obtain these results, it has had to work on minds. It has had to arouse everywhere a taste for material well-being, a desire for comfort, and an aspiration for prosperity and even for wealth. It has succeeded thus all the more to the extent that it has been able to satisfy the appetites it aroused. Hence its action in depth. The fundamental governing values of human life no longer have any importance by themselves but only in terms of material values. Intellectual values are directed towards production and spiritual values are only remembered insofar as they are necessary for social tranquility as a condition of economic progress. Thus the order of values has been reversed; success is acquisition of wealth; prosperity, the raising of individual and collective living standards; civilization is economic power.

Progressive though it may be, this economy has not, however, ensured the same proportional quota of well-being to every social class. It has even witnessed the spread, under its aegis, of one of the era's most disturbing social phenomena — that of the industrial proletariat. As it is founded on the extensibility of needs, and since it resorts to all the resources of propaganda to quicken such needs as exist and to create new desires, its inability to satisfy the appetites so whetted becomes, for the mass, a pretext for ever more radical demands. For public authorities who, in a democratic régime, are subjected to the votes of the people, it has provided the justification for meeting such demands.

In addition, this economy is unstable and subject to alternating acceleration, with periods of prosperity, of recession and of depression. At all times, it casts a latent threat of unemployment over the masses and thereby incites them to accentuate the radicalism of their demands. Hence arise the socializing tendencies of our era, in reaction against the economic system but in harmony with it as regards inspiration. To correct the evils due to the economy's insufficiencies, the field of state intervention is constantly being enlarged, because the state is being made responsible for the economic security and living standards of each of its subjects. But the state cannot accept any such responsibility without restricting individual initiative. It is not so much a matter of doctrinaire socialism, but of a technical socialism whose incidence on Man will, nevertheless, be exactly the same in the long run.

This economy has upset the traditional institutions of the social order. Work was the first to be affected, then property, then family, then ways of life – and now it is ideas. If well-being is the objective of living, the objective of education has become *efficiency*. The accent has to be put on those dispositions of mind and character which success, as understood in our time, requires; these include the ambition to succeed, a spirit of initiative, resourcefulness and cleverness. But forgotten and even considered detrimental are the Christian virtues of justice, charity, patience, sacrifice, etc.; the accent is laid on professional training to the detriment of culture. Thus arises conflict between education of a Christian and human inspiration as taught in families and in schools, and of the requirements of the social milieu and of the culture which is lived.

In summary, under pressure from a materialistic, technical, quantitative and collectivist economy, social institutions born of a spiritual personalist and qualitative concept have been shaken and overturned. Now, in socialism's line of development, and as one of its natural requirements, there is what is called "mass" civilization, which, insofar as it can be judged up to now, is the very antithesis of civilization because the latter, by definition, is the fruit of liberty and of the development of the individual.

Nevertheless, we can scan even further horizons. The prodigious scientific progress of the last half-century has brought about the technical conditions for world unity. Social integration, a consequence of the last half-century's economic progress, has been effected at the level of individual relations with society and is now proceeding on the level of human communities. Without a meeting of minds on the plane of permanent and universal values, it is only force which can ensure the union of peoples and the maintenance of peace. The problems thus presented transcend both the economic and political domains. The question is to know according to what idea of their own vocation men will henceforward organize their lives. But one does not pose the problem of Man's vocation without asking oneself about his relations to God. We have to choose between the Christian concept and materialism, either in its pragmatic or philosophical form. This option dominates our era and it is laid upon the conscience of Man as Man, and is not left to the sole virtuosity of state leaders.

CONCLUSIONS

In summary, and in addition to reasons of a geographical, economic and historical nature which are common to all the Canadian provinces, the Province of Quebec has special motives for preserving its autonomy:

1) having, by history, become the national focus and, by law, the fundamental milieu of French Canada, as a political unit the Province is charged with a mission without equivalent in any other province;

2) taking geography, economy and ethnic composition into account, the autonomy of the provinces generally, and that of Quebec in particular, is a condition of peace for the whole of Canada. If they were placed under the authority of a unitary or strongly centralized state, the values of language, traditions and cultures special to the two human communities of which the country is composed would, far from being causes of mutual enrichment, become causes of misunderstanding, opposition and struggles which would be harmful to the common prosperity.

What Canada needs, to relax the state of tension which the events of the last quarter of a century have provoked, is a renewal of political thought – for in many quarters there is a strong tendency either to forget the lessons of history, or else to confuse, the orders. External security is, without doubt a necessity, but internal peace and security are the primary conditions for it. Economic stability and security are, without doubt, major requirements for a system evolving towards integration at ever-increasing speed. But it rests with politics to direct the economic activity, whose objective is welfare, and to create the conditions for progress which maintain it in accordance with the requirements of good living – which is the prime objective of a society's life.

The French-Canadian case, however acute it may be, is only a modest episode in the vast drama in which all the peoples of the same cultural filiation, who are truly concerned with Man's future, are now engaged. The world of tomorrow will be materialistic or it will be humanist and Christian, according to how modern men, within the intimacy of their consciences, decide. As for French Canada, its choice is already made.

5. SOCIAL SECURITY

Earlier we brought up the great question which dominates our age, that of knowing according to which concept of Man – Christian and individualist, or materialist and socialist – society will henceforth be organized. On the political level, in facing decisions to be taken day by day, it is in connection with social security that the most immediate choice presents itself. Tomorrow's society, in its inspiration and institutional forms, will result from the solutions adopted for the different problems. Even though in its present meaning social security is a relatively new notion, most of what it means has been, at all times and in all countries, the object of social enterprises, both private and public. New policies cannot ignore the spirit of these, not underestimate their achievements. This is particularly the case in the Province of Quebec.

SOCIAL SECURITY AND CONSTITUTIONAL ORDER

We previously established the distinction between intellectual culture, regarded as knowledge, humanitarian culture, regarded as wisdom and real culture, regarded as the integration of the two preceding cultures in manners, practices, customs, traditions, laws, the established modes of collective life, and the way of living and acting. In the structure and working of the collectivity, the educational system corresponds to the first two, and the social regime to the last. Educational and social institutions, which are living expressions of culture, are both essential elements of the ethnic milieu. Of this we have said previously that it is the agency which renews and perpetuates every national community. Thus we have them closely connected as aspects of one single reality. It would be impossible to imagine a peculiar culture continuing to live and bear fruit in a social setting which was foreign to its genius. From the point of view of the Province of Quebec, social policy and culture thus raise the same problem – with this more serious difference that the majority, who are not always ready to divine it, are more easily mistaken about the deep significance of social measures than about the significance of purely cultural measures: such as language, schools, etc.

If the Province of Quebec wishes to fulfil effectively its constitutional mission as guardian of French-Canadian culture, it is obliged to conceive and organize its social life in conformity with the permanent demands of that culture. It must at all costs preserve its constitutional jurisdiction in the matter. It must also try alone to take the initiative in measures whose administration it has agreed to share with the federal government, upset as it has been by events. This must be done unless the federal government, conforming with the wish expressed above, enters definitely into the spirit of federalism, and agrees to make its own policy fit in with the fundamental demands of French-Canadian culture.

CONTEMPORARY SYSTEMS OF SOCIAL SECURITY

If the Province of Quebec wishes to fulfil effectively its constitutional mission as guardian of French-Canadian culture, it will have to develop a social policy which conforms to the fundamental demands of that culture. The reason for this is very simple: social institutions, being the sociological expression and the living form of culture, exert on it either a preserving and enriching influence, or one that alters and impoverishes, according to whether or not they are in harmony with its spirit. In order to judge the conformity or non-conformity of a measure or social system with the demands of a given culture, we must compare the concepts of life from which both arise.

At this moment of its evolution, the western world offers three principal social security systems, more or less clearly distinguished, and corresponding to the three great concepts of social order which divide thinking minds.

Liberal and Neo-liberal System

The modern economy was organized under the rule of liberalism. This considers the value of the individual as supreme and the natural mechanisms for organizing social life as superior. Thus, in practice it would not admit that any rational or authoritarian form of organization could answer needs better than nature itself. Looking from this point of view, the most effective social security must arise from the free play of individual and social solidarity.

However, as nothing human works perfectly, and as adaptations of collective life are always slow, certain individuals can experience *temporary* difficulties. The state then intervenes according to the fiscal limitations which cause the least disturbance to the operation of productive forces. But as beneficence continues to be itself harmful to productivity, the state encourages the development of *insurance plans.* Liberalism in its pure form rejects all other solutions – not through egoism, but because it believes them to be less effective, and even, in the long run, harmful to the best human interests.

However, the free direction of human institutions under the pressure of technical progress has upset the natural order and raised obstacles to its harmonious operation. These artificial obstacles must be overcome by artificial compensatory measures. Thus we have recourse to the state, which is henceforth admitted as a necessity. In spite of appearances, this attitude is typically liberal. For, in the spirit of liberalism, state intervention, in fixed circumstances and within fixed limits, is less likely to affect the forces of competition and trade than an organic effort to raise up systems of agreement and to reorganize professional classes, etc. By its definition, liberalism is opposed to corporative solutions to economic or social problems, and hostile to all forms of organization or coalition of forces.

Thus, a certain degree of state control of social security, a sort of *Welfare State,* is accepted by modern liberals, even though they reject the term. Liberals are thus in agreement with socialists over the state control of social security, but the agreement does not go further. For the Socialist State has as its goal the organized coalition of forces, which liberalism condemns both in theory and in practice.

In short, a liberal system of social security only allows state control for the correction of defects which attend the natural mechanism of distribution. It does not put under its control the free sector of insurance or assistance; it does not accept right away the general extension of State Social Security, either to all individuals or to all risks. It upholds a genuine distinction between assistance and insurance, so as to encourage individuals to turn away from assistance and to rely as much as possible on insurance.

Furthermore, social security which offers the preceding characteristics makes for the creation of a liberal state of affairs, that is to say, a form of organization which is extremely personalized up to the point of individualism and disregard for social solidarity. After underestimating the social aspect of human personality, it ends up in state control while seeking to avoid it as much as possible.

From the above picture it may be said that the first social security measures of the federal government (old age pensions, pensions to the blind, etc.) were of the liberal type.

Socialist System

This system is situated at the opposite extreme, and it is on the idea of freedom that the inversion exists. The liberal is an individual who possesses freedom as a man, and has the right to the assistance of society and the state in order to exercise his freedom to the full; the socialist is a "freed" man, that is to say, made fit by society and the state to exercise his freedom. In liberal thought, the individual is supreme, and the solutions which, within the bounds of the law, he himself brings to his own problems are the only really effective ones; in socialist thought society is supreme, and the best solutions to the problems of individuals are those which it lays down while looking towards the good of all. In liberal thought, the common good results from the initiative of individuals freely exercised within the limits of the law; in socialist thought the state is the creator of the common good, the dispenser of benefits necessary to Man for the fulfilment of his own life. In liberal thought the individual is held responsible for his own lot – security is his duty, and he has the corresponding right to the help of society; in socialist thought, society is responsible for the lot of everyone – security is a right of the citizen, and he has the corresponding duty of contributing to the initiative of the state in order to achieve it. For the liberal, security is the fruit of freedom; for the socialist, it is a condition of it, its foundation. From there come the characteristics of social security according to the socialist concept. It must be

a) *universal,* that is to say, granted to all citizens as such, without distinction of fortune, social rank, etc. It is the result of the connection which socialism establishes between security and freedom; since all citizens have a right to freedom they have, *ipso facto,* a right to the security on which it is conditional;

b) *compulsory* – Obligation is the counterpart of the right to security. It satisfies the demands of equality according to the Socialist concept. The right to stay outside the established system, that is, not to contribute to it because one refuses its benefits, is incompatible with the socialist concept of Man's relation to society. Furthermore, when the insurance formula is substituted for the assistance formula, compulsion is the administrative result of its universality: it is necessary to demand from each his contribution to a scheme which responds to the right and good of everyone;

c) *general* – The right to security as a foundation of freedom does not acknowledge the limitation of organized security to certain risks only: that would be to lessen by so much the freedom of the citizen. As for restricting organized social security merely to the needs of the citizens, there can be no question of this, since in socialist thought citizens cannot achieve freedom outside the system which it advocates. If some gain it, it is at the expense of the others. Since the need is total, the means of satisfying it must be also;

d) *distributive,* that is to say, organized so as to ensure the distribution of goods in such a way that each one may count on the essential minimum at all times and in all circumstances. This characteristic, like universality, is bound up with socialist equality, and with the fundamental obligation which is incumbent on the socialist state of providing each one with the satisfaction of his essential needs before anything else is fulfilled — because there lies the very basis of all freedom;

e) *free* — The absence of charge follows from the above-mentioned outlook. How could the citizen pay for a minimum of benefits which he does not have and which are his due? His contribution is demanded as a member of society and considering his capacity to pay at the moment when funds are collected. He will get it back at the right time according to his needs;

f) *state controlled* — Since the first function of the state is to ensure economic security, the basis of freedom, state control of social security, is the result. Liberal state control, a precautionary measure, will be as limited as possible in scope, but radical in its materialization. Socialist state control, the general form of organization, will frequently be more basic and more decentralized in the way it is carried out.

Every social security system which offers the preceding characteristics is socialist in inspiration, whatever persons and groups advocate it; merely from its existence and its operation it tends to shape minds and to bring about the development of a social organization according to the socialist concept. It is unnecessary to mention that by its fundamental materialism and its implicit totalitarianism, it is in complete contradiction to the Christian concept of Man and Society.

Looked at in this way, it may be said that the recently established social security of the federal government is clearly socialist in spirit and in form: family allowances and old age pensions, which are general and financed from taxation, etc.

System of Catholic Inspiration
The Catholic concept of social security differs essentially from the two others — even though in practice certain of its solutions

seem to identify it sometimes with the one and sometimes with the other. That is because it arises from a quite different philosophy of Man and his relations with society.

Liberalism and socialism, each in their own way, limit their view of Man in his relations with society to earthly horizons, one may say to economic horizons. Catholicism considers Man as called to an eternal destiny of which the present life is but a prelude and a preparation. All its philosophy springs from this, including its social philosophy.

On the one hand, the achievements of the temporal life – causes of worthiness or unworthiness for the eternal life, according to the spirit in which they are carried out – are essentially of a personal and individual nature. It is Man who makes his salvation, and he makes it because, as a reasonable and thus a free being, he chooses, in the intimacy of his own conscience, to act according to divine grace in each and every one of his actions. He does this by the judicious use of his faculties, and by the well-regulated exercise of his calling as a man. Thus, there is a transcendence of personal purposes – with a corresponding autonomy and responsibility.

On the other hand, society is indispensable to him, not only in the fulfilment of his temporal life but also, from the general disposition of this, in the pursuit of his eternal destiny. "Political society has the duty of leading the human being to spiritual perfection."[1] From this concept of a transcendent order which Man must achieve in his person and which society must aid him to reach, the key ideas of social philosophy draw their meaning: they are freedom and the common good. Each of them is defined in terms of the person; the first, as the faculty of choosing and of using oneself all the available means of fulfilling one's aptitudes as a man, and of reaching one's natural and supernatural purpose; the second is defined as the most widespread benefit, common to all men, and one which everyone must enjoy in order to fulfill his vocation. In short, Man himself, considered in the entirety of his being and purpose, is the all-important basis of the social order.

A Catholic-inspired system of social security is thus a specific application of the Catholic concept of the social order. It arises from the same general principles:

1) The first initiative and responsibility comes from the individual. This is on the ground of the connection which the Catholic concept establishes between the accomplishments of

the temporal life and the fulfilment of the calling of Man –
both natural and supernatural. The duty of each one is to provide for his own subsistence, and for his own protection against
the various eventualities of life. Thus his duty is to work, save
and use forethought. To this duty there corresponds for every
man the right to demand, in the name of the common good,
that society afford him access to work, and the chance to save
and make provision. Thus there should be placed at his disposal
the means of carrying on his business in reasonable conditions
of security and benefitting from them. Lastly, he should be able
to organize his protection.

2) **Principle of "subsidiarity."** The Catholic philosophy regards society as a complete organism into which Man is placed
through the medium of institutions, groups and communities
which he creates himself through a natural need; these include
families and various asociations which contribute to the fulfilment of the common good, each according to its own purpose.
The role of the state is not to take the place of these natural
groupings, but to help them to achieve their purpose.

From the point of view of social security, Man's duty is thus
to create for himself organizations which will ensure the full
effectiveness of his action; trade unions and various associations
in the realm of work, and mutual benefit societies in that of
providence. On its side, the state must encourage the development and good operation of these organizations, and must
arrange them and co-ordinate their functions. It must assume
direct responsibility only when it is sure that all the intermediate groups are fulfilling their role completely.

3) Finally, the suppletory principle. This principle is derived
from the preceding one. The state is not the creator of the
common good; it is its guardian. It alone is not the whole of
society; it is the first of the various societies that Man creates
according to his needs, on his own initiative. It does not replace
private, personal or organized initiative; it stimulates, surrounds and controls it, co-ordinates its movements, and, where
necessary, takes its place more or less completely. It employs
direct action only in the case where individuals and groups
suffer from an insufficiency, which cannot be remedied. Its rule
is justice, that is to say, the continual search for a group of
conditions that enable each person on his own, or with the aid
of those like him, or, if circumstances demand it, with the
direct help of the state, to acquire the benefits necessary for the

fulfilment of his life. It cannot allow anyone, through a defect of social organization, to be thwarted in his life and lessened in his person.

Social security, according to the Catholic concept, has no practical rules going along with the theory. Following the demands of the common good, the state takes no action if private, personal or organized initiative answers the needs.

TRENDS OF SOCIAL SECURITY IN CANADA

With the progress of the idea of social insurance and public pensions, the Anglo-Protestant provinces began to make their way towards the institutionalizing of public charity. The Province of Quebec already possessed at that moment a system of private organizations, the equivalent of which the other provinces did not have. It was, in fact, more advanced and did not have the same needs. It met new situations by creating new institutions subsidized by the state.

In 1921, with the Public Charities Act, the Province began to turn towards a form of assistance which was clearly of Liberal inspiration. For the first time the word "Public" Assistance was written in the laws. Industrialization had profoundly altered its sociological set-up. In an urbanized and proletarian environment it had spread Anglo-Saxon influence far and wide. After 1921, and with the 1930 crisis, which overran the limits of subsidized charity as it was then organized, evolution towards the Liberal concept took place more rapidly.

In the Anglo-Protestant provinces, during the same period, the evolution towards a growing extension of state assistance continued. There was still hesitation as regards the socialist trend of social security: minds turned more towards the establishment of public charity (i.e. pensions). However, with the entry into the country of large numbers of immigrants, socialism began to spread its ideas. Political groups were formed which found their way into the electoral mechanism, and though without any hope of immediate success, they served as an excellent form of propaganda. "Intellectuals" with socialist leanings infiltrated into the universities and even into the Civil Service. In 1940 the federal government passed its first social insurance law: i.e. unemployment insurance. In 1943 appeared the Marsh Report, the Canadian version of the Beveridge Report. As a result of that came federal state-controlled family allowances, old age pensions, which are contributory, general and state-controlled, as well as state-controlled pensions for the disabled. There also came constant pressure in favour of a state-controlled health plan. Two provinces, under the direct influence of socialism, have already put such a plan into operation.

The general trend of the recent legislation of certain provinces and of the federal government thus marks the evolution of Anglo-Canadian thought towards socialism, at least in the usual manner of the Anglo-Saxon character, towards the socialist practice of social security without adhering to the corresponding theory. Universal, obligatory and general measures, the distributive nature of grants, and financing by means of taxation leave no doubt on this subject. The sole trace of liberalism which persists is the absolute state centralizion, which is applied in all spheres. While experiencing in part the effect of federal legislation, the Province of Quebec remains at heart faithful to its Catholic-inspired social traditions. In fact, the two systems are the expressions of sharply different and incompatible philosophical concepts. Social institutions exercise a transforming influence on the cultural environment where these are developed, tending to identify it with the spirit from which they themselves arise. If the Province of Quebec rejects socialism as a social doctrine, it must keep away from institutions which take their inspiration from it, and it must also take care to give itself a social security system consistent with its religious convictions, culture and the social tradition of its population.

Cleverly prepared socialist propaganda throughout the world has ended by identifying social security in the minds of the masses with its institutional and state-controlled forms. This, however, is an ideological and political position which the intrinsic demand of social security in no way postulates. In fact, it is quite possible to conceive and organize a social security system which will be very effective and totally different in manner from the liberal and socialist systems. Otherwise, it would have to be admitted that, since liberalism itself is outmoded, socialist solutions to the social problems of modern times are unavoidable – that henceforth any really free society is unimaginable, and that to enjoy economic security, Man will have to give his personality into the hands of a state, which is sole judge and master both of the material and spiritual welfare of the citizen.

The moment has come for the Province to define its position

clearly. Two attitudes are possible, on the political and constitutional level on the one hand, and on the ideological and
social level on the other – one involves the other:

1) To let the evolution of the last thirty years follow its
course; in other words, leave the initiative for large-scale social
security measures to the federal government, which is sympathetic to the idea of a *Welfare State*. The federal government
enacts its law at a time which it considers opportune, prescribes
its form and spirit, decides its own share of the financial burden,
and leaves the rest to the provinces, who fall into line and pay
their share from their current income.

The provinces have the theoretical right to refuse to participate. However, if any of them adopts this attitude, it takes
away the advantages of the federal measure from a population
which in any case has to pay for the provinces which derive
benefit from it. They can also support the system, then declare
that they have not sufficient income to carry out their responsibilities, and bring pressure to bear on the federal government
to take over the entire burden of social legislation. This, in a
few words, is the history of constitutional-fiscal relations of the
last ten or fifteen years.

The consequences of such a policy which would come sooner
or later – if Quebec decided to adopt it definitely – are easy to
foresee. In less than a generation, probably, its social system, in
its main lines and general inspiration, will be integrated with
that of the rest of Canada. Provincial autonomy will at one
and the same time have lost one of its pillars and one of its
chief justifications. For, if the Province of Quebec has its own
religious convictions and culture, psychologically speaking it is
not made differently from the rest of humanity. If politics
impose upon it a way of life which is out of harmony with its
culture and social tradition, the Province will end by thinking
in the same way as it is made to live. It will ask for the disappearance, in law, of the differences which social institutions
no longer allow in fact, and the meaning of which it will itself
have lost. Already signs can be seen of such a turn of mind.
In many circles, particularly the working class, when social
security is spoken of it is in terms of federal laws. That may be
explained, thanks to the method of distributing family allowances to all mothers of children and pensions to all persons,
regardless of means.

All this marks the influence which social laws of federal
origin have already had on thought, and indicates in what

direction it is proceeding. If the Province persists in its policy of the last thirty years, we must not be surprised if, on its side, public opinion allows itself to be won over to the idea of the complete centralization of social legislation at Ottawa. As far as the assimilation of French Canada is concerned, thirty years of social history will thus have had more effect than a century and a half of political history.

2) To administer its own social jurisdiction alone and to utilize its fiscal powers to this end. On the purely constitutional level, this attitude would raise no problem, if it could obtain from the federal government the assurance that it would keep to its own jurisdiction. But, because of the attitude of the rest of the country, very serious political and fiscal problems arise, which can only be settled in conformity with the constitutional rights and demands of French-Canadian culture, if the government of the Province can rely upon a public opinion which is enlighted and well aware of the importance of what is at stake.

The liberal concept of the social order has long been out of date, outmoded, and impracticable as such, not only in the sphere of social security, but in economic and social relations as a whole. Thus, for the Province of Quebec the only possible choice lies between a state-controlled socialist system of social security and one of Christian inspiration. The choice of state control and socialism would mean that henceforth the Provincial Government would have to create, administer, and finance by means of taxation the social services which the development of the social and economic situation impose. This choice would mean that the government would have to organize a Provincial *Welfare State*. From the constitutional point of view, it has the right and the power to do so. From the social and cultural point of view, such a choice would clearly bring the same results as the present system. For what gives sense and value to provincial autonomy is not that a certain function should be carried out by the Provincial Government but that it should be carried out in a certain spirit.

A social policy of Christian inspiration, in accordance with traditional forms, is thus the only one which justifies Quebec in demanding respect for its autonomy, and at the same time meets its legal prerogatives and its fiscal and financial capacities. On the other hand, its legal prerogatives and fiscal and financial capacities, as defined by the Constitution, are wide enough to allow the Province to construct a social security system of a technical standard as high as that of any country of socialist theory or practice. Its human quality would be far superior; for, over and above administrative techniques and rules, this system brings together the man who gives and the man who receives. This can be achieved, it must be re-stated, provided that its initiative is not halted by a federal fiscal policy which exhausts all sources of revenue.

ADJUSTMENT AND ORIENTATION

It is obviously not for us to lay out a detailed programme of social security for the Province – the most we can do is to indicate its principal lines. We recommend the reading of it to anyone who wishes to have an idea of what a system of social security, founded on the traditional ideas of a Catholic population, would involve in practice.

This system would be embodied in an organized code of laws giving form and direction to the three great branches of individual and community activity found in every organized society: work, provision for eventualities, and assistance. While guaranteeing the individual the security he needs, it would tend to make this very security the first fruit of personal initiative practised freely and voluntarily. Thus it would aim to form Man and to encourage his improvement while at the same time seeking to improve his material living conditions. For, let us remember that every civilization is first of all a certain quality of Man; there is no real progress even of a material nature, no civilization in the strict sense of the word, unless the functioning of community life tends of itself to improve Man, by urging him constantly to use his particular talents to the full.

The first sort of social security demanded by modern Man is security of employment, occupation and earnings – three aspects of a single aspiration which is bound to the law of work itself. This latter has far more significance than those who look upon restricted horizons generally understand. It is not only a condition of subsistence and material progress, but it is also a condition of the full realization of Man himself.

By security of employment, we mean an economic state such that every man, conscious of his responsibilities, has the assurance that he can in all circumstances be usefully employed, and thus make provision himself for his daily subsistence and that of his family. Such a concept of security demands that the state, the guardian of the common good, should utilize to the full all the means at its disposal in order to stimulate individual and community enterprise in the setting of an economy regulated for the good of all.

Security of occupation is the great preoccupation of the industrial worker and the salaried worker. It refers to the legal position of the employee in the establishment, and to the system of work, that is, to the collection of laws governing labour and of varied organizations which are developed in their settings. On the other hand, the stability of the employee in the business presupposes the stability of the business itself. It is once again the whole economic policy which is involved.

Economic policy comes, in second place, from a certain concept of the social order. If left merely to the interplay of natural forces, in accordance with the Liberal concept, the economy tends to become concentrated in the hands of a certain number of key enterprises, and geographically speaking, in the most favoured regions. There are two alternatives: either the state takes over direction and establishes a socialist type of economy, with all social and human consequences of such a choice; or it organizes the direction, first of all ensuring the collaboration of the forces of production, both employers and employees. It is the Christian concept of the economic order which demands the intervention of the state, but above all in order to encourage and co-ordinate all private enterprises, and to regulate them for the common good. Such a combination of private forces and public authorities can, without turning into state authoritarianism, and by controlling its natural mechanisms, ensure the maximum efficiency and stability to a given economy. From the point of view which we are considering here, that of security of employment and occupation, it is the first condition to be fulfilled. The rest is a matter of adaptation and of arrangement of the social and legal system of labour; these are easier to fulfil inasmuch as those who benefit from them are already accustomed to generous collaboration on the level of higher interests of state and society.

Finally, there is security of earnings. Even in the best regulated economy ups and downs have to be foreseen and thus the demand for labour fluctuates. For the independent worker, security of earnings means protection against a fall in prices; for the wage earner, compensation in case of loss of wages.

Taken as a whole, security of employment, occupation and earnings involves the struggle against every fall and wrong direction of production; thus it is an economic policy which comes from a knowledge, kept continually up to date, of all the movements of economic life at home and abroad. The time has long since passed when the economy could be left to the spontaneity of private enterprise, left to its own impetus; however, the assumption by the state alone of the general direction of the economy leads inevitably to some form or other of totalitarianism, incompatible with the basic demands of the social order and of the dignity of Man. Between the two, the only choice, at the same time favourable to prosperity as our age understands it and to the full flowering of human values, is that of the collaboration of political and social forces within the limits of the law.

The second form of security demanded by modern Man is protection against the risks inherent in existence itself: old age, sickness, disability, death, etc. At the time when independent work was the usual pattern, and every family was an economic unit, this form of security was spontaneously assured by natural family, professional, or parochial solidarity. Today subordinate work is the usual pattern; since the lot of each person is henceforth bound up with a social structure, the movement of which is out of the hands of personal control, the family is no longer a haven of protection for its own members; it must make provision for their security by means which society alone can put as its disposal. After which fashion? Here again appears the choice of which we have spoken many times.

According to the Christian concept, the first initiative and responsibility for his own protection belong to the individual himself, acting on his own or by means of natural groups: the family, mutual benefit societies and various associations. The state must ensure that all is arranged in such a way that private, personal or organized initiative can act as completely as possible in this sphere as in others. The state must intervene directly only in those cases when the latter is powerless.

From the point of view which concerns us at the moment, the general spread of insurance must be one of the main objectives of social policy; not, however, as in the liberal system, merely at the pleasure of insurers and at their initiative, but according to a general plan which aims to adapt insurance to social ends, and thus to cover the ordinary risks of human existence, on terms accessible to the mass of individuals and families. The task is to work out an insurance programme covering, by the appropriate means, the ordinary risks of human existence in an industrialized society; this programme must be achieved through the means of private, commercial or mutual societies, at terms which can be met by the savings of the ordinary person; the government itself can, in certain well defined cases, pay a certain subsidy into the fund. There is no question of organizing assistance under the pretence of insurance in accordance with the Socialist formula, but of really placing insurance within the reach of all those who can and wish to protect themselves.

In certain circles it is claimed that the lower classes, and particularly the working class, do not want, or no longer want, insurance, and that they feel that they alone are bearing the burden of it and are thus affected in their living conditions. If such a state of mind exists – and it assuredly does in certain circles – we must see in it, on the one hand, a reaction against the disorganizing state of affairs which sprang from the Liberal, individualistic concept of earlier times. On the other hand, we must see in it the result of the propaganda which in all parts of the world is endeavouring to secure the triumph of state-controlled and socialistic forms or social security. If we wish to secure the acceptance of different forms of security, based on personal initiative and responsibility fitted into a system which is at the same time considerate of all needs and respectful of all freedom, we shall have to counteract adverse propaganda, and bring about the systematic education or re-education of the public.

Taken on the whole, the social security system of the Province, as opposed to the liberal concept, thus admits and would admit habitual and constant intervention by the state, but intervention for organization and regulation. As opposed to the socialist concept, it is aiming at, and would aim at, reducing state action to a minimum. On the contrary, it endeavours to encourage personal initiative to the full, and to arouse, urge and induce organized forms of social action to give of their best, as well as co-ordinating their movements.

The laws in which would be embodied a complete system of social security, in accordance with the ideas outlined above, already exist for the most part. They have been worked out over the years and interpreted by circumstances, and the movement of ideas. They form today a comprehensive and very varied collection, which, as is quite evident, differs totally from the system of corresponding laws in the other provinces. However, in it, particularly because of federal intervention, divergent trends may be traced, whose doctrinal inspiration, often uncertain, does not always appear to be in harmony with the spirit from which the whole system has come in the course of history. Thus it may be necessary to re-unify the whole, both as regards ideas and structure, and to take advantage of the opportunity to specify the ideological, constitutional, political and administrative position of the Province, both in itself and in relation to the federal government and the other provinces.

PART TWO:
FEDERALISM

6. THE GENERAL THEORY OF FEDERALISM

The question of federalism lies today at the very heart of the conflict which places Ottawa and Quebec in opposition. If Canada had been a state of unitary form or, if Quebec had willingly agreed to disappear as an autonomous political body, no such conflict would have been possible. The question is of all the more present interest and acquires all the more importance since both sides, in order to justify the political attitudes they have adopted, lay claim to federalism; one party in the name of the traditional concept thereof, while the other invokes a "new" concept, or, rather, what they themselves call a "new federalism." In any case, whether one wishes to maintain it wholly, to give it a new form, or even work secretly to destroy it, federalism is under inquiry and constitutes one of the very first questions on which we must, in this inquiry, state our position.

In the concrete and most general sense, federalism, as the word's etymology makes clear, means a regime of association as opposed to a single regime. Since the term was first applied to the system of association between states, it took on a political and juridical significance which today remains closely attached to it. Little by little, however, the possibilities of federalism became known and it was discovered that there was advantage, not only for states but also for social groups within the states, to practice the system of association. As a result of further sociological studies it was finally agreed that federalism was not only a political and juridical fact but also a social fact and that there was even inter-dependence between these facts. Thus a doctrine of federalism was evolved which offers it as a system for the general organization of society.

The Special Nature Of The Federative System

At the origin of most unions between public groups or states, two more or less contrary tendencies manifest themselves; the tendency towards unity or towards the disappearance of previously existent political bodies and the tendency towards pluralism or towards the maintenance of these pre-existent public bodies' independence. At the moment of negotiations for union, three situations may present themselves; either the tendency to pluralism takes the ascendant, in which case an alliance, league, or, at best, a confederation is formed in which each party keeps its integral independence and satisfies itself with executing jointly reached decisions; or the tendency towards unity completely carries the day, and, in that event, there results therefrom a state of unitary design, possessing only a single supreme centre of government for all the populations of the new territory; or, finally, the two tendencies are reciprocally balanced, one and the other being equally strong and seeking to prevail without, however, being able to dominate. Then the solution, if recourse to violence and a definite rupture is not desired, is a compromise which, while giving satisfaction to the parties on essentials, none the less calls for serious sacrifices from each.[1]

In what does this solution actually consist? Primarily in this, that there is admitted and established within the new state two orders of government which are equal and co-ordinated, one of them represented by a central government charged with the general interests of the new collectivity and the other formed by the regional governments whose mission it is to watch over

---

[1] Dicey analyses at length the conditions requisite for the establishment of the federative state. The inhabitants of the country concerned, he notes, must hold a particular sentiment in common: "They must desire union, and must not desire unity. If there be no desire to unite, there is clearly no basis for federalism . . . If, on the other hand, there be a desire for unity, the wish will naturally find its satisfaction, not under a federal, but under a unitarian constitution . . . The sentiment therefore which creates a federal state is the prevalence throughout the citizens of more or less allied countries of two feelings which are to a certain extent inconsistent—the desire for national unity and the determination to maintain the independence of each man's separate state. The aim of federalism is to give effect as far as possible to both these sentiments". (A. V. Dicey: *The Law of the Constitution*, pp. 141-143).

For his part, K. C. Wheare, after having undertaken a similar analysis concludes it in these terms: "It would seem that federal government is appropriate for a group of states or communities if, at one and the same time, they desire to be united under a single independent general government for some purposes and to be organized under independent regional governments for others. Or, to put it shortly, they must desire to be united, but not be unitary'. (*Federal Government*, p. 36).

the particular and special interests of the original political communities. Therein lies the prime and distinctive feature of the federative system. Since this feature is to be found in all federative systems established on the model of the United States, it has been concluded that therein lies the essential feature of federalism, and there has been drawn from it a general principle which has been specifically called the federative principle.

Concerning this principle, there are several definitions. In brief, the federative principle requires the distribution of governmental powers between political units which are, at one and the same time, inter-connected and also independent of each other. It is no doubt important that the two orders of government should be able to act directly on the people but it is even more important that each should be limited to its sphere and, within that sphere, should enjoy independence with respect to the other.

Thus, in our turn, we may define the federative system properly so-called as being the system of association between states in which the exercise of state power is shared between two orders of government, co-ordinate but not subordinate one to the other, each enjoying supreme power within the sphere of activity assigned to it by the Constitution.

Essential Characteristics Of The Federative System

From the general principle we have just recalled there emerge three main characteristics which clearly mark the federative system and distinguish it from the unitary system. These are the distribution of power, the supremacy of the constitution and the authority of the courts as interpreters of the constitution; and all these characteristics, with greater or lesser modifications, are to be found in every truly federative state.

THE DISTRIBUTION OF POWERS

Whereas, in a unitary system, all powers of the state are concentrated in a single supreme centre of government whose legislative powers are without limit and with all other branches of government subordinated to it; in a federative system there is necessarily a distribution of powers and limitation of these powers through the very fact that they are divided between a general authority and regional authoriities, each master of its own house, but within a well-defined field. As Dicey says, the federative system not only involves distribution but definition and limitation of the powers of government which is not met with in a unitary system:

> The object for which a federal state is formed involves a division of authority between the national government and the separate States. The powers given to the nation form in effect so many limitations upon the authority of the separate states, and as it is not intended that the central government should have the opportunity of encroaching upon the rights retained by the States, its sphere of action necessarily becomes the object of rigorous definition . . . The tendency of federalism to limit on every side the action of government and to split up the strength of the state among co-ordinate and independent authorities is especially noticeable, because it forms the essential distinction between a federal system such as that of America or Switzerland, and a unitarian system of government such as that which exists in England or Russia . . .

All this is clear and enables us to better understand the scope of the federative principle. It may be noted in passing that this principle, if strictly applied, requires the two orders of government to be independent of each other, even in the economic, financial and fiscal domain. Hence the necessity of ensuring, in the division of powers, a practical basis for this independence. For it is not sufficient, in fact, to establish a central government and regional governments; to each of them must be given the means of living and of living in independence, otherwise the federative system itself will not long exist.[2]

[2] "It is not enough that the general government should be able to finance itself; it is essential also that the regional governments should be able to do likewise . . . If a general government is to be established and supported – and that is the first assumption of any union, federal or non-federal – will there be sufficient resources also to support independent regional governments? If there are not, then no matter how a federal constitution is drawn up, in practice federal government will not be possible. Soon the regional governments will be unable to perform their functions or they will be able to perform them only at the price of financial dependence upon the general government, that is, at the price of financial unification". (*K. C. Wheare: Federal Government,* p. 53).

Professor Wheare explains this requirement of the federative principle:

> Now if this principle is to operate not merely as a matter of strict law but also in practice, it follows that both general and regional governments must each have under its own independent control financial resources sufficient to perform its exclusive functions. Each must be financially co-ordinate with the other . . .
>
> Grants, if they are to rank as independent sources of revenue, must not depend, of course, upon the good will of the contributing government. They must be obligatory contributions about which the contributing government has no discretion . . .

THE SUPREMACY OF THE CONSTITUTION

The second characteristic of the federal system, which, though less evident on a first view, is no less important than the distribution of powers, is the supremacy of the constitution. Here we are confronted by the system's master instrument: it is the constitution, and the constitution alone, which assures the juridical foundation of the state and guarantees its federative form. It is thus what one is pleased to call "the supreme law of the land" — that which takes pre-eminence over all other laws and to which reference must be made to decide the validity of the legislative acts performed by each of the two orders of government.

From this essential characteristic of federalism, Dicey draws three conclusions. The first is that the constitution must be a written one. The second is that it must be rigid and not easily modified. It is the system's fundamental law and there must always be a serious reason for touching it. In any case, neither of the two orders of government should have the right to modify the constitution by themselves, at least insofar as the distribution of powers and the status of each is concerned. The best method, especially if it is desired to ensure permanence for the federative character, is to associate the two, and even the people, in this process of revision.

The third and final conclusion regarding the consequences of the constitution is that every legislative assembly in a federal system, whether in the central or regional governments, is a body subordinated to the constitution; and, as a consequence, its laws are valid or invalid to the extent that they are situated within or outside the authority which the constituion precisely confers upon it.

AUTHORITY OF THE COURTS

A third essential characteristic of the federal system is the authority of the courts as guardians and interpreters of the constitution. For it does not in fact, suffice to proclaim the constitution supreme; means must also be provided to have it respected by everyone, beginning with the governments themselves, and to have its true meaning interpreted in case of conflict. Since this role requires an impartial arbitrator outside of and independent of politics, it is natural and normal that recourse should be had to the courts and that what has been called jurisdictional control should be instituted.

What especially interests us here is not so much the role as the formation or, if one prefers, the juridical status of the Supreme Court. Therein resides a requirement of the federal system that neither of the two orders of government may, to the exclusion of the other, touch the distribution of powers, once the latter have been fixed in and by the constitution. It follows that neither of them is fit to decide by itself, the quarrels which may arise on this point. Hence the necessity of having recourse to an outside tribunal.

In a federal system, theory and common sense alike demand that a tribunal completely independent of the parties to the suit shall decide, in final resort, quarrels concerning the division of powers. And if this requirement proves either too difficult to meet or contrary to national susceptibilities, at least appointments to the Supreme Court must not be the exclusive appanage of one of the two orders of government.

Born of a compromise between two contrary tendencies and founded on a delicate and meticulous equilibrium between two orders of government, the federal system can only function badly and will grate painfully when one of the governments shuns all compromise or strives to tip the scales in its favour.

Taking a wider view, we would even say that federalism, as a political and juridical system, will be able to maintain itself and give satisfaction only on the condition that it spreads its roots into the life of the society itself and there encounters sociological and even philosophic bases on which it can firmly stay itself. In other words, the veritable spirit of federalism must be sought far deeper than in political and juridical structures. That is why we must here deal with the second aspect of federalism, that is to say with that more sociological and philosophic aspect under which it presents itself as a general system of social organization.

7. FEDERALISM AS A SYSTEM OF SOCIAL ORGANIZATION

We are now approaching the heart of the question. For it must be carefully noted that, if debate in the constitutional realm has, in recent times, assumed such gravity, it is only because it reflected and translated a much deeper conflict in the ideological field. Thus it would be a proof of naivety, while cherishing a dangerous illusion, to pretend that the first can be settled without taking the second into account.

Moreover, juridical technique alone is powerless to resolve a conflict of ideas in effective and definitive fashion. For the real question which currently presents itself concerns the philosophy of man and society. What kind of man and what kind of society do we want? What kind of civilization do we claim to be building? On the answers we make, in practice, to these questions in our daily life depends the fate of our political system because, as we shall presently see, federalism implies a certain concept of Man and Society and it can only expand and maintain itself where this concept flourishes.

What then, after all, is federalism? We have said it is the system of association as opposed to the system of singleness; it obtrudes itself each time we desire neither unity, destructive of individualities, nor independence, destructive of unity. It is thus a general formula, effective not only between states but in all fields of social life. Thus considered, it appears as a system which, in simultaneous reaction against unitarianism and individualism, proclaims association between individuals and between social groups as a central organizing principle of society.[1]

---

[1] One of the Swiss authors who has best grasped the veritable spirit and character of federalism, writes, in this connection: [Trans.] "How can federalism be defined? Every federation is, first of all, an association. Association, therefore, is the first principle of federalism. This principle possesses a value and a force which goes beyond this political federation between small states, and between cities, to become a concept of social life and, in consequence, of man himself.

This concept finds practical expression thus: wherever the intervention of the state does not obtrude itself as absolutely necessary, substitute for the system of statism that of associa-

Philosophic and Sociological Bases

By this phrase we mean the deep-seated foundations on which the whole system normally rests and from which it draws the best of its spirit. These bases are four in number: the Christian concept of man and of society, the fact of social life's variety and complexity, the idea of a common good and the principle of the subsidiary function of every community. On each of these, long explanations might be given, but we shall content ourselves with the essentials.[2]

The Christian Concept of Man and of Society

At the base of the federalist doctrine one encounters a concept of man and of society which, in its principal features, draws its inspiration from the great Christian principles upon which our western civilization has been built.[3] According to this concept, man is above all a spiritiual being, intelligent and free, endowed with an immortal soul; in short, a person and, as such, exceeding in value all the material universe while having charge and responsibility for his own destiny.

---

tion. Federalism is a social principle. It is a social principle before being a political principle. To protect, harmonize and develop social life – such is its raison d'être and such is its purpose." (Gonzague de Reynold, *Conscience de la Suisse,* pp. 106, 110).

[2] [Trans.] "It by no means suffices that we understand by federalism a political form, a system of government; the principles by which it roots itself in human life must also be disengaged. For principles are not abstractions but roots; they are in no wise *above* life but they are in life as roots are in the soil; they do not in the least integrate themselves in life from the top downwards, by the force of laws and constitutions, but it is life which receives from them the sap without which it could not flourish in its integrity." Gonzague de Reynold, *Conscience de la Suisse,* p. 105).

[3] The *social* federalism whose theory is here explained is wider than the political federalism previously described. It may be found realized and, indeed is met with in countries and in states which have nothing *politically* federative in their structures. On the other hand it does not always exist in states which officially call themselves federative. In definitive, what counts is not so much the external appearance as the spirit which animates a system.

Made in the image of God, he has for his mission to mark the earth and society, in turn, with his own image: that is to say, to humanize them by introducing and making to reign therein the values which constitute his own greatness and dignity, namely, the values of the spirit. Being a person, man can neither serve as an instrument nor a means to anyone or anything whatever, and must cause to be unfolded within himself the life of the spirit in all its forms and must develop himself in the fellowship and love of his fellow-beings.

From this it follows that society itself must be regulated for him and must be organized in such fashion that he may develop as a person, that is to say, spiritually and morally. To that end, the forces of his spirit and the dynamism of his liberty must be able to come into play so that he may participate actively in the social organization, of which, in short, he must be the artisan and not the slave.

This evidently supposes that society itself will treat him as a man and will assist him in the stern apprenticeship of his freedom, educating him with a view to obtaining his free collaboration in the common good. Here the aim is not so much to manage man as to teach him to manage himself by assuming his own initiatives and responsibilities, for, according to a saying of Nicolas Berdiaeff, "freedom is difficult and it is slavery which is easy."

It is on such a concept that federalism is founded. The men it needs are neither slaves nor amorphous beings, without personal life, but rather persons, that is to say, social beings, capable of initiative, decision and responsibility, able not only to construct society in their own image but also to retain the mastery thereof and to prevent it, once organized, from becoming a monster which devours them.

Federalism also desires to conserve for society its human character, so that it may truly be a society of persons and consequently sensitive to the play of spiritual forces and moral values, and not exclusively dominated, as are the animal societies, by regard for material welfare and by the instinct of the species' survival.

Some may say this explanation is scarcely "scientific." To those we are content to note, along with the great English historian Arnold Toynbee, that science alone is impotent to resolve our present problems, because they are moral problems and science is amoral. Nor should we forget the spectacle which communist and totalitarian states offer us today; the more "scientific" pretentions such systems may advance, the more is human personality crushed.

The Variety and Complexity of Social Life

One of the great merits of federalism is, moreover, that it shuns abstraction and pure ideology. Its conception of man is immediately associated with the natural and multiform facts of human sociability, of social life's complexity and variety; and it is the recognition and acceptance of such facts that it sets, in the second place, at the base of its programme of social organization.

Answering the pressing invitations of his own nature, man does in effect enter into relations with his fellow beings and progressively founds a host of groups, assocaitions, communities and societies which extend from the family to international society. There is a law of his very being which impels him to insert himself into multiple groupings of which, however, none, and not even the state, exhausts the social needs and possibilities of his nature. The more civilization develops and becomes refined, the more do social affinities multiply, by that fact increasing the number of groupings and institutions.

That is a truth of experience, noted by all the great social observers since Aristotle, for whom man was "by nature a political animal," to Harold J. Laski, who defined him as "a community-building animal." Human society thus definitely appears as an immense network made up of a multitude of diverse associations, each of them encompassing man in a certain aspect as, for example, as a father or as a worker, as a sportsman, a believer, and so on.

There are certain systems, for instance the totalitarian system, which take umbrage at such richness and cannot endure such complexity. Thus they endeavour to suppress one and the other by reducing, first of all, social life to the individual's relations to the state and by absorbing it thereafter in political life. In other terms, statism erected into a system seeks to reduce everything to the unity of simplicity and seeks to "politicize" everything so that man himself may be more effectively controlled and subjected.

As for federalism, it stems from social life as it exists and admits it in all its variety and complexity. Its purpose is not to enslave but to co-ordinate; it does not seek to unify but to unite. Nothing is more foreign to it than abstract simplifications and oppressive unifications. It does not intend to sacrifice, by organizing it, any human portion but it seeks to conserve for social life its freedom and vitality. Because it rests entirely on the principle of association, and because it sees society as a vast network of associations, it can only oppose any single dictatorship, even that of the state, and it can only claim for the various groups the right to expand while putting a pluralism respectful of man and of life at the base of its social organization.

The Idea of the Common Good

Respecting, as it does, both man and life, federalism manifests a similar respect when it then proposes the idea of the common good as the organizational idea of social life.[4] According to it, not only does the common good constitute every society's objective but it should be conceived in the very image of social life, that is to say, as varied and complex as is that life itself.

Whatever society he may found, whether it be family, union, state, etc., man is always drawn thereto by the lure of a benefit, either real or apparent. It is this good, sought in common, which unites wills, determines society's ends and imposes obligations on each of its members.[5]

But no matter how grand or how complete it may be, no good sought in common by men can in itself suffice to exhaust the social activities of human nature. In other words, there is not just one common good, but many; the common good of humanity carries within itself many different aspects.

We have already seen that man, while exercising his social activity, quite naturally founds a series of communities or societies, each of them embracing his common good and each, in consequence, claiming a part of man's activities and reciprocally providing man with a social milieu for the nourishment of his social life. The common good, then, must not be considered as a given monolithic block, completed at one stroke,

---

[4] [Trans.] "There is philosophy of federalism. Federalism has sense, value and solidity only if it remains attached to this philosophy like the lustre to a ring. But what ring? The Christian concept of man and, consequently, of human life." (Gonzague de Reynold, *Conscience de la Suisse,* p. 114).

[5] On this role of the common good, see J. Messnes' *Social Ethics,* Book I, Part *III,* No. 46: "The Ordering Power: The Principle of the Common Good" (St. Louis and London) pp. 194-196.

but rather as a whole, organized in concentric circles around the human personality and reaching from the family to international society, while realizing itself by degrees, by stages and by levels.

The totalitarian state holds a definitely monistic concept of the common good and it seeks to realize it solely through the state's acivity. It thus tends to absorb the more particular "common goods," like those of families, professional associations, cities, provinces, etc., with the result that, little by little, these groups lose their personal life and become cogs in a vast administrative mechanism.

As for federalism, on the contrary, each community and each society has its own common good which is the source of its rights and of its duties. Instead of making everything depend on the will of the state alone, it wants to make everything flow from the search for the common good pursued by each group; which is to say, that it founds right, not solely on the state, but on the social requirements of human nature itself.

Here is how a Swiss expert, who appeared before our Commission, describes this central idea of federalism:

[Trans.] Each group personifies its own common good . . . Every society which incarnates the common good is vested with special rights. To the extent it personifies this common good, each community has the right, drawn from itself by reason of its own patricular purpose, to provide itself with the rules and institutions which realization of this purpose requires. To the extent that it ensures service of that common good which is its own, it has the right to demand that this right be recognized to it and that it be respected by all other communities. Its particular right (as are all individual rights) is opposable to all. In place of considering that the state . . . alone has the right to rationally determine the principles of the common good . . . every community which has under its care a portion of the common good is recognized as having the right to promulgate such rules . . .

The state's role and task are in no whit affected or diminished by reason of the existence, in its midst, of local or regional communities, each, for its part, assuming a portion of the common good, any more than its properly understood external sovereignty is affected or diminished through the existence of a more or less universal international community to which is also assigned the care of one aspect of the common good, of the universal good.[6]

If federalism insists on this idea of the common good, after having insisted on the diversity and complexity of social life, it is because it is convinced that both one and the other are necessary to man's free development and because it believes, with Jacques Maritain, that "the development of the human person normally requires a plurality of autonomous communities, having their own rights, their own freedoms and their own authorities."[7] Through the medium of these basic communities there is, in fact, created a whole zone of private law, withdrawn from the observation and reach of the state and within which the concrete freedoms of the person may come into play and flourish. Hence the importance of a pluralist concept of the common good.[8]

The Principle of the Subsidiary Function of all Collectivities

To complete its basic doctrine, federalism finally puts forward an organizational principle which tends to decide between activities and responsibilities in the functioning of social life. This principle might, in a general way, be enunciated as follows: with respect to individuals and lower groups, every collectivity must be satisfied to exercise a suppletory and subsidiary function, abstaining, consequently, from doing in their stead what they are able to do for themselves.

Such a principle is only the logical complement of the three other bases we have just described. In any case, it flows from the Christian concept of man and of social life. Every man, in

---

[6] [Trans.] "The idea of the common good is at the basis of all social life and not only of political life. Every society pursues a good common to its members; that is a fundamental assertion of sociology. And so it is with the family as with economic or professional groups." (J. T. Delos, O.P. "La fin propre de la politique; le Bien commun temporel," Semaine Sociale de Rheims, 1933, proceedings, p. 221.

[7] Joseph Piller, *La conception fédéraliste; sa réalisation dans l'ordre juridique,* in *Politeia,* vol. *I,* fasc. 3-4, 1949, p. 253.

[8] Jacques Maritain, *Les Droits de l'homme et la loi naturelle,* p. 25.

fact, has the right and the duty to seek self-development according to his nature, to expand his personality. But, to be intelligent and therefore able to foresee his needs and the consequences of his acts, to be free and therefore able to decide what he shall or shall not do, he can only really develop himself as a man by assuming his responsibilities and, in consequence, by having the chance to assume them. That is why he must utilize his own resources, before getting help from others for otherwise he will not be able to develop what is really human in himself, because he will not be exercising his creative powers nor directly assuming command of his own destiny.

On the other hand, since he does not have within himself all the resources required for the accomplishment of his personal vocation, man must seek assistance and help from society. But society does not exist merely to render service to men; if it relieves them of the responsibilities which are normally theirs, not only does it not render them service but it causes them great wrong by treating them in a manner contrary to their natures. In other words, man's first duty is to act in conformity with his nature and to assume the responsibilities to which this fact obliges him. And his first right is to be treated in conformity with his nature and thus be encouraged and assisted to assume the responsibilities which are his. That is why society's role is not so much to do things by itself as to create conditions which permit its members themselves to act as men.

The same reasoning applies, to a proportionate extent, in the case of superior collectivities with regard to smaller ones. If it is desired to conserve the diversity and complexity of social life and the pluralist character of the common good, the right of inferior or intermediate groups not only to existence but also to action must be recognized; each must be granted its fair share of activity and responsibility in the functioning of social life, so that, definitively, man may assume his responsibilities at all levels and educate himself to living as a social and political being, which he could not do if the higher collectivity substituted itself for the lower collectivities in the fulfilment of their task.

That is what must be understood by the principle of "subsidiarity," a principle which *L'Institut international des Sciences sociales et politiques* enunciated in its declaration on federalism in these two propositions: "All needs which can be met by individuals, family or association, local or professional, should be left to these to satisfy, acting either alone, or in voluntary collaboration. In all cases, the higher authority should limit its activities to those matters with which the lower are incapable of dealing."

In his encyclical on the restoration of social order, Pope Pius XI strongly emphasized the salutary effect of such a principle:

> Just as it is wrong to withdraw from the individual and commit to the community at large what private enterprise can accomplish, so too it is an injustice, a grave evil, and a disturbance of right order for larger and higher organization to arrogate to itself functions which can be performed efficiently by smaller and lower bodies. Of its very nature, the true aim of all social activity should be to help individual members of the social body, but never to destroy or absorb them.

If this principle enjoys such importance today, it is because the state, through its repeated meddlings in the social domain and through its claims to a monopoly of the common good and of social functions, is in process of killing men's personal lives, their initiative, their sense of responsibilities and, in fact, everything which represents spiritual expansion. We shall have occasion to return to the role thus enacted by the state.

Against this ruinous interference and in order to remedy any such hypertrophy of state functions, federalism asks that the principle of subsidiarity be applied to the entire social order. Its special formula might very well be thus stated: Wherever the system of association between individuals or groups suffices for the accomplishment of a certain task, it must be preferred to direct state intervention.[9]

Definitively, what federalism, supported on the four bases we have just described, aims to establish is a social and political order which will be human, an order made in the image of man, to the measure of man and for man, and consequently penetrated and animated at all stages by the life of the spirit, ponsibility, self-decision and self-government.

---

[9] At the Semaine Sociale de France, in 1932, Fr. Delos showed how the notion of the common good flowed, at one and the same time, from a principle of individual responsibility and initiative and from a principle of authority as far removed from statism as from the social dictature of collectivism:
[Trans.] "The rule may be laid down that, wherever there is a collective good to be ensured, it is incumbent upon the

Its final objective is to truly *organize* society and not merely to *mechanize* it as statism eventually does by concentrating all life and all initiative in the hands of a central authority, which, like the mainspring of a watch, then sets into movement, from above and afar, both individuals and groups like so many anonymous and unconscious cog-wheels. On the contrary, the order which federalism aims to establish is a living and organic order which, gathering communities, primary and intermediate, into one single whole without destroying them, permits, on the one hand, to each of these the possibility of working for its members' good within the limits of its competence and of its specific purpose; while, on the other hand, it asks collaboration from each with a view to realizing the general purpose of the whole and complete organism – namely, the creation of a sphere of life which allows man to develop himself in conformity with his nature.[10]

To recapitulate, the federalist order seeks to translate practically the Christian concept of man, while taking into consideration the diversity and complexity of social life; it does not

---

interested parties to provide for it by use of their freedom and under their responsibility. What does Christian thought and reason tell us? The common good is the necessary condition for the individual good; the same obligation which forces Man, as a free and intelligent being, to tend towards his own good, throws upon him the obligation to procure the collective good, which is the condition of his individual good. The human person is responsible for his social purposes as he is for his individual purposes.

This responsibility affects him, first, in his conscience: then towards the collectivity of those with the same interests; for the common good is the good of many and each of them may demand that the others make their contribution to him.

Thus, at the source of social organization, we see freedom, individual responsibility, initiative, because we find therein Man, aware and responsible, confronted by one of his obligatory ideas, the common good." (*Le Bien commun international et les enseignments du Saint-Siège,* compte-rendu, p. 200).

[10] According to the pluralist principle everything in the body politic which can be brought about by particular organs or societies inferior in degree to the State and born out of the free initiative of the people should be brought about by those particular organs or societies. Jacques Maritain, *Man and the State,* p. 67.

intend to sacrifice any group, any community or any particular society which is useful to man, but wishes to integrate them all, by virtue of the idea of the common good and the principle of subsidiary, into a living and organized whole, all the more human by reason of its greater respect for the lives of its members, both individuals and groups, and because the latter will collaborate more spontaneously towards the good working of the whole.[11]

REQUIREMENTS OF THE SYSTEM IN POLITICAL LIFE

What we have said so far of federalism, as a system, is valid for the entire social order. But since federalism first made itself known as a political system and as it is still under this political aspect that it chiefly interests us, at present, we think it necessary to explain, at somewhat greater length, certain of the system's concrete requirements in political life. The three following divisions seem to deserve particular attention: the pluralist and decentralized organization of the political order, the juridical recognition of local and regional autonomies, and the union of national groups rather than their unification.

The Pluralist and Decentralized Organization of the Political Order

As soon as there is a claim to apply federalism to the political order, this first consequence imposes itself automatically, in the sense that the system's living sources – the Christian concept of man, the fact of the complexity of social life, the idea of the common good, the principle of subsidiarity – all call for a pluralist and decentralized organization, even in the political order.

The same reasons previously given with respect to the social order here retain all their force. Federalism, in proposing a

---

[11] [Trans.] "The social order conforms to natural law: it is not at all that individualistic order in which a scattering of autonomous individuals are gathered under the sole constraint of the state; no more is it that collectivist order in which the group alone provides for all the needs of the individual; actually, the term "social order" is pluralistic; it includes as many groups as, at a given stage of civilization, life worthy of man requires; each of these groups has its purpose, its nature and, consequently, its own law; and all are the content of an organic society which ensures the complete good of the life of its members." (J. T. Delos, *Cours à la Semaine Sociale d'Angers,* 1935, compte-rendu, p. 313).

pluralist and decentralized organization, tends to establish a more human order than that of any other system, and certainly more human than the centralized and monistic orders that most states know these days.

This order is more human, primarily, because it denies none of the works of man, that "political animal" and "community builder," but integrates them all while leaving to them vitality and initiative. It seeks to have the greatest possible number of communities and societies participate in political life; it is a pluralist and living order which builds itself from the ground upwards, erecting its tiers according to the idea of the common good and the principle of subsidiarity. Thus it may be clearly recognized in the description of the political order given by philosophers. For example, Jacques Maritain writes the following:

> Not only is the national community, as well as all communities of the nation thus comprised in the superior unity of the body politic, but the body politic also contains in its superior unity the family units whose essential rights and freedoms are anterior to itself, and a multiplicity of other particular societies which proceed from the free initiative of citizens and should be as autonomous as possible. Such is the element of pluralism inherent in every truly political society. Family, economic, cultural, educational, religious life matter as much as does political life to the very existence and prosperity of the body politic. Every kind of law, from the spontaneous unformulated group regulations to customary law and to law in the full sense of the term, contributes to the vital order of political society. Since in political society authority comes from below, through the people, it is normal that the whole dynamism of authority in the body politic should be made up of particular and partial authorities rising in tiers above one another, up to the top authority of the State.[12]

---

[12] [Trans.] "Among the conditions which the society must fulfil to be in a position to produce civilization, there is one that must be emphasized and it is that the society be sufficiently differentiated so that it may possess all the organisms necessary for a full and superior life. This condition cannot be fulfilled by a uniformed society, without elites, without social authorities and in which there has been atrophied, if not destroyed, the essential organisms; the family, the "corps", the cities. It is therefore plain that a state organized according

But the human character of federalism springs especially from its specific aims of liberating and evoking the *human* from its members by a constant appeal to their initiative and their responsibility. What it seeks to assure is this: an organism, of which all the parts should be full of life and self-operating, and not a mechanism with an all-powerful central mainspring.

Such liberation and education of the political being in man has much more chance of succeeding in a society which leaves to its members management of and responsibility for their own affairs rather than in one which takes everything from the cradle to the grave upon itself, and which considers that the citizen has fulfilled his political duty when he has, for example, cast his vote once every four years.

One hears, these days, repeated like a refrain: Democracy is dying, the people are becoming more and more uninterested in politics and show very little concern about democratic living That is all true. But an evil like this will not be cured merely by asking the citizens to vote and take a greater interest in public affairs. Things will only get worse so long as there is persistence in playing the game of centralizing statism, and so long as the state is left with a monopoly of political functions and is, over and above, invited to assume social functions.

It is necessary to start with the clear undersatnding that the centralized state cannot be an acceptable solution. The philosophers tell us it is "a bad thing in itself",[13] aiming, above everything else, at output and efficacy; inclined to consider itself an

---

to the system and principles of federalism — if this federalism is able to remain faithful to its essence and is consequent with its principles — will form a much more favourable environment for the development of civilization than a centralized and bureaucratized state, obsessed with its egalitarian prejudice which is a leveller of all intellectual or social superiority and where economic considerations dominate all others." (Gonzague de Reynold, *Conscience de la Suisse,* pp. 130-131).

[13] Cf. the appendix: Charles de Koninck, *La Confédération, rempart contre le grand Etat,* p. 16. The author, after referring to Aristotle, quotes therein this passage from Bertrand de Jouvenel: [Trans.] "The Big State is a bad thing in itself, for a fundamental reason, drawn from the very nature of the human mind which is incapable of considering the innumerable relations linking a great quantity of objects, which it only manages to handle by reducing them to a small number of classes, and

end in itself and to seek its own prosperity and its own power, it can only work against what is human. Bertrand de Jouvenel writes:

> [Trans.] The administration of a state is necessarily all the more blind to individual realities as the state's size increases. It is more inhuman, more geometric, more automatic. It cannot recognize individuals and their faces, but only their files, classified according to a determinant social character. If, in a small state, there may be injustice through favour, consisting in unequal treatment of similar cases, the Big State presents another form of injustice – injustice through classification and consisting in treating different cases in a uniform way . . .
>
> The Greeks believed that the dignity of the individual only finds assurance in a small state, where each may make himself heard and where each is taken into consideration. The Empire, said the Greeks, is the work of barbarians as the city is the work of civilized men.
>
> The vices of the Big State are all the more appreciable the more centralized it is and the more things the central government busies itself with. These two characteristics are in full development in our times . . .[14]

The centralized Big State is not an acceptable solution because it allows its subjects to live only on the condition that they renounce the good life, that is to say, the life of the citizen, since the state transforms public functions into simple administrative functions, because it only offers a remote and abstract common good, beyond the reach of common mortals, because, in a word, the society which it forms is not political but despotic, as the philosopher Charles de Koninck shows:

> [Trans.] That man should be, by his nature, a political animal is one of those necessities which liberty pre-supposes

---

> even this number is pre-determined by the mind's capacity. If, therefore, the quantity of objects is greatly augmented, the classes must each include an increasing number of objects, so that, if the objects have an individuality, the classes set up by the mind will be views further and further removed from reality." (p. 23)

[14] Quoted by Charles de Koninck, appendix, pp. 17 and 22.

but which the Big State can tolerate only nominally. The Big State collides with the past, with customs and all sorts of contingencies which have formed persons and people as well as their diversity. It is these very complex, heterogeneous materials which are men, subject to the most contrary passions even within one and the same individual, which the Big State is constrained to homengenize. It is unable to tolerate what cannot be "streamlined", and its vital condition is to succeed in uprooting people and to arouse in persons contempt for the principles of their being . . .

From the fact that it has to be efficient, it is bound — by the nature of the order that it cannot elude, as of the sway that it is constrained to exercise — to make more and more generic and abstract simplifications, so that it already effects a sort of revolution against the political order and against human nature which is never fulfilled save in individuals always differing, one from the other, under very different respects and living in more or less contingent circumstances . . .[15]

To this threat, which causes centralized statism to hover above society, there is a natural antidote — federalism, understood not only as a juridical and political regime, but also in the sense of a general system for organizing society. Without a doubt, the political order will thereby be more complicated, but it will also be more human, more to the measure of man, more susceptible of developing his initiative, his creative faculties, and his sense of responsibility. In a word, all that is most precious in him, his personality.

Juridical and Practical Recognition of Local and
Regional Autonomies
If we desire to satisfy all the requirements of federalism in the political order, we cannot be satisfied with administrative decentralization. Federalism implies a general concept of man and of society, and, at the same time, an original concept of law. According to doctrine current since the 19th century, the state is the unique holder of political power and its will, expressed by laws, is the foundation of the law. It is the state which fixes and determines not only the rights of individuals

---

[15] Charles de Koninck, *La Confédération, rempart contre le Grand Etat,* pp. 18 and 20.

but also the juridical status of social groups and it may modify such status at will, according to reasons of which it remains the sole judge. It may abandon to inferior bodies a certain number of powers, but then it is its will which operates and what it grants today it may equally withdraw tomorrow.

Federalist thought is unable to accept a system which subordinates everything to the state. Such thought holds that man, the human person, must be the starting point, the centre and the goal of everything in society and even in the state. It is man who is the first subject of law and after him all communities and societies, from the family to international society, which his social nature demands for its development. Law is definitively based upon the social exigencies of the human person, and each community, each society, by the fact that it is charged with a good corresponding to these exigencies, is endowed with its peculiar rights and can give itself the rules and institutions which realization of this good requires.

Thus we come back to the central idea of the common good to which we have previously referred. Because federalism refuses to grant the state the monopoly of the common good, it can therefore only refuse it the monopoly of law, powers and public functions. It does not begin by totalizing all powers in the state and then asking it to be good enough to grant some of them to other societies, thus effecting some decentralization; on the contrary, it lays down that each society has its own power, which it draws from its reason for being and from its purpose and not simply from the state's good pleasure. That is why the decentralization which it claims is based on the autonomy of the different social groups and particularly of local and regional collectivities.

According to the federalist system, these collectivites are actual political societies, each having its special task to accomplish and enjoying a natural autonomy prior to any intervention of the state. The latter's role, when it intervenes as supreme guardian of the juridical order in a determined territory, is not, therefore, to create them, at one stroke, and to concede to them, with more or less good grace, certain governmental powers but it is rather, on the one hand, to endow them with a juridical status adapted to the political role they have to play and, on the other hand, to permit them the practical means, especially financial, which will allow them to satisfy the exigencies of the common good with which they are charged.

Two important consequences flow from these explanations.

The first is that the federal order, to be soundly constituted, must be built from the bottom upwards and must therefore rest, as on a base, upon the local collectivites, that is to say, on autonomous and fully living communes or municipalities. To these municipalities must be conceded the right, the powers and the means of self administration, of managing their own affairs, of collecting the revenues needed for their expenses, with the state intervening only in subsidiary fashion and in cases of urgency.

The second consequence might be stated thus: the various degrees, circles or centres of political life which the federalist order admits, do not build themselves on ruins but upon mutual respect. In other words, when a certain number of groups, each by itself incapable of satisfying its common needs, join together to create a new centre of political activity, the latter's duty is not merely to perform the special task for which it was established, but also to protect and assist these groups which called it into being to accomplish their functions.

Union of National Groups Instead of their Unification

The ethnic composition of the Canadian community disposes us to say a word about another requirement of federalism which is special to collectivities where several national groups participate as such in the state's organization.

It may be said immediately that such a fact does not in any way alter the state's role in respect to the groups which live within its territory; its first role and duty is always to organize the juridical protection of the rights and liberties both of individuals and of social groups, and always to institute an order which ensures the rule of law and permits human values, including national values, to maintain themselves and flourish in peace and justice.

However, this role is complicated in federations resulting from the union not only of territorial collectivities but of national communities, particularly when the latter, officially recognized by the constitution, participate as such in the system's functioning. In such case, actually, the political federation is duplicated by a national federation, with the result that union is thereby found more difficult to realize and to maintain, and the government thereof becomes more delicate and complex, differentiated nationality being more of a divisive than a unifying factor.

A federation of this kind has a chance to operate well only

on condition that, at all levels of the political order, there reigns the veritable federalist spirit, that is to say, the spirit of partnership, of collaboration, of respect for the variety and complexity of social life. This spirit is all the more necessary when a majority group finds itself in a position to practically control the governmental apparatus and to have it serve to the almost exclusive advantage of its own people. The temptation then becomes great to utilize the state power, not only as an agent of union between all groups – but as an instrument of unification and assimilation, and perhaps also of domination and oppression.

To yield to such a temptation is a denial of federalism, which is the system of association, and a move onto the road of unitarianism, which is the system of single domination. To have recourse to such means is not, as is said, to work for national unity but it is rather to prepare its ruin, for men are not handled with impunity and therefore are not unified like things.

Such are the requirements of federalism in the political order. They all tend to give and preserve for that order a properly human character. Therein is to be found the feature which fundamentally characterizes the federalist system. Whether with regard to social or political life, it aims less at a technical efficiency, tending to give security at the expense of liberty, than it aims at a human efficiency, obtained through putting men's moral forces and spiritual values to work, through a social and political education effected in and by the communities which surround such men and primarily in and by those which touch him most closely, which are made to his size and measure and which offer him a concrete, attractive, tangible and realizable good.

It is a social and political order of this nature that we would wish to see established in the province of Quebec and in the whole of Canada. Without doubt, it represents an ideal and a certain luxury for our present population, much more anxious about security than liberty; but it is also an ideal and a luxury which man needs if he is to live as a man and lead a life in conformity with his nature as a spiritual, thinking, free and responsible being.

PART THREE:
CULTURE AND FEDERALISM
IN CANADA:
1867-1955

8. CONFEDERATION: ITS CAUSES

Union between states requires certain prior conditions, such as geographical propinquity, similarity of social institutions and allegiance to the same sovereign, or membership in the same political community. Union often takes place as a result of the three following causes: common defence needs, a common desire for independence, and the hope of economic advantages to be gained. One only has to look at the British North America of 1864 to discover all these pre-requisite conditions and causes. These conditions had existed for a long time. But, after 1860, other causes came into play to bring about a rapprochement. First was the common need for security. The small British provinces, separted from each other, but all in contact with their powerful neighbour, were wide open to attack and England admitted itself powerless to defend, one after the other, this string of colonies without the help of their inhabitants.

Lower Canada could not look with disfavour on this common front which might mean safety because, more than any other province, it feared absorption by the neighbouring republic, and it certainly had more to lose through such an event. French Canadians had to choose between Confederation or annexation. The first undoubtedly seemed to them much more re-assuring than the second, so far as the survival of their national group was concerned.

The second classic cause – desire for freedom and independence – played a much less important part than it had played a century earlier in the formation of the United States. Union did not come from a movement of revolt against the mother country, but there may, nonetheless, be discerned among the men who worked for it a conviction that the action they were contemplating would be an important step towards independence and an inauguration of a great destiny for all the British provinces.

To these two causes was added a third – the hope of greater material prosperity. The two Canadas and the Maritime Provinces were then going through economic and financial difficulties. By wiping out provincial boundaries and by allowing all the provinces to be welded into one, Confederation would simultaneously suppress customs duties and also activate inter-provincial trade. It would open up immense new fields for exploitation, and require much new capital especially for the construction of railroads which the new state urgently needed if it was to create, affirm and ensure its unity. Consequently, big-businessmen, financiers and railroad builders worked for union and exercised pressure in Canada as well as in England to bring it about as quickly as possible. When the Maritimes threatened to withdraw from the scheme these interests intervened with the British government so that the latter, in turn, might induce the recalcitrant provinces to see reason.

These general causes had long existed. Why, then, did union negotiations start in 1864? Two events at that time combined to incite men to immediate action. The first was the political crisis in United Canada which had reached a high pitch, while the second was the Maritime leaders' decision to meet in Charlottetown.

The province of Canada had become ungovernable. Ministries followed each other and, one after the other, fell. All manner of party combinations were attempted, but all failed. Every political expedient was attempted, but without success. To make matters worse, racial and religious passions had been aroused and threatened peace between the two sections of the Province. The sole solution which presented itself was in federating either Upper and Lower Canada or all the British provinces. On June 30th, 1864, there was formed a coalition which made this solution its sole programme.

With Confederation decided upon, the problem of how to accomplish it still remained. However, at this junction it was learned at Quebec that a conference consisting of delegates from the Maritime Provinces would open on September 1st at Charlottetown to discuss the advisability of a union between Nova Scotia, New Brunswick and Prince Edward Island. For the Canadians it was an unexpected opportunity. They got themselves invited to the conference, set out their views, obtained support and brought all these delegations back to Quebec for the month of October.

CAUSES OF THE FEDERATIVE CHARACTER OF THE UNION

The union of the British provinces was to be made on a federative basis. But this was not easily decided upon, for a good number of the delegates preferred a legislative union or a unitary state which would merge all the provinces under a sole and single government. John A. Macdonald especially favoured this latter method of union. It was only with reluctance that he finally accepted, at least outwardly, the federative plan.

Impracticable and impossible – these two words echoed like a refrain in the mouth of speakers as soon as they tackled the question of legislative union for the British provinces. Cartier's answer to the partisans of legislative union was that no other project except the federal system was possible.[1] And Brown specifically declared: "There was another reason why the union was not made legislative – it could not be carried. We had either to take a federal union or drop the negotiation. Not only were our friends from Lower Canada against it, but so were most of the delegates from the Maritime Provinces. There was but one choice open to us – federal union or nothing."[2]

Macdonald did not conceal his opinion: "I have never hesitated to state my opinions. I have again and again stated in the House that, if practicable, I thought a legislative Union would be preferable." But, he added . . . "On looking at the subject in the Conference, and discussing the matter as we did, most unreservedly and with a desire to arrive at a satisfactory conclusion, we found that such a system was impracticable."[3]

But why was legislative union then considered impraticable and impossible? A first answer would be to say, quite simply, that the provinces, particularly the Martimes and especially Lower Canada, did not want it. But what were the reasons why the provinces rejected legislative union? Let us distinguish between certain general reasons and Lower Canada's special and more particular reasons.

General Reasons

The provinces which agreed to unite each had a fairly long and special political history and all of them enjoyed responsibile government. The Maritimes particularly sought to preserve their individuality. Upper Canada and Lower Canada, though apparently constituting only a single unit, were, in

[1] *Confederation Debates*, 1865, p. 57.

[2] *Confederation Debates*, 1865, p. 108.

[3] *Confederation Debates*, 1865, p. 29.

reality, two sections leading separate lives, and Lower Canada aspired to see the day when it could recover the separate existence it had known from 1791 to 1840 and the mastery – but this time, a real mastery – of its own political destiny. In a word, the provinces were glad to unite but they also wanted to survive as autonomous political bodies.

Moreover, divergent economic interests and the state of isolation in which most of them lived, made maintenance of a local form of government necessary. It may also be recalled that, according to George Brown, the federative system would permit each province to be financially autonomous, that is to say, in a position to pay its own expenses itself and not those of the other provinces. Accordingly to him, Lower Canada under the Union had been sponging financially on Upper Canada which had, alone, paid three-fourths of the total expenses. Brown, therefore, desired a separation. Thereto were added geographical exigencies.

One decisive reason finally made federation the only possible system – the population to be united were too different in language, in religion, in ethnic origin, in the juridical sysems respectively in force, in national culture and in social institutions. No doubt all these provinces were part of the British Empire, but each of them had grown up in isolation, living in social and political life after its own fashion and providing itself with a body of laws adapted to its own needs and whose renunciation would be painful to it. This reason was valid not only for Lower Canada, a separate and non-assimilable bloc, but also for the Martime Provinces which clung to their laws and institutions. But the decisive factor was, beyond doubt, the presence in Lower Canada of a differing national group.

Lower Canada's Special Reasons

These general reasons were valid for the entire new community in the aggregate. However, it may perhaps be of some interest to examine the special reasons which impelled Lower Canada to demand a union of federative character. Let us make it clear from the start that we are speaking of the French-Canadian element which formed about four-fifths of the total population of old Lower Canada, and not of the Anglo-Protestant minority.

The French-Canadian leaders, while trying to reassure the minority by all kinds of promises, nevertheless strongly and obstinately demanded a political set-up which would ensure the majority's survival and its freedom to expand. At that time this majority already constituted a homogeneous nationality, full of vitality and aware of its distinctive origin. In a word, the French-Canadian nation, far from agreeing to disappear, wanted to live and govern itself. The road to total independence being closed, there only remained for it to obtain, in the midst of the new state about to be founded, the maximum of political autonomy.

It had known and could not accept the régime of legislative union; it had tasted its fruits for a quarter of a century. Yet that had only been a union of two in which Lower Canada had a numerical equality of representation. The new plan being put forward envisaged union of all the British North American provinces and plainly carried with it the principle – long refused by Cartier but now become a necessity to which all must bow – of representation by population. To accept such a system under such conditions would have meant agreeing to its own disappearance in the near future.

Even with gauarantees, it must not be thought that the French-Canadian population of Lower Canada was enthusiastic over the plan of Confederation. For them it was an adventure and a grave risk. A considerable number of them even saw it as a prelude to their total assimilation. Only one thing could quiet their fears but could not, however, fully reassure them, and that was the prospect of a provincial state whose government it would control by its votes and to which could be entrusted the guardianship of its ethnic, religious and cultural interests. This was the repeated argument used by all the French-Canadian leaders.

Such a prospect could not fail to be attractive in the eyes of the French Canadians and could make them forget, or at least put into the background, the sacrifices made elsewhere. In addition, the word "confederation" deliberately used, it would seem, in an equivocal sense by most of the Fathers, allowed them to hope for very wide autonomy, and perhaps even independence, in the new union.

It is not without interest to recall, in this regard, that as early as 1857, the "Courrier du Canada" had, through the agency of J. C. Taché, explained in a series of thirty-three articles, a whole confederation plan for the British colonies in North America.[4] *Le Canadien* of September 8th, 1847, had previously enjoined its readers not to be fearful for their future in the event of a grouping of all the British colonies in North America. On the contrary, it wrote, a federation would give French Canadians "a greater freedom of action, and greater security for their local interests than under the direct action of a remote government ignorant of their needs and desires."

It is clear that the French-Canadian population of Lower Canada would never have accepted any other kind of union than a federative union. For them, it was not so much a question of economic interests to be safeguarded, as was the case in Upper Canada, nor was it only that political and administrative individuality had to be maintained, as was the case in the Maritime Provinces. Their vital social, religious and national interests were at stake. Their destiny was to be fulfilled on a wider scale and in an adventure where, in reality, they took all the risks and had only one guarantee – that of an autonomous provincial government established at Quebec, charged with the protection and promotion of their interests.

⁴ J. C. Taché, *Des provinces de l'Amerique du Nord et d'une Union fédérale.* (Quebec, 1858).

9. THE NATURE OF CONFEDERATION

We may start by taking as wide a view as possible of Confederation, for that will help us obtain and present a right idea of it. At the very outset, one point has to be noted – Confederation is not a single fact but something extremely complex which the historian, sociologist, politician and legalist can each study in turn, but which none of them can wholly explain by looking at it solely from his special angle.

Seeking, therefore, to obtain an over-all view of it, we might describe Confederation as that complex aggregate of events, principally historical, political and legal, which culminated in and gave birth to the union of the British North American provinces in 1867. Considered in this light, Confederation appears as an essentially Canadian project which, however, was consummated only in Great Britain as a project sponsored by men who spoke, not as individuals, but as representatives of already existing national groups and political units.

Consequently, whoever seeks to obtain a right idea of the nature of Confederation cannot and should not overlook any one of the Canadian, Imperial, national and political aspects of the work carried on between 1864 and 1867.

INTENTIONS OF THE FATHERS OF CONFEDERATION

What kind of a system did those men who have been called the Fathers of Confederation, during their labours which lasted from 1864 to 1867, desire to establish? We might be tempted to try to summarize, for perhaps the hundredth time, a study of what were the intentions of the Fathers of Confederation as regards the federative quality of their work. However, we believe any such study would be only partially useful and it might cause us to lose sight of the precise object which primarily interests us, namely, our search for the kind of a system which Lower Canada wanted and what had been promised it in order to have it decide to enter the new union.

It would appear that these promises may be summarized as follows: first of all, that the union would be federative and, secondly, that within this federative union Lower Canada would enjoy all the autonomy needed to preserve and develop its own national life.

Everyone, it appears, agrees as to the first promise. There

remains to be seen what kind of federative union had been promised Lower Canada. The authors of the 1864 project could use, with whatever degree of precision, the expressions "confederation," "federation," "federal union," "the federal principle" but, fundamentally, all of them very well knew that for Lower Canada federalism meant, first and foremost, the possibility of being mistress in its own house and of organizing its national life as it saw fit.

CONFEDERATION, AN ESSENTIALLY CANADIAN WORK

It is well-established historical fact that, in its origins and salient characteristics, Confederation was the work of Canadians themselves. Contrary to what happened in 1791 and 1840, both the initiative and the constitutional plan came from British North American public figures.

One need only read the text of the Quebec resolutions – repeated in almost identical form in the London Resolutions – to become immediately aware that all the main questions regarding union of the provinces had been settled by the Canadians themselves. Moreover, they insisted that there should be, in the Act itself, a phrase emphasizing that the union was not solely an obligation imposed on them by Great Britain but a definite act of the provinces themselves: "Whereas the Provinces of Canada, Nova Scotia and New Brunswwick have expressed their desire to be federally united. . . ." John A. Macdonald constantly spoke of "our" constitution,[1] and Cartier, after his return from London in 1867, declared England had merely given its sanction to the work accomplished by Canadians.[2]

This suffices to show that Confederation was, first and foremost, an essentially Canadian work. History has recognized the fact by giving the title of "Fathers of Confederation" not to British statesmen but to the representatives of the various provinces who had met in conference at Quebec and in London.

CONFEDERATION, THE WORK OF TWO NATIONAL GROUPS

However, to learn the full nature of Confederation, one must penetrate to the heart of this word "Canadians" and make sure

[1] See the speech of February 6, 1865, *Confederation Debates*.

[2] See the speech of May 17, 1867, in the Tassé collection, pp. 523-524.

to whom, at that period, it referred. For a long period, the only Canadians, called by that name without hint of hyphen or qualification, and even after the English conquest of 1760, were the former settlers of New France and their descendants. However, after 1840 the colony, with the Act of Union, officially resumed the name of Canada and all its inhabitants could claim title as Canadians from the political and legal viewpoint.

But the policy of fusing races or national groups soon ended in failure. By 1842, Bagot found himself forced to turn to the French Canadians, as such, and (as he himself admitted) as constituting a race and people and not only a party. This gesture inaugurated the Union's transformation into a federation of nationalities. The legal and official system, no doubt, subsisted as a legislative union, but the *de facto* situation, more eloquent than any mere legalism, had practically established a system of federal unions, as Macdonald himself recognized.

About 1860, the two groups were equally anxious to rid themselves of the legal double-harness imposed on them twenty years earlier, but one could not take any action without the other. An understanding, an agreement or a compromise became necessary.

The facts reveal that the French Canadians only gave their support on two clear conditions: that the union should be federative and that, in this union, they should be recognized as a distinct national group and that they should be placed on the same footing as the other ethnic group. The French Canadians did not want to enter upon this new union as conquered and second-class citizens but as partners and associates with special and distinct rights as regards everything, notably their language, their religion and their civil law, which might affect their survival as a nationality.

The constitution of 1867 bears, in several places, the mark of this determination of the French Canadians to have themselves recognized as a distinct national group with an official place in the Confederation. Thus, for example, Section 133 mentioned use of the English and French languages in Parliament and that was included to give effect to a resolution expressly adopted by the delegates of all the provinces at the Quebec Conference. Maintenance of the French language, John A. Macdonald was careful to point out, had previously been left to the good will of the majority, but that was an inconvenience, and ". . . in order to cure this, it was agreed at the

Conference to embody the provision in the Imperial Act. This was proposed by the Canadian government for fear an accident might arise subsequently, and it was assented to by the deputation from each province, that the use of the French language should form one of the principles upon which the Confederation should be established, and that its use, as at present, should be guaranteed by the Imperial Act."[3]

The same spirit and the same desire for equality are to be found in Section 93, designed to protect the two religious minorities, both Protestant and Catholic, against the possibility of injustice at the hands of the provincial authorities. Moreover, Lower Canada only consented to enter the Union on the express condition that it would conserve control over its civil and social organization. This is why sub-heads 8 and 13 of Section 92 reserve legislation on municipal institutions, property and civil rights to the exclusive jurisdiction of the provinces.[4]

Consequently, anyone who searches for the true nature and sense of the 1867 union cannot overlook the existence of this prior agreement between the two principal races or national groups; an agreement which aimed at giving each of them official status in the Confederation, along with equality of treatment. No one has better defined the spirit of the Canadian federation in this respect than did Sir John A. Macdonald, in 1890, during a celebrated debate in the House of Commons in Ottawa, regarding the legal position of the French language in Canada:

I have no accord with the desire expressed in some quarters that by any mode whatever there should be an attempt made to oppress the one language or to render it inferior to the other; I believe that would be impossible if it were tried and it would be foolish and wicked if it were possible. The statement that has been made so often that this is a conquered country is *à propos de rien*. Whether it was conquered or ceded, we have a constitution now under which all British subjects are in a position of absolute equality, having equal rights of every kind, of language, of religion, of property

---

[3] *Confederation Debates,* op. cit., p. 944.

[4] Cf. D. G. Creighton, *British North America at the Time of Confederation,* a study prepared for the Royal Commission on Dominion-Provincial Relations, Appendix 2, p. 60.

and of person. There is no paramount race in this country, there is no conquered race in this country, we are all British Subjects, and those who are not English are none the less British Subjects on that account.[5]

Such was the presiding spirit when the 1864-1867 agreement between the two main races was being drawn up. There was no question of victor or vanquished, nor of a superior or inferior race; both were to be associates and partners, with each possessing equal rights with respect to the survival of their ethnic groups in the Canadian union. It has been in this sense that the Province of Quebec has always interpreted and understood the spirit, and, therefore, the nature, of Confederation.

CONFEDERATION, THE WORK OF THE PROVINCES

If Confederation can be called an essentially Canadian work, it is scarcely less true that it owes its origin and distinctive features to the provinces themselves. Met in conference at Quebec in 1864, the delegates of the various provinces drew up a series of 72 resolutions which they undertook to submit to their respective governments.

These Resolutions were presented to the Parliament of the United Canadas at the 1865 session as a pact and treaty entered into between the various provinces and to which, consequently, no amendment could be entertained. It was Sir John A. Macdonald who was the most insistent and inflexible on this point. The government, he declared in his first speech to the House, would use its entire influence to have the scheme adopted without any alteration, for the very good reason that it was "in the nature of a treaty settled between the different colonies, each clause of which had been fully discussed, and which had been agreed to by a system of mutual compromise."[6] The other members of the government were no less categorical and Taché,[7] Cartier,[8] Brown [9] and D'Arcy McGee,[10] each in turn maintained that it was a treaty.

[5] Canada, House of Commons, *Debates,* 1890, Vol. 5, p. 745.
[6] Speech of February 3, 1865, *Confederation Debates,* p. 15.
[7] Speech of February 16, ibid., p. 240.
[8] Speech of March 7, 1865, ibid., p. 713.
[9] Speech of February 8, 1865, ibid., p. 109.
[10] Speech of February 9, 1865, ibid., p. 134.

So there is no doubt that the Quebec Resolutions were presented in the Canadian Parliament as an inter-provincial compact. Newfoundland and Prince Edward Island refused for the time being to ratify them, and they consequently remained out of the 1867 Union. As for the two other Maritime Provinces, New Brunswick and Nova Scotia, after many postponements, changes of attitude and discussions during which there was constant reference to the Quebec scheme, they finally appointed delegates to carry on union negotiations at London.

We freely admit that everything is not clear in this affair, that there were some not wholly loyal manoeuvres, and that the Maritimes had reason to complain, but we fail to see how all this alters the fact that Confederation was, in principle, the work of the provinces and can be considered as an inter-provincial compact. In any case, it was as such that it was presented to the Imperial Parliament.

CONCLUSION

An essentially Canadian work, Confederation was at one and the same time an agreement between the two principal national groups, a compact between the provinces, and also an Act of the Imperial Parliament. Within the past twenty-five years, an extremely violent attack has been directed by every means against what is referred to as the "so-called compact theory of Confederation."

Why and how has this happened? Why is there, even today, so much eagerness to demolish a concept which seems to fit in so well with the historical and political facts? It is for the simple reason that this is not a purely theoretical, speculative or even an historical question, but one which has considerable practical importance for each of the governments of the Canadian state – namely, the greater or lesser facility of amending the Constitutional Act of 1867.

That is the controversy's vital centre. Since the Constitution did not provide any general formula for amendment, application has to be made, each time, to the British Parliament. But who should make such request, and on what terms? The provinces, and particularly Quebec, claiming that the Act of 1867 was only the legislation of an interprovincial compact, put forward the principle that the central government could not, without their consent, ask London to amend the Constitution. Obviously, this would make the Constitution a very difficult one to amend.

Up to 1940, it would seem, the federal government did not have any very definite policy in this regard. Sometimes it acted alone and the provinces, considering they had no interest, allowed them to do so; at other times, they obtained the provinces' consent. But, ever since the beginning of the Second World War, the central government has adopted a much clearer and more categorical attitude which might be summarized in these terms: for amendment of those parts of the Constitution which concern it, the federal government no more has to seek authorization from the provinces than the latter need Ottawa's permission to amend their own constitutions. This was the declaration of a new principle, completely contrary to federalism in general and unknown to Canadian federalism.

In conformity with this new principle, the central government, despite protests from the Province of Quebec, proceeded alone with the amendments of 1943, 1946 and 1949. In the latter amendment, it even had London admit its claims of being able, alone, to amend the Constitution of Canada in matters wherein it considered itself the only interested party.

By such action, Ottawa notified the provinces of its firm and determined desire to set aside, in future, at least insofar as constitutional amendments are concerned, any claims solely founded on the fact that an interprovincial compact existed prior to the Act of 1867. Shutting itself up within a narrow and exclusive legalism, the central government reduces all of Confederation to the British North America Act and it forces the provinces to follow it in this practice.

Therefore, Quebec should reaffirm its traditional concept of Confederation's true nature, but without confining itself to this argument alone. The central government's gesture forces it to fall back onto its own legal and constitutional positions. While continuing the struggle on the political plane, the Province must, in future, base itself to a greater extent on properly juridical and legal arguments, while solidly and scientifically organizing its defences on this subject of growing importance so that, when the crucial question of a general formula for constitutional amendment again arises, it may be able to secure adoption of one which will not only be in accordance with the true nature of Confederation, but will also respect the particular character of our federalism as well as Quebec's special position in the Canadian federation.

10. THE FINANCIAL SETTLEMENT AND SUBSIDIES

It was not sufficient to create a new government while allowing the old ones to continue. The resources necessary for the performance of their functions had to be insured to one and the other. Theoretically, many solutions were open to the authors of the federation project. To the provinces could be left the task of financially maintaining the central government, or the latter might be entrusted with the task of meeting the needs of the provinces. Or, again, each order of government might be given revenue sources which would make it financially capable of fulfilling its obligations without any inter-dependence.

The two first solutions were unacceptable, because they denied the federative principle in the financial domain. The third solution fully respected the requirements of that principle, and it was, in fact, the ideal solution to which most of the interested parties were inclined but which they could not adopt in all its purity because of the practical difficulties deriving from the administrative and financial situations of the various provinces.

DISTRIBUTION OF TAXING POWERS

The federal government, which assumed the most costly obligations, (debt service, transport, defence, etc.), saw itself exclusively entrusted with the most productive revenue sources of the period, that is, customs duties and excise taxes, and it received, in addition, a right of access to the other forms of taxation, although what was meant exactly by this latter faculty was never precisely stated.

The provincial governments, on the other hand, only assumed obligations, doubtless of great importance, but whose financial cost at that period seemed to be relatively modest. For instance, expenses relating to public education in 1866 barely exceeded 10 per cent of the provincial budgets since private initiative, the religious institutions in Lower Canada and the municipalities defrayed the major part of educational costs. It was the same with regard to social welfare, to which governments of the middle nineteenth century paid scant heed.

However, these governments had to live, and calculations made by the financial experts showed that, even by reducing their expenses to the minimum they could not properly fulfil their obligations with the revenue sources placed at their disposal. Furthermore, since the Maritime Provinces had not developed their municipal system, they found themselves at a disadvantage through this distribution of revenue sources.

How could the gap be closed, especially in a way to satisfy everyone? At least three solutions suggested themselves to leave the provinces with a right of access to the indirect tax; to ask them to use the direct tax insofar as it might be necessary to fulfil their obligations; or to require of the central government that it grant them subsidies.

However, the first solution could not be considered since one of the purposes of union was precisely to encourage trade between the provinces and thus lower tariff barriers, and the Fathers of Confederation feared that this end could not be achieved if they left indirect taxes to the provinces. As regards the second alternative, most of the Fathers considered it impracticable at that time though some, like Galt, believed it to be the ideal solution. There consequently remained only the solution of subsidies to the provinces and all finally resigned themselves thereto.

THE COMPROMISE OF SUBSIDIES

The subsidies certainly constituted a departure from the federative principle which requires that each order of government should be autonomous and responsible in the financial domain as in other legislative fields. On the other hand, their adoption made Confederation possible by ensuring revenues to the provincial governments and by granting favoured treatment to the poorer provinces. They may, therefore, be rightly classed as an *expedient* and as a *compromise* necessitated at the time.

It is therefore, a mistake to pretend that the general system of subsidies to the provinces is, at all points, in conformity with the spirit and the letter of the federative pact. It rather constitutes an exception to the principle of autonomy and of the financial responsibility of each government. The negotiators, for the most part, only consented thereto with the greatest repugnance and they considered their work as an expedient and as a makeshift. This expedient has an interesting aspect: it does not merely comprise a single formula but three or four and it seeks to adapt itself to the financial needs of the provinces. What was sought was equality of advantage to all, even if there had to be recourse to differing and complicated formulas in order to do justice.

From the very start, there was an admission that, in a federative system, certain provinces could receive not only different but even preferential financial treatment. The union was conditioned thereon and the Fathers of Confederation do not seem to have considered it a serious obstacle that their settlement formula might later be found singularly complicated. Perhaps, in these present days when, above all else, mechanical simplicity, even in the government of men, is being sought, it might be well to draw our inspiration from such breadth of view and from such a spirit.

THE CONTINUING PROBLEM OF SUBSIDIES

The provinces had difficulty understanding and admitting the fixed nature of the subsidies paid them by the federal government in return for the sacrifice they had made by granting it a monopoly of the customs duties and excise taxes. The revenue from these levies was growing constantly but the amounts paid out by the federal government is subsidies did not increase at the same pace. It was not, then, surprising that the provincial governments sought to have the sums they received annually from Ottawa under the provisions of Section 118 increased. This was one of the principal objects of the inter-provincial conference convened in Quebec by Honoré Mercier in 1887. Resolution 17 adopted by the delegates favoured a new basis for subsidies and this the Government substantially accepted twenty years later. The Resolution asserted that the provinces were not in a position, either by means of direct taxes or otherwise, to meet the expenses required for their governmental operations. They consequently requested the federal government to increase the annual allowances according to a plan which would take into account the increase of population up to a certain point.

It was only some years after Laurier had come to power that the question of federal subsidies was again discussed. In 1902, Premier S. N. Parent of Quebec, after consulting Laurier, organized the second inter-provincial conference at Quebec, its principal object being to study the problem of increasing the federal subsidies. In the month of December, 1902, the conference opened in Quebec with representatives from all the provinces, with the exception of the two Prime Ministers of Ontario and British Columbia who could not attend personally. The Ontario Premier had, however, communicated his views on the question in a confidential memorandum and the Prime Minister of British Columbia later made his views known.

However, it required yet another Conference, held in October, 1906, to bring about a general settlement of the problem. This time it was the federal government which took the lead and it called the provinces to Ottawa. All accepted and were there represented. The resolutions of the Quebec Conference of 1902 were taken as a basis for discussion, and these resolutions were finally accepted by all except British Columbia, which asked special treatment by reason of its geographical situation.

Laurier, who, in the past, had often denounced the very principle of subsidies and who, again in 1905, had just declared that he favoured each government's own financial responsibility,[1] none the less desired, for political reasons and in order to keep the peace, that the Conference might be successful. But, in order to forestall any subsequent claim on the part of the provinces, Canada's Prime Minister resolved to proceed by means of an amendment to the constitution, and to insert in the text of the Address to the Queen a clause on this subject declaring it to be a "final and unalterable settlement."

The provinces did not long consider the settlement as final and they again sought federal government aid. In 1913, another inter-provincial conference met in Ottawa and adopted the following resolution: "That, in the opinion of this Conference, an additional subsidy equal to ten per cent of the Customs and Excise duties collected by Canada from year to year should be granted to the Provinces, payable semi-annually in advance, in addition to all other subsidies to which they are now or may hereafter be entitled. . . ." This request by the provinces went unanswered, the war of 1914 soon obliged the federal government to devote all its financial resources to conduct of the war.

START OF CONDITIONAL SUBSIDIES

With the Conservative Party's advent to power in 1911, there opened a new phase in the policy of subsidies. Until then, Ottawa had been satisfied to turn over to the provincial governments the amounts prescribed by Section 118 of the Constitution without any condition as to their use. Now, however, the

[1] "If there is one admitted principle in finance and all the more so in government business, it is that those upon whom falls the duty of spending a country's revenues should be also be charged with the responsibility of raising these revenues." (*House of Commons Debates*, 1905, p. 1493).

federal government declared itself ready to grant other subsidies, but for specified purposes and on certain conditions. The policy of conditional subsidies had a modest beginning in a field in which the two orders of government enjoyed concurrent jurisdiction. This was the field of agriculture.

In 1913, the federal parliament passed an Act for the Purpose of Aiding the Furtherance of Agricultural Instruction in the Provinces; this federal measure offered to distribute the sum of $10,000,000 to the provincial governments, over a period of ten years, to develop agricultural education. The widest latitude was allowed the provinces as to how this money should be spent, provided the general purpose was respected.

The provinces availed themselves of this offer, and Quebec took advantage of it to establish its system of agronomy. On the whole, the provinces showed themselves satisfied with this help, but, after ten years' experience with it, the federal government, for political and financial reasons, refused to continue its programme of subsidizing agricultural education.

Meanwhile, Ottawa had assumed other obligations towards the provinces along the lines of conditional subsidies. Even before the first world war, it had set up a Royal Commission with a view to studying what assistance might be given to industrial and technical education. In the report presented to the federal government in 1913, the Commission used an argument which was new at that time, but which was subsequently to become familiar. Its reasoning ran along the following lines: industrial and technical education was of national importance, and, since the provinces did not have the financial resources necessary for its complete development, the federal government's help would consequently be necessary. The Commission, therefore, recommended creation of a federal fund designed to provide the provincial legislatures with the assistance needed in this respect.

The war of 1914 postponed execution of this recommendation; but, as soon as the fighting was over, the federal Parliament took it up again and, in 1919, passed the Act for the Purpose of Encouraging Technical Education in Canada. This time, however, Ottawa required the provinces to co-operate, and it undertook to turn over to them an amount only equal to what each of them would spend for that purpose within its own territory and satisfied itself with offering an amount of $10,000,000, to be distributed over a period of ten years.

The proposed Act met with strong opposition in the House

of Commons from the Liberal Party which maintained the view that this was an intrusion by the federal government into the affairs of the provinces. Despite this opposition, the bill was adopted and all the provinces, in turn, finally accepted the federal government's offer. The Province of Quebec did so with only moderate enthusiasm at first, but, from 1923 on, with determination and energy.

In 1918, the federal government, adopted an Act to Co-Ordinate Labour Employment Offices, which offered subsidies to the provincial governments, following agreement, with a view to helping them set up and co-ordinate their labour employment offices. It was said that the consequences of demobilizing hundreds of thousands of men had to be provided for, and every thing ought to be put in readiness to ensure them employment on their return. It was none the less true that Ottawa, for the first time, was about to spend its money for a purpose exclusively within provincial jurisdiction.

Encouraged by its successes and by the conciliatory replies of the provinces, the federal government, in the following year, made a new offer of subsidies; this time to help the provinces to combat venereal disease, following agreement and upon certain conditions. At the same time, it set up a Department of Health at Ottawa whose mission was to co-ordinate Dominion and provincial activities with respect to health matters.

Ernest Lapointe intervened to denounce such a measure:

> That government is gradually encroaching on the provincial area and it has done so in many matters. Take the question of the Department of Health which has been created this year. I have read in Hansard of many years ago a debate when a resolution to create such a department was proposed in the House of Commons, at the time Sir John A. Macdonald was Prime Minister. Sir John A. Macdonald, Sir Charles Tupper and other leading statesmen of that time stated emphatically that under the British North America Act this government could not establish a Department of Health. This year, with all the precedents which the minister had adduced, a Department of Health has been created.[2]

---

[2] Speech of June 20, 1919, *Debates of the House of Commons,* 1919, — p. 3804-3805.

Immediately following the war's end in 1919, the federal government brought down legislation whose object was to encourage the building and improvement of highways, and whose main clause carried an offer to distribute the sum of $20,000,000 over a period of five years to provinces which would sign an agreement with Ottawa and conform to the conditions laid down.

Once again, Ernest Lapointe pointed out the dangers of such intrusion and the injustice which would, in such case, be caused any province which might refuse to sign the agreement required to obtain the federal grant.

> This government, according to the resolution, is to have control over the quality and the standard of the roads which are to be built," he declared. "Suppose that quality or standard does not coincide with the quality or standard which has been adopted by the province of Quebec and that province refuses to change its plans, would it be fair that the people of the province of Quebec should be required to contribute money for the construction of works in other provinces which ought to be carried out by the people of those provinces? Why not leave to the provinces those rights, powers and responsibilities which have been given to them by the British North America Act? (....) I protest against the interference of the government in local works; if they interfere with matters of education or of highways, they might do so in connection with other matters which are purely local and provincial.[3]

This opposition did not prevent the project from becoming law or being generally accepted by the provinces.

Thus, little by little, there was established a new system of federal subsidies, never foreseen by the Fathers of Confederation and under which Ottawa spent its money for exclusively provincial purposes. A remarkable fact is that, if one makes an exception in the case of agricultural education, it took only a year or two to establish the new system solidly. The offer of help to organize and co-ordinate provincial labour employment offices came in 1918 and it was in 1919, the very next year, that, one after the other, there came subsidies to fight venereal diseases, to assist technical education, and to encourage the construction and improvement of highways.

[3] Speech of June 23, 1919, *Debates of the House of Commons*, 1919, p. 3906.

11. BETWEEN THE WARS

The era which, historically, has become known as the "between-wars" period, can be divided, from the viewpoint of federal-provincial relations, into two phases. The first extended from 1920 to 1930 and was marked by the preponderant activity of the provincial governments, while the second covered the rest of the period and was characterized by a resumption of federal direction.

GENERAL OUTLINE

Wearied by its gigantic war effort and a little awed by the magnitude of the resultant debt, from 1920 onward the federal government seemed little disposed to rush into vast undertakings. The new fields offering themselves for governmental action largely belonged to the provinces, by virtue of the British North America Act.

The provinces, whose finances had been little affected by the war and whose needs had been progressively augmented, soon entered, with the support of solid electoral majorities, upon vast programmes. Little by little, their prestige increased in relation to the federal government. During this period, Ottawa mostly showed itself conciliatory towards the provinces and even seemed anxious to get a definite settlement of long outstanding problems which had been causes of friction between the two orders of government.

Thus, to pacify the Maritime Provinces, which were dissatisfied with the lot assigned them by Confederation, it appointed a Royal Commission (the Duncan Commission) in 1926, charged with inquiry into their grievances. After a brief inquiry, the Commission recognized the justice of the Maritimes' claims. It recommended to the federal government that it should proceed with a fuller study of the subject, with a view to arriving at a complete revision of the financial agreements with these provinces. It asked the federal government, meanwhile, to increase the annual subsidies it was paying to each of them. The federal government accepted these recommendations, paid the subsidies and even had its action approved by the provinces which met in conference at Ottawa in 1927.

It was during this same period that the federal government and the Prairie Provinces began to reach a settlement on the question of lands and natural resources. After a great deal of discussion and bargaining, they eventually received the promise of complete satisfaction, having been supported in their claims not only by the Maritimes but also by the central provinces.

It must not, however, be thought that the provinces, intoxicated with their growing power, had wholly lost all their inquietude concerning acts done by the central government. This was the period in which social policy plans and labour legislation were beginning to be elaborated, first at the International Labour Office and then at Ottawa. These projects the Province of Quebec regarded with some distrust because they reflected an inspiration foreign to its own way of life and to its already existent institutions. This was also the period during which the federal policy of conditional subsidies to the provinces was being amplified. This policy, with some fluctuations, was to reach its peak with the Old Age Pensions Act of 1926.

Old Age Pensions Act

In July, 1924, a special House of Commons committee had expressed a wish to have established a system of old age pensions as soon as possible for the benefit of needy persons aged seventy and over, with the federal and provincial governments equally sharing the cost of operating such a system. Before proceeding to draft its Act, Ottawa consulted the provinces and its Department of Justice. Replies from the former were not unanimous, with certain provinces declaring they were ready to accept Ottawa's offer and even to allow it to carry the entire financial burden of the new system, while others showed themselves much more reluctant. The Department of Justice, for its part, replied that institution of an old age pensions system appeared to it to be within the category of subjects covered by "property and civil rights," and, consequently, to be within provincial jurisdiction.

If it persisted in legislating in this field, the federal government had no alternative but to abandon the idea of a contributory and obligatory old age insurance plan and revert to the policy of conditional grants. The federal government offered to pay half of the cost to every province which would, after signing an agreement with it, establish an old age pensions system.

The government of Quebec not only entertained serious doubts as to the federal Act's constitutionality, but also held that it did not correspond with the spirit and structure of the social assistance system already in force in the province. It was with a view to finding a better solution in that direction that, in 1930, it had instituted a commission on social insurance and had particularly requested it to study the subject of old age assistance.

The Commission delivered itself of the following judgment on the federal Act:

[Trans.] While recognizing the legislators' laudable desire to assist old people in need, your Commission cannot refrain from expressing the opinion that this system, which, far from equalling that of contributory insurance, is in many cases a premium on improvidence, on carelessness and idleness, and accustoms the individual to depend solely on the State, prevents the development of a spirit of thrift and risk and, in its application, may lead to abuses and fraud which it is not always easy to uncover. The system of contributory and obligatory insurance, on the contrary, encourages from early youth those who will derive benefit from it to save and provide for their old age. Once that old age is reached, the beneficiary will only have a better opinion of himself and will say, when receiving his annuity, that it is right he should enjoy it because he will have acquired it himself.

In 1867 it had been agreed that the whole social domain should lie exclusively within the competence of the provinces and that was done more particularly to enable the French-Canadian citizens of Quebec to preserve their own way of life and their own institutions. But now, under the influence of socialist ideas and groups, Ottawa was setting out to legislate in the social field, and this confronted the Province of Quebec with the alternative of either renouncing its ideals of social organization and accepting a plan of foreign inspiration, or remaining faithful to that ideal by paying a high price for it.

The Old Age Pensions Act was only one more manifestation of the policy of conditional grants through which the federal government busied itself with exclusively provincial questions. But this time it was a clear and unadulterated invasion of the social field and an invasion which, moreover, had all the earmarks of permanence never before displayed in federal-provincial agreements. An amendment to the British North America Act had to be made in 1951 to regularize the situation which had arisen between the two orders of government. For these reasons, it is fitting that attention be called to this Act, which, in truth, constitutes an important milestone in the history of federal-provincial relations, and clearly illustrates the process whereby a subject of provincial competence may be transferred to federal jurisdiction.

DOMINION-PROVINCIAL CONFERENCE 1927

Convened in the sixtieth year of Confederation, not to study any particular or acute problems, but to examine practically all questions touching relations between the Dominion and the provinces, this Conference lasted one week and was carried on in the fullest harmony. It discussed such matters as Senate reform; the procedure to be followed for amending the British North America Act; the formation and operation of companies, including trust, loan and insurance companies; immigration; the claims of the Maritime and Western Provinces; provincial liquor laws; federal grants for the construction of highways, for technical education, agricultural instruction; aid to the jobless; and so on. Certain opinions expressed on that occasion may be recalled. For example, when Senate reform was discussed, the report noted, "Throughout the discussion, the right of the provinces to be consulted on such an important matter as this was frequently emphasized."[1]

Before terminating its sessions, the Conference discussed the subject of conditional grants. The report notes the following: "On the question of aid for highway construction, practically all the provinces, with the exception of Quebec, favoured assistance from the federal treasury. . . Quebec did not ask any assistance. That province had its own system by which the roads were paid for on a 50-50 basis with the municipalities. . . ." He then made this declaration: "The question of unemployment relief was but briefly dealt with; with the possible exception of Manitoba, no speaker urged federal aid in this direction. Several of the representatives, in fact, were of the opinion that unemployment relief on any fixed basis was simply an encouragement to unemployment."[2]

Complete harmony ruled as the Conference adjourned. "The Agenda having been completed," the reporter noted, "the repre-

---

[1] *Dominion-Provincial Conference,* 1927, Official précis of discussions, pp. 9-10.

[2] Ibid., p. 31.

sentatives engaged in mutual felicitations, each of them expressing his satisfaction at the success of the conference." This was, indeed, a happy period.

THE ECONOMIC CRISIS

Effects of the world crisis which occurred in 1929 soon made themselves felt in Canada and seriously tested the proper operation of the federative system. During the previous period, the provinces had claimed their rights, they had obtained marked advantages, and had opened new fields of activity while contracting considerable expenditures and increased debts; but they had not failed to preserve good relations with the federal government. But the depression would show how weak was the basis on which provincial finances rested.

Governments, taken by surprise by the new scourge of unemployment, believed, at first, that such traditional means as private charity and action by the municipalities – the latter being responsible for aid to indigents – would suffice to remedy the situation. But it soon proved so serious that the higher governments had to intervene directly and assume progressively heavier responsibilities.

The first plans, suggested by the federal government and agreed to, by Quebec in particular, called for payment of part of the cost of relief and of works by the province and municipalities. For example, during the fall of 1930, Quebec and Ottawa had signed an agreement for the purpose of assisting unemployed in the province. In five years, from 1931 to 1936, the federal government paid in the form of direct relief in the Province of Quebec $29,410,619.33. In the same period, the federal government spent $8,070,922.05 in the province for public works.

The result of such a system was to bring most of the municipalities to the verge of bankruptcy, while it obliged the provinces to come to their rescue. Since some provinces were already having persistent financial troubles, the federal government had to grant them special assistance. In 1932, the Minister of Finance, Mr. Rhodes, declared in his budget Speech that, in order to preserve the reputation of Canadian credit abroad, and especially on the New York market, the federal government had had to assist certain provinces.

The crisis thus revealed one of the thorniest problems of Canadian federation, that of the economic inequality of the provinces, or the "poor provinces" problems. In 1937, Quebec received from the federal government in statutory and special subsidies $0.81 per inhabitant, whereas Saskatchewan got $6.10; in the same year, subsidies and contributions by the federal government to Quebec amounted to $4.82 per head, but to $30.51 in Saskatchewan.

At the Federal-Provincial Conference of 1935, Mr. Taschereau, Premier of Quebec, while requesting that drastic measures against unemployment be taken, asked, at the same time, that Quebec be put "on the same footing as the other provinces." In his opinion, increase of the federal contribution would not constitute an effective remedy for unemployment, since it would only "be an appetizer to the class of professional unemployed." He believed it would be necessary to come to the aid of the municipalities and of the provinces by granting them loans on advantageous terms, so that they might suitably discharge their own obligations.

The economic and social crisis was to engender a crisis of confidence with regard to federalism. A whole school of intellectuals had already begun to re-interpret the Act of 1867 in favour of the central government, and they were striving by every possible argument to convince it that it should take the lead without letting itself be deterred by considerations of respect for the Constitution or for the autonomy of the provinces.

The central government asked for nothing better than to go into action. In 1932, it instituted the Canadian Broadcasting Corporation, and, in 1934 the Bank of Canada, both of which were soon to become valuable auxiliaries in pursuit of its policies. In 1935, it had a whole series of clearly unconstitutional social Acts passed. In 1936, it effected centralization of harbours, by suppressing the local Commissions. Finally, in 1937, it set up the Royal Commission on Dominion-Provincial Relations, whose Report would both confirm and stimulate its centralizing policy.

One of the main effects of the economic crisis was to focus attention on constitutional problems and particularly on the procedure to be adopted for amending the British North America Act. The question had previously arisen at the Dominion-Provincial Conference of 1927. However, divergent opinions among the provinces had prevented any solution.

In 1930, the provinces, led by Ontario, informed Ottawa with regard to adoption of the Statute of Westminster that they were opposed to amendment of the 1867 Act without their consent. Mr. Howard Ferguson, Premier of Ontario, wrote the Canadian Prime Minister to remind him of the provinces' existence and of their right to be heard. The letter was accompanied by a memorandum in which the Ontario Premier, resuming the ideas held by his predecessor, Mowat, officially and at length set out what was soon to become known as the "compact" thesis, or theory of confederation.

> The British North America Act, 1867, is usually referred to as the Compact of Confederation. This expression has its sanction in the fact that the Quebec resolutions, of which the Act is a transcript, were in the nature of a treaty between the provinces which originated the Dominion.

Proof of this assertion was offered and the Ontario Premier denied there was validity in any precedents the federal government might have set regarding amendment of the Constitution. The memorandum concluded with this passage:

> While this subject is under discussion it would not be opportune to give Imperial statutory authority to incidents which have been allowed through inadvertence or otherwise, to find a footing in our constitutional procedure. Such an enactment has been and is likely to be a source of friction and weakness to the Dominion of Canada. It is, therefore, earnestly represented that no re-statement of the procedure for amending the Constitution of Canada can be accepted by the province of Ontario that does not fully and frankly acknowledge the right of all the provinces to be consulted, and to become parties to the decision arrived at.

This energetic intervention by Ontario, to which Quebec added its own, induced the federal government, in 1931, to convene a Federal-Provincial Conference for the purposes of studying the provinces' views regarding certain clauses of the Statute of Westminster. After examining the question the Conference agreed on a text which was to be incorporated in the Statute itself and become its seventh Article. The provinces had thus obtained recognition of their sovereignty.

The same year, however, was marked by the first serious attempt to demolish the theory which, up to then, had been traditionally accepted by both politicians and jurists – namely that Confederation constituted a pact and a treaty. In an address given before the *Canadian Political Science Association* in 1931, Mr. N. McL. Rogers attacked what he called the "compact theory" and also its logical corrollary, "the doctrine of unanimous consent," which were preventing the Constitution's development.

From 1930 to 1935, modification of the British North America Act came to be studied with more and more attention. On a motion of Mr. Woodsworth, Leader of the C.C.F. Party, the House of Commons in 1935 instituted a special committee to study the best method of amending the British North America Act. The Committee, in its report to the House, recommended that a Conference be held as soon as possible to give the provinces an opportunity to express their views. However, the Committee refrained from making any suggestion as to the procedure that should be followed with a view to amending the British North America Act.

This same year, 1935, witnessed one of the most dangerous assaults on provincial autonomy, from a political as well as from a juridical point of view. The federal government passed certain social Acts, the most important of them dealing with a weekly day of rest, with minimum wages, and with the eight-hour day. To those who opposed such Acts on the grounds that they were unconstitutional, inasmuch as they dealt with matters within provincial jurisdiction, the government replied by invoking the obligations it had incurred as a participant in the general convention of the International Labour Organization.

A new problem thus arose in Canada – did their having signed international agreements allow the federal government to legislate on classes of subjects expressly reserved to the provinces? The entire future of Canadian federalism rested on how this question would be answered. The Privy Council, to whom the question was put by a reference to it of the litigious Acts, declared itself distinctly opposed to the stand taken by the federal government. It first pointed out that, since Section 132 of the British North America Act applied to treaties made by Canada as a part of the British Empire, there could be no reliance thereon in this matter, and there was no other section in the Constitution to legitimate the steps taken by Ottawa in social matters.

The Privy Council continued its argument by denying that the social Acts in question could be justified under Section 91 of the Canadian Constitution. Treaty-making legislation, it pointed out, did not exist as such: "The distribution (of legislative powers between the Dominion and the provinces) is based on classes of subjects; and as a treaty deals with a particular class of subjects so will the legislative power of performing it be ascertained".[3] Did this mean that Canada could no longer, because of its Constitution, bind itself by treaty? No, the judges concluded, Canada possesses all the powers needed for the execution of treaties:

> But the legislative powers remained distributed, and if in the exercise of her new function derived from her new international status Canada incurs obligations they must, so far as legislation is concerned, when they deal with Provincial classes of subjects, be dealt with by the totality of powers, in other words by co-operation between the Dominion and the Provinces. While the ship of state now sails on larger ventures and into foreign waters she still retains the watertight compartments which are an essential part of her original structure.

THE FEDERAL-PROVINCIAL CONFERENCE OF 1935

All the period's problems became crystalized in the discussions of the Dominion-Provincial Conference of 1935. The atmosphere was no longer as it had been in 1927; the country was in the grip of a crisis and most of the provinces were in financial straits.

Meeting in various committees, the Conference members studied several important questions, among them unemployment, finance, and amendment of the British North America Act.

With regard to unemployment, the Conference recommended a new distribution of responsibilities between the Dominion, the provinces and the municipalities, as well as institution of a federal employment and relief Commission to be vested with extensive powers.

The committee on financial matters discussed the financial condition of the provinces, a National Loan Council, duplication of taxes and possible reallocation of tax sources between the Dominion and the provinces. The committee devoted special attention to a detailed study of the following proposals:

---

[3] *Attorney-General of Canada. v. Attorney-General of Ontario et al.*, A.C. 1937, p. 326.

a) abandonment of the income tax field by the Dominion, so as to leave it entirely to the provinces; b) collection by the federal government of provincial taxes on individual incomes and on estates, with subsequent remittance to the provinces.

The committee on constitutional questions contented itself with affirming that Canada ought to possess power to amend its Constitution, provided a method of procedure of doing so, satisfactory to the Dominion Parliament and to the provincial legislatures could be devised. It recommended, in consequence, that a group of experts be called together to be charged with perfecting the details of this formula, which would be submitted to a Federal-Provincial Conference soon to be held.

The government, at the 1936 session, proposed an address in the House of Commons in which the British Parliament was asked to amend the British North America Act with regard to taxes and the guarantee of provincial debts. It was sought to amend Section 92 in order to allow the provinces access to indirect taxation. The Canadian Parliament was also asked to authorize the federal government's guarantee of the payment of principal, interest and sinking funds of all obligations of the Canadian provinces. The House of Commons approved the measure, but the Senate rejected it.

CONCLUSION

Many financial and constitutional questions had arisen in Canada some years before the last war without the answers having been found. The Province of Quebec and the Province of Ontario had got through the years of economic crisis fairly well, but the Maritime Provinces, despite the special assistance given them by the federal government, were still at grips with their age-old difficulties. The western provinces especially had been ruined ever since the onset of unemployment, and due to the further handicap of poor harvests. All these difficulties constituted a serious threat to the autonomy of the provinces which were incapable of fulfilling their obligations with the slim revenues at their disposal. To an era of splendour there had now succeeded a period of decline.

12. THE ROYAL COMMISSION ON DOMINION-PROVINCIAL RELATIONS

The Liberal party, during the half-century which followed Confederation, had been the great defender of provincial autonomy. Indeed, Laurier, in 1918, could truthfully write: "To all these attempts, the Liberals offered inflexible opposition and, from the outset, constituted themselves the champions of provincial autonomy."[1] This same party had found, in Ernest Lapointe, during the period from 1920 to 1937, a no less solid defender of the rights of the provinces.

Nonetheless, during the ensuing period it was the Liberal party in power which was to take the "Macdonaldian" idea for its own. Two world catastrophes of tremendous importance were responsible for the new federal imperialism: the economic depression of 1929, and World War II. The first event would not, perhaps, have had such influence on the trend of Canadian politics, had it not been responsible for the setting-up by the central government of the Royal Commission on Dominion-Provincial Relations.

THE ATTITUDE OF QUEBEC

The Commission sat in Quebec from May 12th to 16th. In the name of the Government of the Province of Quebec, Mr. Emery Beaulieu, K.C., presented a re-statement of the issue of which we feel that we should recall the main ideas, as these reflect the traditional attitude of the Province of Quebec, and because they will on many occasions be re-expressed in different forms.

[Trans.] "The Government of this Province," said Mr. Beaulieu, "feels obliged to declare solemnly that it does not recognize the right of the federal government to confer, on its authority alone, either to a Commission or to an individual, the right of inquiring into the financial position of the provincial governments. Under the rule of our present federal system each province in the spheres which are proper to it is an autonomous state, enjoying all the prerogatives of a sovereign state and in no way subject to federal authority.

[1] *La Revue Trimestrielle Canadienne*, November 1918, p. 221.

The Federal Government cannot arrogate to itself the right to make an inquiry, through the intermediacy of its agents, into the financial position of the provinces any more than the latter could inquire into the financial position of the federal government. To recognize the authority of your Commission would be, to a certain degree, to recognize the supremacy of the federal authority in matters pertaining to the provincial field and, notwithstanding all the respect which it feels for the members who make up the Commission, the government of this province would deem itself failing in its duty if it were to admit any concession implying such recognition."

While refusing to recognize the Commission's powers, the Quebec government thought it nevertheless fitting to give its point of view on the possibility of amending the 1867 Act of Confederation. "It is not from the Central Government," it declared, "that the provinces' powers and prerogatives come; it is rather from the voluntary agreement between provinces that the central government was born." The government emphasized the "contractual character of the federal pact" with this all-important consequence. "Partaking of the nature of compacts, the federal pact can neither be amended nor modified without the consent of all parties; that is to say, of all provinces."

The brief later stated: "The centralization apparently desired in certain quarters opposed to provincial rights is a national and social evil. The country's prosperity does not depend on a greater centralization of legislative powers. On the contrary, the closer the contact existing between the legislator and the localities for which he must legislate, the greater will be the chance of such legislation's being truly fruitful."

The Quebec Government was of the opinion "that the federal subsidies payable to the provinces should be readjusted, and that the sources of revenue be redistributed between the central government and the provinces, taking into account the populations of the different provinces, their present needs and also the sacrifices which certain of them have made for the development of the country." Quebec's brief ended thus:

To sum up, the position taken by the Province of Quebec is neither complicated nor ambiguous.

In its view, Confederation is a pact voluntarily agreed upon and which can be modified only by the consent of all parties. Quebec intends to respect all its terms, it expects others to do the same.

It is at the same time a form of government freely chosen in preference to legislative union, because it is better designed to ensure protection for minorities and the peaceful and harmonious development of the country. This choice of government was decided upon after mature deliberation by statesmen belonging to our two great races and both political parties. The incontestable vision and foresight of these men were not obscured by the disorders of a troubled period. The Province of Quebec believes that this system is still the one best suited to the needs of a vast country peopled by many races.

Finally, the Province of Quebec is prepared to collaborate in any matter of general interest not incompatible with provincial rights; to assist in implementing any reform which might be just and reasonable within the framework of the constitution, and to co-operate generally with the federal authorities and other provincial authorities for the good of all and respecting the rights of each.

RECOMMENDATIONS OF THE REPORT

The Commission's major decision, reached in its study of financial conditions, was that "many provinces whose financial position is not the result of emergency conditions are unable to find the money to enable them to meet the needs of their citizens." The fundamental question confronting the Commission, it was added, was therefore, that of finding a method allowing the improvement and stabilization of provincial finances, failing which the finances of the federal government, on which the efficiency of all provincial agencies depends, might have to suffer disastrous consequences.

The Commission first recommended that the federal government be entrusted with the support of able unemployed and of their dependents. It recalled that other commissions, such as the National Employment Commission and the Social Insurance Commission of Quebec, had already expressed the same opinion, and it added: "So firmly is the Commission convinced of the validity of this conclusion that, even when it comes to consider the situation which will arise if its main recommendations are not implemented, it proceeds on the assumption that the relief of the unemployed who are able and willing to work will become a federal function."

The second important recommendation of the Commission was that "the Dominion should assume all provincial debts (both direct debts and debts guaranteed by the provinces) and that each province should pay over to the Dominion an annual sum equal to the interest it now receives from its investments." As in the Province of Quebec, the municipalities had undertaken obligations which had elsewhere been assumed by the provincial governments, the Commission recommended that the Dominion pay 40 per cent of the combined provincial and municipal debt service in Quebec.

In return the Dominion would receive the sole right to collect succession duties and income tax from individuals as well as from corporations. The Dominion would reciprocate by agreeing "to refrain from competing with the provinces in respect of sources of revenue left to them and should leave the provinces free to collect these revenues in whatever way appears to them most efficient even if the method of indirect taxation should be involved."

The Commission suggested that the present form of subsidies to the provinces be abolished. "The subsidies," it was observed, "have been based on no clear principles and it has been impossible to say whether or not different provinces have received equal treatment." In addition, the Commission recommended another system of subsidizing the provinces "on a national basis," revisable every five years, and calculated in such a manner as to allow the provinces to give their population an assurance of nearly equal services throughout Canada. Such a system would presuppose an equal burden of responsibility for all.

We think it well to recall two other minor recommendations. Had they been adopted, they would have greatly changed the legal basis of federal-provincial relations. The Commission recommended that "the Dominion should have power to implement conventions of the International Labor Organization." This would have amounted to an indirect way of relinquishing to the federal government an important part of provincial jurisdiction. It also stated that it was in favour of introducing powers of delegation in the relations between the two orders of government, so that the Dominion might "delegate any of its legislative powers to a province and vice versa." This amounted to allowing the governments to mock the Canadian Constitution, and deny the federal principle which asserts the supremacy of the Constitution.

We do not propose to undertake here any critical appraisal of these recommendations, as we wish merely to report the facts. It may, however, be useful to point out the strange concept held by the Commissioners regarding the federal system in general and provincial autonomy in particular. Instead of suggesting a guarantee of a sound basis for the fiscal and financial autonomy of the provincial legislatures, so that they might be allowed to fulfil their obligations in complete independence, they recommended a still greater concentration of fiscal powers in the hands of the central government, leaving to the provinces only rights of lesser importance. The Commissioners were confident that their recommendations ensured the financial autonomy of the provinces, but this would be at the cost of their fiscal autonomy being rendered insignificant. This solution was in complete conformity with the ideas previously expressed by John A. Macdonald.

THE CONFERENCE OF JANUARY 1941

In his opening speech of January 14th, 1941, Mr. King, although refusing to state that the Report was a final solution, stated, nevertheless, that the federal government regarded it very favourably and concluded that it was necessary that it be adopted, not only to give the greatest impetus to the war effort, but to lay the foundation of post-war rehabilitation.

What followed is well known: on the one hand, the federal government which would discuss nothing but the Rowell-Sirois Report; on the other hand three Provincial Premiers who refused to sit on any committee which would undertake the discussion of the Report. The Conference adjourned on the second day in a complete deadlock. All provinces, however, declared themselves ready to give their best support to the efforts of the central government in the war effort.

For the federal government, this was merely a deferment. As the Honourable Mr. Isley, Minister of Finance, made it clearly understood at the closing session of the Conference, the central government had decided to pursue the financial war policy which he deemed necessary, with or without the consent of the provinces. He relied on the War Measures Act and his allegedly unlimited powers of taxation. "Under the British North America Act," the Finance Minister declared, "our taxing authority is not limited."

13. FISCAL AGREEMENTS AND PROVINCIAL AUTONOMY

Through its decision to participate actively in the War of 1914, Canada was about to subject its federative system to a serious test: conduct of a war requires concentration of all efforts, as well as of all a country's resources in men and money. For more than four years, the federal government assumed the direction of Canada's political, economic and financial affairs, intervening heavily in the nation's life and focussing all attention upon itself.

ENTRY OF THE FEDERAL GOVERNMENT INTO THE DIRECT TAXATION FIELD

Until the War of 1914, the provinces alone had occupied the field of direct taxation, the Constitution guaranteeing exclusivity of its use to them within their territories for provincial purposes. However, by 1915, the federal government, harassed by the needs of war, had studied the possibility of an income tax on individuals but considered it untimely "at least for the time being," since collection costs would be high and especially in view of the fact that certain provinces and even some municipalities were already in that field.

Such was the opinion expressed by the Finance Minister, Sir Thomas White, who added: "My chief objection, however, to an income tax is the fact that several provinces are also likely to be obliged to resort to measures for receiving additional revenue, and I am of the view that the Dominion should not enter upon the domain to which they are confined to a greater degree than is necessary in the national interest."[1]

Next year, while defending the War Profits Act, (1916), Ottawa's first venture into the field of direct taxation, he clarified his thought and indicated the conditions on which he considered encroachment permissible.

It was a *provisional* measure, due to the war, effective for one year and, moreover, it was aimed only at extraordinary sources of income which were not, in normal times, available to the provinces. The Act, in effect, taxed special profits result-

---

[1] *House of Commons Debates,* February 11th, 1915, p. 86.

ing from war activities but not ordinary profits. The Minister explained this in the following terms:

> As I have stated before, it is a temporary measure, not a permanent measure. It deals with excess profits, or profits beyond the normal, derived since the outbreak of the war . . . If we were considering (. . .) a comprehensive system of taxation, vitally different from that upon which we have relied up-to-date, we should have considered the question of land taxation, taxation possibly upon personal or business property, and income taxation; but these would involve many considerations.
>
> We should have to consider the expedient of embarking upon such an extensive system of taxation, having regard to the requirements of the municipalities and the provinces. Under the British North America Act, while the Dominion government is not confined to any particular mode of taxation, the provinces and, by consequence, the municipalities, are confined to direct taxation.[2]

In the spring of 1917, the question of levying a federal tax on individual incomes again arose. But the Finance Minister, Sir Thomas White, again showed a certain reluctance and, to those who cited the case of England where such a tax existed, he replied:

> If we are to compare Canada with England in this matter, we must bear in mind any respect in which Canada differs from England. There they have only one income tax, that imposed by the Imperial Parliament; but in this country, it is possible to have three different income taxes, that of the municipality, that of the province, and that of the federal government. The income tax is peculiarly within the jurisdiction of the province and is a suitable tax for the purposes of the province and the municipality. In my opinion, the Federal Government should not resort to an income tax until it is indispensably necessary in the national interest that it should do so.[3]

[2] *House of Commons Debates*, March 21st, 1916, p. 2001.

[3] *House of Commons Debates*, May 15th, 1917, p. 1441.

The Minister mainly upheld his previous attitude – no federal income tax because the provinces and municipalities already occupied that field and because such a tax was perfectly suited to their needs. Only a case of national emergency would justify the federal government's entry into that field.

However, two months later, Ottawa decided it was necessary to establish an income tax. In presenting the relevant Bill, the Finance Minister sought to emphasize that this was an innovation in our country's system of financial laws, inasmuch as the federal government had previously contented itself with exploiting the field of indirect taxation, with the sole exception of the new War Profits Tax, established in 1916.

The Minister added that the country's financial situation together with the new obligations contracted for conduct of the war made it necessary to have recourse to an income tax. But whereas, when presenting the War Profits Act the year previous, he had spoken of a provisional measure, he was content, in regard to the present project, to talk about the need for revision after the war:

> I have fixed no time limit upon this taxation measure; but I do suggest – and I should like this suggestion to be in Hansard – that after the war is over, this taxation measure should be deliberately reviewed.[4]

These words were received with scepticism by Mr. Rodolphe Lemieux who observed that the federal government, even after the war, would remain in the income tax field:

> The minister states, however, at least that is what I gathered from his remarks this afternoon, that this income tax is only temporary, that when the war is over it will be revised or wiped out. Personally, I do not share the optimism of my hon. friend on this point, because as a student of history, I remember that when the first income tax was introduced in England by the younger Pitt at the time of the Napoleonic wars, a distinct pledge was given that it was only for the duration of the war, but Sir Robert Peel, Mr. Gladstone and all the other great chancellors of England ought to admit that the thin edge had been introduced into the taxation

[4] *House of Commons Debates,* July 25th, 1917, p. 3765.

system of the United Kingdom and the income tax was there to remain.[5]

The sequence of events was to justify the accuracy of this prediction. Not only would the federal government remain in the field of income taxes, but it would occupy so much of it that the provinces would be practically evicted therefrom, despite their pressing financial needs during the economic crisis of 1929, and also despite the spirit and letter of the Constitution which guaranteed them exclusive jurisdiction in this field for purposes relating to their legislative competence.

WARTIME FISCAL AGREEMENTS (1942)

Of all the recommendations making up the Rowell-Sirois Report, none was more attractive in the eyes of the federal government than that which gave it the monopoly to levy and collect income taxes both in the individual and corporate field. Having been unable, at the time of the 1941 Conference, to convince all the provinces that they should willingly and for all time renounce their rights in this dual field, Ottawa was still unwilling to give up. Recalling the great cost of the War, it returned to the charge a few months later to propose the same plan, but for the duration of the war only. The provinces would give up none of their rights, but would merely cease to exercise them for a limited time. The era of fiscal agreements was about to begin.

The Budget Speech in 1941 announced that the federal government was discontinuing the further study of the Report of the Rowell-Sirois Commission until the end of the war, and was proposing to request that the provinces renounce temporarily their rights to both individual and corporate income tax. In return, the Dominon offered to compensate them.

The Province of Quebec accepted Ottawa's offer. It should be noted that Article 20 of the agreement foresaw, that, at the expiration of the agreement, the Dominion would reduce its rate of taxes on incomes of individuals and corporations by an amount which would allow the province to re-enter this double field, and would especially reduce its tax rate on the income of corporations by at least 10 per cent of these incomes.

The agreement was temporary. The Federal Finance Minister had many times repeated this same statement. For example,

[5]Ibid., p. 3776.

on presenting his proposals to the House of Commons, he had formally declared that it was only "a temporary war-time expedient," an expedient which the provinces were free to accept or reject:

> I should like to emphasize that this is not an attempt to get the provinces out of these tax fields permanently . . . I should also like to emphasize that no province is being forced to accept this offer and any province which does accept will have the right of withdrawal from the plan at the end of any year subject to reasonable notice. Furthermore, the arrangement with the provinces will be discontinued and the Dominion will cease making the payments which are contemplated in the proposal and will agree to reduce its taxes in these two fields proportionately, within one complete fiscal year after the war.
>
> The Plan which I have outlined for alleviating the present difficulties is by no means perfect and is not intended to be more than a temporary wartime expedient.[6]

This was a promise which was to be very difficult to keep.

THE RECONSTRUCTION CONFERENCE (1945-1946)

In August, 1945, only a few days before the end of the war, the Federal-Provincial Conference on "Reconstruction" opened in Ottawa. The federal government had long been preparing for this Conference and presented the provicial prime ministers with a detailed plan for post-war policy, accompanied by ten volumes of references.

In his opening speech, the Prime Minister of Canada reaffirmed that his government was in no way seeking to weaken the provinces, to centralize administrative functions, to subordinate one government to another, or to strengthen one government to the detriment of the others; but, rather, to place each government in a position allowing it to exercise its own functions efficiently and independently. "In other words," he said, "we believe that the sure road of Dominion-Provincial co-operation lies in the achievement in their own spheres of genuine autonomy for the provinces. By genuine autonomy I mean effective financial independence, not only for the wealthier provinces, but also for those less favourably situated."

---

[6]*House of Commons Debates*, 1941 session, Vol. III, p. 2345.

The programme contained a three-fold series of proposals. The first series was entitled *National Problems and Objectives*, the second, *Transition Measures*, and the third, *Public Investment Policy, Social Security and Financial Arrangements*.

As regards "Public Investments," the two objectives aimed at by the federal policy were the maintenance of individual incomes and full employment. Social security measures completed this first plan: health insurance, subsidies to health agencies, subsidies for the combatting of mental diseases and financial grants for the building of hospitals, national old age pensions payable to all by the federal government alone at the age of seventy years, and old age pensions payable by the Dominion and provinces to the needy aged sixty-five to sixty-nine years.

Finally, the federal government proposed to renew the financial agreements reached during the war and due to terminate in 1947. In precise terms, its proposal was as follows: "That after the war the provincial governments should by agreement forego the imposition of personal income taxes, corporation taxes and succession duties, leaving the Dominion Government the full and exclusive access to these revenue sources." In return, Ottawa would measurably increase the payments already being made to the provincial governments.

After the reading of the federal proposals, the Conference adjourned to allow the provincial representatives more time to study and prepare their own proposals. The Province of Quebec, in its brief, strongly criticized the financial proposals and attitude of the federal government, a criticism of which we shall give the concluding part here:

> The financial proposals of the Dominion Government tend to replace the system of fiscal autonomy of the Provinces, in the field of taxation, by a system of grants that would allow the Dominion Government to exercise over them a financial tutelage control. Such a system is incompatible with their sovereignty. Moreover, these proposals exclude the Provinces from the most important fields of direct taxation and to that extent deprive them of the exercise of the powers assigned to them by the constitution. Suppose the extreme case of a central government imposing on the inhabitants of a Province all possible taxes, direct and indirect, so as to leave the provincial government bereft of means for its own administration. Is it not a certainty that provincial autonomy

would then be a meaningless word. The process is none the less an encroachment on the provincial prerogatives, if it is meant to deprive the Provinces of its most important sources of revenue and leaves it with the least important and the most arbitrary sources.

The Quebec Government brief next gave its views on the worth of the federal proposals regarding social security. It found them obscure and rather expensive for the provinces from whom Ottawa was at the same time planning to take away the leading sources of revenue. The Quebec Government, finally, did not consider the federal proposals regarding public investment any more favourably, because it seemed to them that they were connected with matters of provincial jurisdiction and would "amount to an indirect and dangerous seizure by the Central Authority of the provincial natural resources."

In conclusion, the Quebec brief first of all re-asserted that the federal proposals favoured centralization and carried a serious threat directly aimed at the inalienable rights of all provinces. The country, it added, needs three things: clarification and precise definition of the powers of taxing of the federal government and of the provinces in accordance with the spirit and letter of the Canadian Constitution; simplification of public taxation to diminish its cost and facilitate its collection; the collaboration of all powers in arriving at a just moderation in the field of taxation.

In order to achieve these three objectives, the Quebec Government proposed the appointment of a permanent committee consisting of representatives appointed by the ten governments of the country and, "during the time necessary for the study and solution of these Canadian problems" a temporary agreement should be made, based on the very foundations of the Canadian Constitution, between the two orders of government, with a view to renting, "in return for fair compensation, not only material but even constitutional, certain of the province's present taxation powers."

In the spring of 1946, the Conference resumed its sittings, but for a few days only. Quebec once more stated its readiness to lease to Ottawa certain sources of revenue, in particular, "the tax on income under certain conditions," but reaffirmed its opposition to the overall federal programme.

The Conference, having arrived at no definite decision, was forced to adjourn on May 3rd, 1946. Its dramatic end recalled in every feature that of the Federal-Provincial Conference of 1941 entrusted with studying and, if possible, adopting the recommendations of the Rowell-Sirois Report. In both cases, the federal government and some provinces, including the largest ones, had clashed completely, and, as no one had been willing to retreat, a completely new beginning had to be made.

THE 1947 AGREEMENTS

The federal government did not abandon the fight. In the very next month, the Budget Speech announced new offers to the provinces, offers of a purely financial nature and quite unrelated to any social security programme. While expressing a wish for unanimous agreement, Ottawa made it clearly understood that it was ready to reach an agreement with any provincial government which requested it.

In 1947, and at the beginning of 1948, seven provinces signed agreements with the federal government, and the entrance of Newfoundland in the Canadian Confederation in 1949 brought this number to eight. Only Quebec and Ontario remained outside of this new financial structure.

On March 25th, 1947, in his Budget Speech, the Quebec Treasurer, the Hon. Onésime Gagnon, after pointing out that, under the federal proposals, Quebec would receive less per person than all the other provinces, qualified the negotiations undertaken with the various provincial governments in these terms: "the most odious bargaining noted in the annals of Canadian history," and he added:

[Trans.] The present policy of the federal government is, in fact, contrary to the spirit of Confederation. Confederation will endure as long as the different parts comprising it study their common problems in a spirit of mutual respect. At the present time, there is no doubt that, if the centralizing policy were implemented, the economic and political future of the provinces would be seriously compromised. The provinces need their sources of income in order to meet their obligations. The best internal policy for Canada would be to favour the provinces in every possible way, so that they might be allowed the full exercise of their rights and the complete fulfilment of their obligations.

At the expiration of the war-time agreements in 1947, nothing remained for the two dissenting provinces but to re-organize their own taxation systems. This they immediately did.

THE FEDERAL-PROVINCIAL CONFERENCE OF DECEMBER, 1950

In December, 1950, all the provinces met in Ottawa for the purpose of studying two questions of prime importance: Old age pensions and the renewal for 1952 of the 1947 financial agreements. At the opening session, the Prime Minister of Canada, the Right Honorable Louis St. Laurent, announced that his government was "prepared to enter again into so-called tax-rental agreements with all provinces in terms similar to though not identical with, the agreements now in force with eight provinces."

On the whole, the provincial prime ministers were inclined to accept the principle of such a renewal. The Prime Minister of Quebec, however, declared that he disapproved, as a general rule, "of a system of federal subsidies to replace the financial powers which are essential to democratic government," further noting that the taxation powers which the federal government declared itself unable to do without were also indispensable to the provincial, municipal, and school administrations.

During the meetings, the Minister of Finance, Mr. Douglas Abbott, set forth the bases of the suggested agreement concerning the rental of fiscal fields. After giving due credit to the moderation and caution of the two provinces of Quebec and Ontario which had signed no fiscal agreements, but whose fiscal policies during these five years had caused "no serious complications to our national economy," the Minister proposed the same two formulas as in 1947, but with guaranteed minimum payments based on the increase per capita in Gross National Product and the increase in population of the province from 1942 to 1948. In other words, the guaranteed minimum payments would be based on 1948 figures.

Then Mr. Abbott stated a third and new formula, particularly favouring Ontario, which by the new formula would receive an amount increased by somewhat more than two million dollars.

During the months which followed the Conference, negotiations continued between the federal government and the various provincial governments, and these negotiations resulted in some changes in detail in the original proposals. Then, during 1952, nine provinces finally concluded a five year fiscal agreement with Ottawa, Quebec being the sole exception.

THE QUEBEC INCOME TAX ACT OF 1954

At the time of the 1947 and 1952 agreements, a section in the federal Act provided that, if a province remained outside the agreements and collected its own income tax, the people of such province would be entitled to a reduction of 5 per cent of the tax payable to the federal government.

In February, 1954, the Legislative Assembly of the Province of Quebec also set up a law imposing, for a three-year period beginning on January 1st, 1954, a personal income tax amounting to about 15 per cent of the federal tax. The head of the provincial government made it clearly understood that Ottawa should credit Quebec taxpayers for amounts thereunder which they paid to the province. This implied a request for full deductibility of the provincial tax. The Budget Speech of April, 1954, revealed the federal government's answer: this answer was negative.

A dispute of several months' duration then ensued between the governments. Following this, in October, 1954, the Prime Ministers of Canada and Quebec met in Montreal and laid the foundation for a temporary agreement, the latter undertaking, among other things, to omit from the preamble of the provincial Act imposing an income tax the statement that the province possesses a right of priority in matters relating to direct taxation.

Finally, in January, 1955, the Prime Minister of Canada made his government's answer known. The proposed deduction, he said, raises administrative difficulties and complications for the taxpayers. Moreover, it "makes the real incidence of the provincial tax depend on the terms of the federal law and makes the total amount deducted from the federal tax depend on the terms of the provincial law." These were his reasons,

> We feel that it would be more satisfactory to reduce the federal income tax by a fixed percentage in any province which imposes and collects a provincial tax and thereby let both federal and provincial taxes stand on their own feet without either government having to provide for a deduction of one tax from the other.

At the same time the Prime Minister announced the two measures which his government intended to take pending the outcome of a new Federal-Provincial Conference: Parliament would immediately be requested a) "to amend the federal income tax law in order to make a reduction of 10 per cent for all taxpayers of any province where a provincial income tax is levied on income for the years 1955 and 1956;" b) "at the same time we will ask parliament to release from its present tax rental agreement any province which would prefer the new arrangement."

Briefly, instead of "deductibility" at 15 per cent, Ottawa was granting Quebec taxpayers a "reduction" of 10 per cent. This left the two governments in their respective positions and did nothing to settle the problem of fiscal relations between them.

The heads of all governments in Canada met in Ottawa in April, 1955, for the purpose of settling their future relations in the fiscal field. Prime Minister St. Laurent indicated that, failing a better system, it may be necessary to foresee a prolongation of the present agreements, with the addition of a few changes of a minor nature. If a province, he added, preferred not to endorse the fiscal agreements, the federal government would in its case apply its rate reduction policy inaugurated for Quebec in January, 1955.

14. AMENDMENTS TO THE CONSTITUTION (1940-1951)

During the period which we have just described, the federal government had been increasing its powers in the constitutional field. From 1940 to 1951, indeed, the Canadian Constitution was to undergo a complete series of amendments whose form and basis are of particular interest to Quebec. The various Canadian governments would seek to lay down an overall formula which would permit amendment of the 1867 Act without in every case having recourse to the authority of the British Parliament.

UNEMPLOYMENT INSURANCE (1940)

The period under discussion began with the constitutional amendment regarding Unemployment Insurance. For the first time since 1867, a transfer of power was to be made between the two orders of government. How could this be done?

In January, 1937, the Judicial Committee of the Privy Council had declared the federal law on employment and social insurance to be *ultra vires*. In the following session, the federal government had declared that it had wished to "be sure of the provinces' support with the aim of bringing to the British North America Act a change authorizing the Canadian Parliament to establish immediately a national scheme of unemployment insurance." On June 25th, 1940, Mr. King announced to the House of Commons that the provinces had accepted the planned constitutional amendment. This decision had been delayed, he declared, but "today, we are able to introduce an Act which carries with it the consent of every single province of the Dominion. That is a great achievement."

ELECTORAL REDISTRIBUTION (1943 AND 1946)

In the matter of unemployment insurance, the federal government had not only consulted the provinces, but had also awaited their consent before doing anything. On the admission of Prime Minister King himself there was no way whatever of doing otherwise.

From 1943 on, a new attitude was to prevail. This new attitude might be summed up in this way: When their powers and privileges are not involved, in any constitutional amendment sought by the federal government, there is no need for provincial governments to be consulted nor to give their consent. By its actions, Ottawa was to show that it deemed itself the sole judge in determining whether or not the amendments which it proposed were harmful to the powers and privileges of the provinces.

The 1943 amendment had as its aim postponement, until after the war, of the readjustment of representation in the House of Commons necessary after each Census, by virtue of Article 51 of the British North America Act. The delay in the alteration of the electoral map was especially harmful to Quebec. A few days after Mr. King's declaration, the Quebec Legislative Assembly protested unanimously and the Premier, Mr. Godbout, made the province's dissatisfaction known to Ottawa in a letter.

It was on this occasion, and in response to the objection that the federal government could not act since the Province of Quebec was opposed to this amendment, that the new Minister of Justice, Mr. Louis St. Laurent, made a declaration of principle.

The Minister of Justice declared that Confederation was not really a pact between the provinces. The provinces exercise soveignty over the matters which were entrusted to them by the Act of 1867 and, if it were a matter of taking from them any one of their powers and transferring it to the federal government, it would certainly be necessary to obtain their consent. But such was not the case in this mater of representation in the House of Commons:

> That is something which is not allocated to the provincial legislature or to the provincial governments. That is something which interests the inhabitants of the provinces, but the inhabitants of the provinces as electors have sent representatives to this national parliament to represent them, and I suggest that when dealing with matters in that category the members elected by the people of the provinces, who are also the people of Canada, are those who have to take their responsibility in determining whether they are in the interest of Canada or otherwise.[1]

---

[1]*Debates of the House of Commons,* 1943 Session, Vol V, p. 4366. This type of argument would bring many protests here. There were, in the Act of 1867, rights and privileges conferred

In other words, the Minister was refusing the provincial legislatures the right to have any say in the composition of the very
organisms of the federal state.

The British Parliament adopted the amendment requested
by the Canadian Parliament. During the debate, Quebec's
opposition was mentioned, but Mr. Attlee merely answered in
the name of the government that he was not aware of such
opposition and that, in any case, as it was a matter of an
Address voted by the two Houses of the Canadian Parliament,
it was difficult for the British Parliament to inquire into the
background of the affair.

The question was to rebound later when the federal government decided to alter the very basis of the system of representation in the House of Commons. To do this, it was necessary
to modify section 51 of the Act of 1867, which stated that
Quebec was to have a fixed number of sixty-five representatives.

Without consulting the provinces, the government presented
to Parliament an Address to this end. The Minister of Justice
took the opportunity to clarify the ideas which he had already
expressed in 1943. The changing of representation in the House
of Commons, he declared in substance, is a question which does
not concern the provinces, because they have jurisdiction only
in matters mentioned in section 92.

In Ottawa, a new theory was prevailing. In London, the
politicians did not claim to have any right to intervene in
Canadian domestic problems and considered the change requested by the Canadian Parliament as a mere formality. The
road was open to legalizing the federal thesis.

THE "FEDERAL REPATRIATION" OF THE CONSTITUTION (1949)
In 1949, the federal government undertook to resolve the almost
century-old problem of a general method of amending the
Canadian Constitution. Until that time, it had on occasion been
necessary to apply to the British Parliament in order to bring
about any change in the Act of 1867. This method was outmoded and ill-suited to the sovereign state which Canada had
become.

---

on the provinces, both by virtue of their sovereign political
authorities and as social and geographic communities; in both
cases only the provincial governments can truly express the
opinion of the provincial communities as such.

On September 14th, 1949, the Prime Minister, Mr. Louis St. Laurent, wrote a letter to each of the provincial Prime Ministers. In his letter he informed them of the federal government's efforts to find a satisfactory way of avoiding this formality in the future. With this end in view, it had been decided that there should be submitted to Parliament during its next session "an address requesting an amendment of the British North America Act by the United Kingdom parliament to vest in the parliament of Canada the authority to amend the constitution of Canada but only in relation to matters not coming within the jurisdiction of the legislatures of the provinces, nor affecting the rights and privileges of the provinces, or existing constitutional rights and privileges with respect to education and to the use of the English and French languages." Such an amendment, the letter went on, "would give the Canadian parliament the same jurisdiction over the purely federal aspects of our constitution that the provincial legislatures already possess over the provincial constitutions." This letter initiated a flood of correspondence between the provincial Prime Ministers and the Prime Minister of Canada.

The Prime Minister of Quebec, in his letter of September 21st, 1949, after re-stating the contractual nature of Confederation, concluded with a statement affirming the necessity of submitting to the consideration and approval of the provinces the projected changes in the Canadian Constitution. "Do you not think that it would be arbitrary on the part of the federal government to decide *ex parte* and of its own authority which are federal rights and which are the rights of the provinces? It seems clear to us that it does not belong to one of the parties to a multilateral contract to declare itself the supreme arbitrator in the interpretation of this contract and to assume on its sole authority rights which profoundly concern the other contracting parties."

In the exchange of letters which followed, the Prime Minister of Canada re-stated his position in these terms:

What we do claim, and what we propose to secure at the present time, is a practical method of having made in Canada, by the Federal Parliament alone, not "all amendments" to the constitution which are the exclusive concern of the federal authority. We believe, we already have the right to have such amendments made without consulting the provincial authorities just as the provincial legislatures have the right, without consulting the federal authorities to make themselves any amendment they consider desirable of those provisions which concern them exclusively.

In spite of the opposition of the Province of Quebec, the Prime Minister of Canada proposed, on October 17th, in the House of Commons, that an Address be sent to the King requesting him to seek adoption by the Parliament of the United Kingdom of such an amendment to the Act of 1867.

It was thus that Ottawa acquired from London the right to amend "the Constitution of Canada," with certain reservations in particular fields. It is not to be doubted that these exceptions were of greater importance than the general rule itself. However, the federal government had nonetheless obtained what it had never previously ventured to demand: amendment in its favour without either consultation with, or consent of, the provinces of Article 91 providing for the insertion of a new paragraph conferring upon it a new power. However, in 1867, it had been expressly stated that the provinces would have the right, with one exception, to change their constitutions. The federal government was given no such powers in the Act.

THE CONSTITUTIONAL CONFERENCES OF 1950

The Prime Minister of Canada called together at Ottawa the Provincial Prime Ministers in the month of January, 1950, for the purpose of discussing a means of amending the Constitution in matters regarding both the federal and provincial authorities.

It was not long before it was realized that everyone was in agreement that the British North America Act should be finally and wholly repatriated to Canada. Several provinces, however, objected to the hasty and unilateral mode of procedure which the federal government had used in having itself granted the power to modify the Constitution in matters within its competence.

What followed is well known. The Prime Minister of Canada stated that the federal amendment of 1949 should not be considered as any obstacle to a mutual understanding among the governments. He was, therefore, not opposed to the idea that the Conference look for a general basis for amendment which would be valid for the whole Constitution. This procedure, once adopted, could render the federal move of 1949 void. However, if the Conference did not succeed in establishing such a procedure there would be no question of asking for revocation of the 1949 Act.

The Conference set to work. In a short time agreement was reached on three points: a) the one hundred and forty-seven sections of the Constitution are not all of equal importance and should not be amended in one and the same way; b) certain sections are of interest not to all eleven governments, but to a few only, with the result that any right to amend them must belong to these few; c) a fair number of sections of the Act of 1867 have become outmoded and useless and should be abrogated.

The Conference, therefore, agreed to divide the Constitution into six sections, of which five would each have their own mode of amendment – the sixth relating to the sections to be dropped. It would follow that the federal government alone could amend the sections which were its exclusive concern, and that the same would be true for the provincial Legislative Assemblies. In matters of interest to both federal and provincial authorities, it would be necessary to determine whether all provinces were interested, and, in such a case, the consent of at least the majority would be required. Otherwise it would be sufficient to obtain the consent of the interested provinces. Finally, for any changing of the provisions concerning fundamental rights "as for instance, but without restriction, education, language, solemnization of marriage, administration of justice, provincial property and lands, mines and other natural resources," it would be necessary to obtain the unanimous consent of the Federal Parliament and provincial assemblies.

The Conference proceeded no further in its work and adjourned after accepting the appointment of a permanent commission representing the federal government and the provincial governments, and having as its purpose continuation of the task already begun.

A few months later, the discussions on the Constitution were resumed at Quebec. They were, however, to be confronted with two extremely difficult problems: that of determining the number of provinces whose consent would be required for any amendment and that of the place to be given, in the schedule, previously prepared for classifying the sections of the Constitution, to paragraph 13 of Article 92 granting the provinces the sole right to legislate on "property and civil rights."

In its preliminary Brief, the government of the Province of Quebec asked for an essentially Canadian Constitution, which would possess the nature of a treaty or agreement and would be drawn up in the two official languages. The Brief next enumerated the powers of the federal and provincial authorities, stating in particular that "matters of civil law, of municipal law and of school law should be adjudicated upon, in the last resort, by a Court of Appeal set up by each Province, the Judges of which should be appointed by each Province."

The Conference of September, 1950, adjourned without having made any important decisions. It had emphasized the opposition existing, not so much between the federal and provincial governments, as between the provinces themselves. This opposition had not been shown so forcefully at any point as it was in the discussion on "property and civil rights". Certain provinces, wishing to have Ottawa assume the cost of social security measures, declared themselves ready to agree that this paragraph of Article 92 be amended by a simple majority of the provinces; but others, more jealous of their autonomy, refused to adopt such a system of amendment. Quebec, in particular, could not easily consent to it without renouncing not only part of its political autommnomy but also its cultural autonomy, that is to say, the power of organizing independently the social life of its population according to its own conceptions of Man and life in society. For Quebec it was not merely a matter of greater material security, but of the maintenance and progress of its social institutions and of the way of life and very existence of the French-Canadian group as such.

15. CONDITIONAL SUBSIDIES

The most recent period in federal-provincial relations has been characterized in all fields by an expansion of federal activity. This expansion has quite frequently been of the nature of true imperialism towards the provinces. Thus, the federal government is already exercising general control in the financial and economic fields, and has succeeded in having its claims in the field of constitutional law legalized. It is now seeking to invade still further the field of provincial affairs by exercising the power it claims to possess of spending its revenues as it sees fit, even for provincial purposes.

There exists for this purpose a standard method, well known since the end of World War I: conditional subsidies to the provinces. The federal government offers the provinces financial help for certain specific purposes and on certain conditions. As we are now concerned with a phenomenon of prime importance, and one which is tending to become a permanent feature in our federal system, it is fitting that we should study it in detail and measure its scope.

THE PROGRAMME OF CO-ORDINATION OF VOCATIONAL TRAINING (1942)

The Vocational Training Co-ordination Act, 1942, initiated a vast programme of help to the provinces in this field. This programme assumed seven different aspects: 1) youth training; 2) aid to students through bursaries; 3) apprentice training; 4) training of the unemployed; 5) assistance to the provinces for vocational schools; 6) training of military personnel; 7) training of workers for defence industries.

The most important of these fields is undoubtedly that concerning the aid to vocational schools. In 1945, nine provinces signed a ten-year agreement on the matter with the federal government, an agreement which was to be studied again during the Federal-Provincial Conference of October, 1955. By virtue of this agreement, the federal government has paid to the provinces for vocational schools an amount of about $113,000,000.

FAMILY ALLOWANCES (1944-1945)

In 1944, the federal government once more intervened in the

provincial field. However, it did not on this occasion trouble to reach an understanding with the provinces.

During the debates in the House of Commons, the problem of the law's constitutionality was presented. The Opposition, while approving of the purpose and principle behind the law, maintained that it was not constitutional, that it infringed upon provincial powers, that it related to basic social relations, and that it would affect the provincial systems of social security. It was said, in other words, that the law in question "proposed to do things which this parliament had no power to do and this without even consulting the provinces first."

As Minister of Justice it was the duty of Mr. Louis St. Laurent to defend the constitutionality of the projected law. This he did mainly in a long speech in the House on July 25, 1944. The Minister of Justice concluded his arguments with statements which have since become standard and which we have even found reappearing in certain Briefs presented to our Commission:

> If the legislation which disposes of the fund is in reality legislation regulating matters which are within provincial control, then the object of the legislation is not to raise a fund and dispose of it but to impinge upon the exclusive legislative jurisdiction of the province.

However, according to his statement, the family allowances' law aimed in no way at "regulating" a field of provincial jurisdiction. It merely allocated a certain monthly provision of money to each child "the only condition attached being that the person to whom the money is paid shall apply it for the maintenance and better upbringing of that child." And the Minister insisted:

> There is nothing else whatever; no obligation of any kind is imposed. The bill is not drawn in such a way that if it were shown that a person had received the allocation and mis-applied it, he would commit an offence. Offences are set out in the act, but that is not one of them. No obligation is imposed upon anyone; no contractual right is interfered with; no family right is affected.

In Quebec, the new law brought many objections. The Quebec Prime Minister wrote a letter to the Canadian Prime Minister protesting the federal initiative. Going still further, during the 1945 session, he caused to be adopted a provincial law on family allowances. This law was never brought into force.

As to the federal law, in spite of Quebec's protests it went into force in July, 1945, and is still in force. At the present time it subjects the federal government to an expenditure of more than $300,000,000 per year, a sum of which the Province of Quebec, because of its many children, receives a good share (more than $100,000,000), but in the distribution of which its government, it appears, has absolutely nothing to do nor to say.

THE NATIONAL PROGRAMME OF HYGIENE AND HEALTH (1948)

In 1945, at the time of the Reconstruction Conference, the federal government suggested a very ambitious programme of social security including, among other measures, a plan for health insurance, subsidies to health services, and financial aid for the building of hospitals.

The federal government, by the Act on national physical fitness, in 1943, had already initiated a system of conditional subsidies to the provinces. Foreseeing rapid developments during the years to come in the health field, it also set up, in 1944, a Department of National Health and Welfare, especially charged with supervising the preservation and improvement of public health, in collaboration with the provinces.

To this Department was entrusted the task of administering the national health grants program adopted in 1948. This programme, in effect, established ten grants which included, in modified form, three of the four types of assistance offered in the 1945 proposals. The Prime Minister qualified these as being "fundamental pre-requisites of a nation-wide system of Health Insurance."

The original first grants were for the following: 1) health services; 2) building of new hospitals; 3) general public health; 4) mental health; 5) anti-tuberculosis measures; 6) the controlling of cancer; 7) the fight against veneral diseases; 8) crippled children; 9) professional training; 10) research in the field of public health.

The provinces were to submit their plans in these fields; if they received the approval of the Minister of National Health and Welfare, a fixed sum, derived from federal funds, would be available for the carrying out of such plans. As a result of this programme, the federal government, from 1948-1953, placed at the provinces' disposal more than $160,000,000.

We cannot doubt that such a programme has contributed greatly to the improvement of health and hygiene services in the various provinces, and that it has especially facilitated the building of hospitals. We must, moreover, acknowledge the fact that all provinces eagerly accepted the financial offers of the federal government in this matter. From the constitutional and federative point of view, we must note that the federal generosity had other practical results: on the one hand, they allowed the central government to justify in some measure its policy of monopolizing the field of direct taxation; on the other hand, they offered it the opportunity to busy itself once more in the affairs of the provinces and to prepare the ground for a future claim to jurisdiction in this regard.

OTHER FEDERAL SUBSIDIES ACCEPTED BY QUEBEC

We should once more mention certain other subsidies granted by the federal government to the provinces, and accepted by the Quebec government, especially those regarding the aged, the blind and the invalid.

In the 1951 amendment to the Canadian Constitution, the federal government obtained the right to legislate on old age pensions. It did so immediately and its law became effective during January of 1952. At the Federal-Provincial Conference of December, 1950, Ottawa proposed, in addition, to pay half the cost of a programme of aid to needy persons between the ages of 65 and 69. All provinces agreed to this, and in 1952 the new programme came into effect. Since 1952 a similar system for aid to the blind has been in existence except for the fact that the federal contribution amounts to 75 per cent of $40 per month for anyone eligible under the terms of provincial law. This involved for Ottawa the spending of about $3,000,000 for the year 1953-54.

These two programmes were completed by another set up in 1954 and brought into effect in Quebec in 1955: the programme of assistance to disabled persons. The federal government reimbursed the province for 50 per cent of a monthly subsidy of $40 paid to any person recognized as an invalid under the conditions of the provincial law.

FEDERAL SUBSIDIES REFUSED BY THE QUEBEC GOVERNMENT

The system of conditional subsidies works without too much difficulty when all the provincial governments accept the federal offer, but, if a few or even one among them refuse it, there

arise many criticisms and recriminations, and not without reason. The taxpayers of the unwilling provinces, indeed, find
themselves paying just the same for the application in other
provinces of a programme from which they receive no benefit
in their own province.

From 1927 to 1936, the Quebec government refused to participate in the plan for old age pensions established by the
federal government. In these last years there are two typical
examples of a refusal of this kind: they concern subsidies for
the building of the Trans-Canada Highway and grants to
universities.

Regarding the Trans-Canada Highway, a first Federal-Provincial Conference was held at Ottawa in December, 1948, and
ended, it seemed, on a note of general agreement in principle. In
the following year, moreover, the federal government adopted
its law on this matter – an Act which allowed it to reach an
agreement with the provinces on the building of the Highway
and to spend for this purpose over a five-year period an amount
not to exceed $150,000,000. As in the other previous pro-
grammes, it offered to reimburse the provinces up to 50 per cent
of the costs incurred by them in the project's realization. In
1950, all the provinces signed or expressed their desire to sign
an agreement of this nature, "but Quebec declined to sign because, in that province's opinion, the Agreement did not include
sufficient guarantee for the protection of the Province of
Quebec."

There is, finally, another federal subsidy in force for only a
few years, and which the Province of Quebec refuses to accept:
it is that relating to universities. It came about as a result of a
special recommendation of the *Royal Commission of Inquiry
on National Development in the Arts, Letters and Sciences in
Canada* – known as the Massey Commission. In its Report,
which had high intellectual value, the Commission began by
making what they claimed to be an essential distinction between
formal education and *general*, or *non-academic* education, that
is, between *education proper* and *culture*. They then stated that
"there is no general prohibition in Canadian law against any
group, governmental or voluntary agency, contributing to the
education of the individual in its broadest sense." They further
added that there was for governments a sort of duty to intervene, and "if the Federal Government is to renounce its right to
associate itself with other social groups, public and private, in
the general education of Canadian citizens, it denies its intellec-

tual and moral purpose, the complete conception of the common good is lost, and Canada, as such, becomes a materialistic society."

The Commissioners claiming that the universities "serve the national cause in so many ways, direct and indirect, that theirs must be regarded as the finest of contributions to national strength and unity," finally recommended federal aid to the universities in proportion to the population of each Canadian province: they added, "that the contributions be made after consultation with the government and the universities of each province, to be distributed to each university proportionately to the student enrolment."

The Massey Report had scarcely appeared and become known to the general public when the federal government stated its readiness to furnish financial assistance to the Canadian universities. In fact, as early as June, 1951, it voted a budgetary credit allowing it to spend slightly more than $7,000,000 on university subsidies. Out of consideration for the feelings of Quebec Province it agreed to the formation of a Federal-Quebec Commission which would be entrusted with the distribution of the subsidies. Quebec accepted the federal aid, but for one year only.

In the following year, the Provincial Government opposed the federal subsidies giving as its reason that education, including university education, is an exclusively provincial matter in which the federal government has no right to meddle. Finally, to compensate for the losses incurred by the Quebec universities as a result of this refusal, it began to grant them special subsidies from the funds derived from its law on personal income tax established in 1954.

No other federal move in the field of conditional subsidies, it seems, has underlined to any greater extent the delicate situation in which Ottawa's repeated generosities for provincial purposes has placed Quebec. The other provinces may accept them without danger, but this is not always the case for Quebec, especially when such gifts concern such a sensitive and important field, from the spiritual point of view, as education. There is no doubt that it can always refuse them, but in that case, its own citizens are the ones being punished, since these latter pay for the maintenance in all provinces of a system of subsidies from which they themselves receive no benefit.

Conclusions on Conditional Subsidies

In Canada as elsewhere, wars and economic depressions have proved harmful to the federative system. The First World War saw the federal government invade the direct taxation field for the first time. As a measure of compensation it offered the provinces additional subsidies. The 1930-1935 depression showed the vulnerability of provincial finances. There followed a chaotic situation which the Rowell-Sirois Commission proposed to remedy by entrusting to the federal government all the main sources of income. The Second World War finally gave Ottawa a commanding position, allowed it to present its centralizing plans in the name of efficiency, simplicity and economy of administration, and to develop a whole new system of conditional subsidies, thanks to which it could closely follow a fair number of provincial activities. The result of all this was a great deterioration of the federal spirit and a rebirth of the imperialist idea after the Macdonald pattern.

The history of federal-provincial relations, as well as Canadian geography and sociology, teach us, however, that it must not be too quickly proclaimed that this march towards centralization is "irrevocable" and "inevitable." Let peace be restored to the world and present prosperity be maintained and the federal government will have lost most of the arguments which it has invoked for dictating provincial fiscal and financial policies. All provinces, meanwhile, should recognize their own dignity as major governments in this country, and offer a united front in demanding their rights. It was in this manner that they succeeded in winning their political and juridical autonomy; it is in this manner that they must proceed to insure their fiscal and financial autonomy. We repeat that we believe neither in determinism nor fatalism in history. On the one hand, it seems to us more fair to acknowledge that "the federal government and the provinces have in turn played leading roles," and to think, on the other hand, that "these continual oscillations will, without doubt, continue to be an important feature in Canadian federalism."

Quebec's attitude may be harmful to itself for two reasons: firstly, it isolates it in the Canadian scheme of federation and allows its opponents to insinuate that Quebec is opposed to the progress of the whole country; secondly, it creates a situation which ultimately exerts on the people and government of the Province a nearly unbearable pressure, by inducing the people to wish for, and the government to be resigned to accept, the financial benefits of federal acts which are only to some extent in agreement with the way of life and concept of Man and Society proper to French Canadians. In this regard, the situation resulting from the federal plan of subsidies to universities closely resembles that which confronted the Liberal Government of Mr. Taschereau from 1927 to 1936, regarding the federal programme of old age pensions.

In spite of these objections, whose seriousness should cause a federal government to hesitate long before offering to provinces or institutions any plan which it knows to be unacceptable in principle to Quebec, at times it remains nonetheless necessary that the latter continue, even though alone, the struggle in favour of provincial rights. By reason of its history, as well as of the cultural character of its population, Quebec is not a province like the others, whatever may be said to the contrary. It speaks in the name of one of the two ethnic groups which founded Confederation, as one of the two partners who officially have the right to live and expand in this country. It is the only one able to represent one of these two partners, just as it alone may determine its reasons for refusing federal largesse.

Throughout its history it has rarely abandoned the cause of provincial autonomy. During the last few years it has even posed as the champion of Canadian federalism, a federalism which is neither so obsolete nor out-of-date as some have tried to describe it. In any case, the history of federal-provincial relations in Canada does not show that the Province of Quebec, by wishing to maintain a true federalism, is waging a battle already lost, and that there is no other alternative for it than that of joining completely in the scheme which the Ottawa Government offers and which certain people speak of as "the new Canadian federalism."

16. THE NEW FEDERALISM: THEORETICAL CONSIDERATIONS.

Since the Second World War a "new federalism" has been erected on the foundations of the previous system. It is a system characterized by the predominant place which the central government occupies (or seeks to occupy) in the life of the Canadian community, mainly on the grounds of national defence, social welfare and security, economic stability and the fiscal system.

This new orientation of Canadian federalism, we are told, is justified by numerous objective factors; it is inscribed in reality and seems inevitable. True, the Province of Quebec does not accept it and, believing it is staying faithful to the original spirit of Confederation, seeks to bring Canadian federalism back to what it was before 1940. But, by refusing "the new federalism," it is said to be fighting a battle already lost, because the new orientation will continue over a long period and "must be considered irreversible." Thus the Province is in a dilemma: "either it accepts the new Canadian federalism or else it refuses and disassociates itself from it." Since separatism seems neither possible nor desirable, "the dilemma which confronts the Province of Quebec is said to call for only one solution: a lucid integration with the new Canadian federalism."[1]

The basis for the "new federalism" is to be found in an idea as old as Confederation itself, an all-powerful central government exercising all the main state powers, controlling the principal revenue sources and extending its control over the provincial legislatures. The "new federalism" exerts itself through the subtle and dangerous use of three powers, of ill-defined and uncertain limits, which lend themselves to multiple combinations. These are the general power to legislate, the "unlimited" power to tax and the no less "unlimited" power to spend. In these we have the practical, constitutional basis of the "new federalism"; and it is important to examine it closely, so as to determine its solidity.

---

[1] Maurice Lamontagne, *Le Fédéralisme canadien* (Quebec 1954) Epilogue, pp. 284 et seqq.

THE GENERAL POWER TO LEGISLATE

The opening clause of Section 91 confers on the central Parliament the power "to make laws for the Peace, Order and good Government of Canada, in relation to all Matters not coming within the Classes of Subjects by this Act assigned exclusively to the Legislatures of the Provinces." Invoked on a great many occasions before the Privy Council in support of the central government, it has received from that Imperial tribunal an interpretation which those who belong to what has been called the "Macdonald-ian School" refuse to accept.

According to this school, the Privy Council has given a too restrictive interpretation to the opening clause of Section 91 – an interpretation neither in conformity with the intentions of the Fathers of Confederation nor with the letter of the Constitution. Their interpretation runs something like this: that the opening clause of Section 91 confers upon the central Parliament a general and preponderant power to legislate in the national interest as well as the main residiary power, or residue of the powers not assigned in the Act of 1867.

In other words, the initial clause of Section 91 is supposed to be the clause which would govern the whole distribution of powers as between the central Parliament and the provincial legislatures, and it would confer on the former a general power which would have primacy over the powers expressly and exclusively assigned to the provincial legislatures by Section 92. Therefore, when the central Parliament makes laws "for the peace, order and good government of Canada," its legislation should, at all times, be preponderant and exclusive and should prevail even if, for example, it trespassed on "property and civil rights," a subject exclusively reserved to the provincial authority. But if any such interpretation had prevailed before the courts, and especially before the Privy Council, the federal system would long since have ceased to exist in Canada. No one has better remarked the consequences of such a position than the authors of the Report of the *Royal Commission on Dominion-Provincial Relations:*

> . . . the bare assertion by the Federal Parliament of a general or national aspect in the subject matter of the legislation would, of itself, justify the legislation under the "peace, order and good government" clause. That clause would then confer tremendous powers on the Federal Parliament, giving it, as Macdonald had proposed, "the general mass of sov-

ereign legislation". The exclusive sphere ensured to the provinces by Section 92 might, if the Dominion so desired, become very small indeed. The power of the Dominion under the "peace, order and good government" clause would become so overwhelming that the federal character of the Constitution would be open to grave doubt. Indeed, under these conditions, the Constitution in its working would approach the legislative union which some of the Fathers desired but which, as they recognized, they could not secure by agreement.[2]

Happily for Canadian federalism the Privy Council rejected this interpretation, notably in its judgment regarding regional prohibition, in 1896.[3] Lord Watson, who delivered the judgment, while recognizing the preponderence of federal legislation based on the powers enumerated in Section 91, none the less refused to admit this same preponderance when such legislation could only be based on the general clause "for peace, order and good government." These words, he declared, do not confer upon the federal Parliament any right to trespass upon any class of subjects which Section 92 exclusively assigns to the legislative assembly of the provinces. In consequence, the general power to legislate is not preponderant with respect to the powers enumerated in Section 92 and it must be strictly confined to questions which are incontestably of national importance and of national interest.

The Privy Council subsequently, in its decisions, followed this rule, to such an extent that in 1930 Lord Tomlin could summarize the whole jurisprudence in this regard in the following general proposition:

The general power of legislation conferred upon the Parliament of the Dominion by Section 91 of the Act in supplement of the power to legislate upon the subjects expressly enumerated must be strictly confined to such matters as are unquestionably of national interest and importance and

---

[2] *Report of the Royal Commission on Dominion-Provincial Relations,* (Ottawa 1940), Vol. I, pp. 57-58.

[3] *Attorney-General for Ontario v. Attorney-General for Canada* (1896) A.C. 348.

must not trench on any of the subjects enumerated in Section 92 as within the scope of provincial legislation, unless these matters have attained such dimensions as to affect the body politic of the Dominion.[4]

In 1896, Lord Watson, after having refused to recognize the general principle of the preponderance of federal legislation founded on the initial clause of Section 91, none the less remarked that certain questions of local and provincial origin might attain proportions such as to affect the body politic of the state and thus justify intervention by the Canadian Parliament with a view to regulating them by legislative means.

From this remark there was to develop the dual doctrine of emergency and of "national dimension" and that is why exercise by the central Parliament of its general power of legislation so closely affects the practice of federalism in Canada today.

The 1914-1918 War was, in fact, the occasion which enabled the Privy Council to elaborate and formulate what has been called the "emergency doctrine." In a succession of cases which immediately followed the war's close, and particularly in the *Reference re Board of Commerce and Combines and Fair Prices Act*, in *Fort Frances Pulp and Power Co. v. Manitoba Free Press Co.*, in *Toronto Electric Commissioners v. Snider*, the Imperial tribunal enunciated the two following rules: 1) in normal times, the general control of property and civil rights remains with the provincial legislatures; 2) in abnormal times, in such special circumstances as those arising from war which imperil national existence, the central Parliament may legislate by virtue of the general powers conferred on it by the opening clause of Section 91, for the peace, order and good government of Canada, and its legislation is valid even if it incidentally encroaches on the powers of the provincial legislatures.

It is noteworthy that, while it formulated this emergency doctrine, the Privy Council refused to recognize equal legitimacy for the second doctrine, that of "national dimension," by which the central Parliament would validly legislate, by virtue of its general power, as soon as its activity had a national bearing, if it had a general aspect or was of national interest. According to some people, the case of *Russell v. The Queen* had established such a doctrine, but in 1925 the Privy Council,

[4] *Attorney-General for Canada v. Attorney-General for British Columbia* (1930), A.C. 111.

faithful to the rule declared by Lord Watson in the case of regional prohibition, set it aside in these terms:

> It appears to their Lordships that it is not now open to treat *Russell v. The Queen* as having established the general principles that the mere fact that Dominion legislation is for the general advantage of Canada, or is such that it will meet a mere want which is felt throughout the Dominion, renders it competent if it cannot be brought within the heads enumerated specifically in s. 91. Unless this is so, if the subject matter falls within any of the enumerated heads in s. 92, such legislation belongs exclusively to Provincial competency.[5]

With the War of 1939-1945, the emergency doctrine immediately came into play, conferring on Parliament all powers necessary to act for the general good of Canada and relegating exercise of provincial autonomy to the background. But the post-war period failed to restore the situation to normal, and it allowed the central government to conserve most of its war powers by invoking the emergency as well as national defence needs.

The emergency doctrine certainly carries a direct threat to Canadian federalism, but at least it is clear, precise and ought, normally, to be temporary. Unfortunately, this is not the case with the second doctrine, brought up since the conclusion of the Second World War, namely, that the initial clause of Section 91 authorizes the central Parliament to legislate, at any time and in any field, provided such legislation has a "national" dimension or has a general aspect and is of national interest. In 1946, by its decision in the *Canada Temperance Federation* case, the Privy Council declared that it is not so much the situation of emergency which must be considered as the real nature of the legislation itself. If it deals with a subject which goes beyond local or provincial concern or interests and, by its inherent nature, interests the Dominion as a whole, then it is within the competence of the latter, as a matter affecting the peace, order and good government of Canada, even though it may, in another aspect, touch on matters specially reserved to the provincial legislature.

Without seeking to minimize the seriousness of this decision, we do not, however, believe it should be given much import-

[5]*Toronto Electric Commissioners v. Snider* (1925) A.C. 396.

ance. In the first place, the case was exactly the same as that of 1882, and the Privy Council could scarcely reject in 1946 what it had maintained at that time. In addition, in subsequent decisions, the Imperial court refused to have revived the theory of the general power to legislate based only on national "dimension." It preferred to base itself on the emergency doctrine, as in the case of the *Japanese Canadians,* and it even reverted to the views it had expressed in 1937 in the case of the *Labour Conventions,* particularly in the two following cases: *Canadian Pacific Railway v. Attorney-General for British Columbia* in 1950, and *Canadian Federation of Agriculture* in 1951.

In fact, the greater danger to the future of true federalism in Canada may be that the Supreme Court should finally allow as a general preponderant principle the doctrine of national "dimension." Supporters of the "new federalism" will not, in any case, fail to invoke such a doctrine in and out of season, basing themselves as well as they can on history, law, the economy, and the social and intellectual welfare of the Canadian people. Thus, for example, the Massey Commission employed this argument several times in favour of federal aid to education, and particularly to the universities. "Universities" it remarks, "serve not only their own region but the nation as a whole in the professions and sciences." And the conclusion follows: "In our view, it can be properly assumed that the national government does in fact recognize certain responsibilities towards problems of higher education in Canada."

Thus the "national" incidence of the question is emphasized and the demand is then made on the "national" government to intervene and to assume greater responsibilities in this field, and the federal government, encouraged by this recommendation, votes grants to the universities. Thus it is that "the new federalism" installs itself.

THE "UNLIMITED" POWER TO TAX

Another theory, no less dangerous to true federalism, is that which claims for the central Parliament an unlimited power to tax. The Act of 1867, sub-section 3 of Section 91, confers on the central Parliament the exclusive power to raise money "by any mode or system of taxation" while sub-section 2 of Section 92 recognizes the no less exclusive right of the provincial legislatures to make laws on "direct taxation within the province in order to the raising of a revenue for provincial purposes."

We therefore find two exclusive powers, one general and

the other particular. That there is at least apparent contradiction between the two is a fact observed by all courts which have had to settle the numerous contestations that have arisen over these two sections. At first sight, the particular would seem to be excluded and withdrawn from the general power, so that the logical solution would seem to be the following: direct taxes in exclusivity to the provinces and all the remainder to the federal Parliament. But this was not how the courts reasoned nor how jurisprudence on these two sections has been established. Basing itself on the restriction included in sub-paragraph 2 of Section 92, viz., "in order to the raising of a revenue for provincial purposes," it has been decided that the two orders of government have equal rights to the direct tax, provided that the one uses it for federal and the other for provincial purposes.

We freely admit that such a distinction manages to avoid legal conflict, but we must observe that a collision, if not a conflict, is inevitable, between two governments which both levy a direct tax, as, for instance, an income tax on their common citizens. And when, moreover, one of these governments claims to have an unlimited power of taxation and arrogates to itself the lion's share, even in the field of direct taxation, which is its colleague's only tax-source, one would have to be blind to deny the existence of conflict.

STATEMENT OF THE CENTRALIST THESIS

The centralist thesis can be easily summed up as follows: the central government has all the taxing powers and can exercise them to the extent that it may leave nothing for the provincial governments. It can impose all the direct taxes allowed the provinces by the Constitution, and others as well. Moreover, the taxes it levies need not be for federal purposes, and there is nothing to prevent it from giving its own taxes priority over provincial taxes. In a word, the central government, according to this thesis, is omnipotent and its power is unlimited.

This latter expression comes up many times in the *Report of the Royal Commission on Dominion-Provincial Relations.* With the "new federalism," this expression has become common and almost classic. And it would seem to mean that the central Parliament has the power to levy any tax whatsoever, for any purpose at all, at no matter what rate, concerning itself only with the country's financial possibilities and the needs of the moment, to the extent that the provinces would not possess any exclusive tax-field but would have to content themselves with whatever the federal government felt like leaving to them.

Critique of the Centralist Thesis

Is the centralist argument admissible *in toto?* To answer that question, one must first confront it with the data of history and of constitutional jurisprudence on the one side, and with the requirements of the federative principle on the other.

To begin with, does history endorse the assertion that the Fathers of Confederation sought to give the Dominion "unlimited fiscal power"? The general impression left from the reading of the debates on this subject is that nobody at that time wanted the direct tax. It was left to the provinces, but in the belief or hope that it would not be of much help to them. When introducing the Confederation Bill to the House of Lords, Lord Carnarvon said:

> The principal subjects reserved to the local legislatures are . . . the raising of money by means of direct taxation. The several Provinces, which are now free to raise a revenue as they may think fit, surrender to the Central Parliament all powers under this head except that of direct taxation.

Here again, it might be argued and maintained that the provinces kept for themselves the whole field of direct taxation. In any case, declarations of this kind are at least sufficient to cast a doubt on the value of the assertion that the Fathers of Confederation desired to give the central Parliament "unlimited powers in fiscal matters."

The historical progress of events is evident; after Confederation, the federal government left the direct tax to the provinces exclusively. Then, forced by the First World War, it penetrated into this territory. Finally, on the advice of the Rowell-Sirois Commission, and owing to the Second World War, it occupied practically the entire field, offering subsidies to the provinces in return. That is how its "unlimited fiscal power" was established and that is how the "new federalism" arose.

If, however, constitutional jurisprudence has any meaning, the federal government's fiscal power is none the less limited. To what, in fact, does all this jurisprudence tend if not to assert with the Privy Council, from the Lambe case in 1887, that "as regards direct taxation within the province to raise revenue for provincial purposes, that subject falls wholly within the jurisdiction of the provincial legislatures." Sub-section 2 of Section 92 imposes a limitation on the general taxing power. The trouble is that, by reducing this limitation to a single question of purpose, the problem, although apparently resolved on the constitutional plane, still subsists on the practical and political plane.

Requirements of the Federative Principle

The federative principle requires a distribution of powers between two orders of government of equal rank and independent of each other, with supremacy of the Constitution in respect of the individual volition of each legislature, either federal or provincial. If these requirements are to be met in practice, each order of government must have at its disposal and under its control the financial resources necessary to discharge its legislative functions and, on the other hand, the fiscal policies of each of the two orders of government must respect the constitutional distribution of powers and must not tend to render them sterile and inoperative.

At the Reconstruction Conference of 1945, the Premier of Nova Scotia declared:

> It is . . . the Dominion's power to levy unlimited taxes in all fields, that is the big club which can be held over provincial heads. If, for example, the Dominion should persist in imposing an initial 30 per cent income tax, should increase its existing rate of succession duties, and should retain a heavy corporation tax, it could render almost completely nugatory the provincial power to impose these direct taxes which are essential to solvency. For any provincial tax imposed in addition to these onerous Dominion levies would impose an intolerable burden on the taxpayers of the province. The province, in short, has lost its bargaining power.

We believe that such a situation, the culmination of federal pretentions to unlimited fiscal power, is contrary to the doctrine of federalism. But in what do federal fiscal pretensions culminate if not in the claim that one of the governments of the Canadian federative state may, on its sole initiative, practically annul and absorb a precise power expressly and exclusively granted to the other governments? One might as well admit that the distribution of powers no longer holds good and that it is no longer the Canadian Constitution which is supreme, but the sole will of the central Parliament.

A choice must be made, for if one admits an unlimited power for one of the governments, the federative principle is sacrificed, first of all in the fiscal field and then in all other fields, since the fiscal power today conditions the exercise of almost all other powers. On the other hand, if one adheres to the federative principle (and we have indicated elsewhere that the only formula acceptable to Quebec and even to Canada as a whole is the federative formula) then one must also adhere to the fiscal autonomy of the provinces, and to an autonomy which must rest, not on the sole good will of the central government nor on its condescension not to use its claimed unlimited powers to the full and to the very end, but on matters and tax-fields which are special and exclusive and over which the threat of a federal invasion does not constantly hover.

THE "ABSOLUTE" SPENDING POWER

In order to build itself up, the "new federalism" is utilizing, more and more, another power. This is the spending power. The central government is of the opinion that it is permissible for it to spend its money for any purpose at all, even for provincial purposes.

Little by little, a vast network of conditional subsidies has been spread which binds the provinces to the central government and which, to a certain extent, provides them with the financial means of discharging their legislative functions, but always at the discretion and on the terms of the wealthy and powerful donor, which prefers this subsidy system, in which it controls everything, as against a reasonable and equitable apportionment of revenue sources.

The Centralist Thesis

What argument is used to justify the central government's attitude in this respect? There is one expression of it which might be termed official, since the courts have already had to deal with a matter of this kind and the two theses, one centralist and the other federalist, have both been sustained. This was the reference to the Supreme Court on the validity of the Employment and Social Insurance Act in 1935.

A majority of the judges declared this Act unconstitutional, but two of them accepted the views of the federal government's attorneys and held it to be *intra vires* by invoking the following reason, viz., under the terms of sub-sections 1 and 3 of Section 81 of the British North America Act, the federal Parliament appears to have an unlimited power to raise money by any mode or system of taxation and to dispose of it as it sees fit.

It was Chief Justice Lyman Duff who sought to justify this viewpoint. Without a doubt, Chief Justice Duff recognized that the federal Parliament could not interfere in the provincial domain on the pretext of exercising a power whose very basis was denied it; but, according to him, the federal Parliament had enacted legislation whose true purpose was to dispose of public funds.

As is known, this view and way of thinking were rejected by the majority of the Supreme Court judges and by the Privy Council itself. It nonetheless continues to influence the central government's behaviour as well as the thinking of a good number of jurists and political men.

Critique of the Centralist Thesis

What should one think of the centralist argument? First of all, let us recognize that it is only the logical complement of the theory of "unlimited" taxing power which we previously examined. If, indeed, the federal government is conceded unlimited taxing powers, it would then be very difficult to deny it the right to spend its revenue as it pleases. In other words, if the federal government can tax, even for provincial purposes, how can it be refused the right to spend the money so collected for the same purposes? The two interpretations go hand-in-hand.

Under a democratic and parliamentary system, it is unnatural that one government should levy taxes for the benefit of another government, even in a federative system. Sub-section 3 of Section 91 does not, it is true, mention that federal taxes should be levied for federal purposes. But this restriction is one of its implicit conditions because it is in conformity both with common sense and with the requirements of the federative principle. What would be the use of a careful distribution of legislative powers, if one of the governments could get around it and to some extent, annul it by its taxation methods and its fashion of spending?

When the federal Parliament spends, it creates, first of all, an obligation which it subsequently discharges, either by, or under the terms of, an Act. If the obligation is one relating to a matter reserved to the legislative competence of the province, the law which gives rise to it, or under whose terms the obligation will arise, must necessarily be a law relating to a matter reserved to the legislative competences of the provinces, and, therefore, is unconstitutional.

In principle, every federal subsidy, especially if it tends to assume a permanent character, which is granted to an institution falling within the exclusive competence of the provinces affects that institution and constitutes an interference in its administration. When, for example, the federal Parliament accords subsidies to the Canadian universities, it is not only disposing of federal property; the prime purpose of such a grant is to assist higher education. Therefore, it is an action which affects education, a field exclusively reserved to provincial legislation.

For these reasons, we believe the right claimed by the federal government to spend its money as it sees fit in the provinces' sphere of activity must be rejected as being unfounded, contrary to the federative principle and to the Canadian Constitution itself. This network of subsidies which the federal government has established has been set up outside the Constitution.

That is where we stand with the "new Canadian federalism." The federal government is now spending, annually, millions of dollars for provincial purposes. It declares itself ready to examine benevolently every new request for financial aid. And the federal government, instead of leaving the field clear to the provinces in the field of direct taxation, so that they themselves can collect the sums required for the discharge of their constitutional functions, is concerning itself with all these questions which are none the less of exclusively provincial concern.

Then it invokes the heavy expenditures which it makes to maintain and even augment its monopoly in the collection of major taxes. By dint of constantly subordinating the provinces to the central government in the financial and fiscal domain, the end result will be complete destruction of the true federative system. The latter requires autonomous governments and cannot be satisfied only with mere administrative divisions at the financial mercy of an omnipotent central authority.

17. THE NEW FEDERALISM:
ECONOMIC, FISCAL AND SOCIAL THEORIES

The "new Canadian federalism" has, as its main objective, assurance to the federal government of complete liberty of action and control over the triple economic, social and fiscal field. One could, no doubt, mention many attempts of like nature during the ninety years which have passed since the birth of the Canadian federation. What is new, however, is the deliberate pursuit of such an objective in the name of the practical demands of economic and social theories all promising prosperity.

During the nineteenth century, and until the outbreak of the First World War, governments generally remained faithful to the maxims of economic liberalism, leaving to private initiative the greatest possible liberty in all fields. In the social field, and according to the prevalent ideas of the time, it was the municipalities that made the first provisions for aid and welfare after confederation. From the beginning of the twentieth century, however, the provincial legislatures entered the field. The federal government also began to be interested in these matters.

Late in the nineteenth century and at the beginning of the twentieth, a wave of immigrants broke over Canada and brought with them the socialistic ideologies of Europe. As early as 1907 a British Columbia representative proposed in the House of Commons that the federal government set up a national scheme of old age pensions.

The War of 1914-1918 gave the federal government the opportunity and pretext of entering the direct taxation field, of exercising certain economic controls and to develop its policy of conditional subsidies to the provinces. In 1919 a federal Ministry of Health was set up and grants for aiding in the fight against venereal disease, and in the development of technical education, were made.

The post-war period was to see the birth of a socialist party in Western Canada. This party in Ottawa lost no time in constituting itself the apostle of social security along the lines of those European concepts favoured by the International Labour Organization. In 1926 the Liberal party in power yielded to socialist pressure and made a firm entry into the welfare field by the passing of its law on Old Age Pensions.

The economic depression of 1929-1930 then rocked the country. Unemployment became general, presenting enormous difficulties for all governments, especially the municipal and provincial governments which, in accordance with the financial and fiscal conceptions of the day, claimed to be in an unfavourable financial position and demanded intervention by the federal authorities. The latter, sharing the same basic concepts, were at first hardly eager to assume such a heavy load. Later, however, as the situation became more serious, the federal authorities ended by providing financial aid, either by giving direct aid to the unemployed, or by public works, or by subsidies to provinces and municipalities.

Canadian thought was gradually becoming pessimistic on the subject of capitalism, at least in its liberal form. It turned, however, to indirect control rather than to the socialist concepts of economic and social control organized in accordance with a single guiding principle. The first step was taken in the monetary field, and there followed a succession of ideas which ended in 1934 with the establishment of the Bank of Canada. Later, full employment became the objective of all minds, and Keynes' theory arrived at the opportune moment to illustrate its workings and requirements. It was at the time of meeting of these currents of thought that the Rowell-Sirois Report appeared. This Report was to furnish inspiration to the federal government's policy of centralization.

There then followed a period completely dominated by the federal government. To allow the latter to legislate on unemployment insurance, the Canadian Constitution underwent amendment in 1940. Ten years later, there followed another amendment in regard to old age pensions. Thanks to the war, fiscal centralization becomes a *fait accompli,* and was to be maintained in the years to follow by means of the system of tax agreements. During the same period, economic centralization was the fashion in the name of theories inspired by Lord Keynes. The central government was multiplying its interventions in the social field: unemployment insurance, family allowances, national health and hygiene programme, pensions to the old between the ages of 65 and 69 years, invalids' pensions.

Upon what theses and theories is this triple centralization – fiscal, economic and social – based, and on what pretext can its continuance be justified?

THESIS OF THE ROWELL-SIROIS REPORT

Although there had been numerous attempts at centralization prior to the Rowell-Sirois Report, the thesis itself had not yet been formulated. It was the Report of the Royal Commission on Dominion-Provincial Relations which gave birth to it in 1940, at least in its historical and legal form. From this capital document, indeed, one draws the impression that the federal government has complete right to priority in the economic and social field, both according to the text of the Constitution and the intentions of the Fathers of Confederation.

The thesis of the Rowell-Sirois Report, in brief, may be thus summed up: Originally, the authors of the Constitution had wished to give the federal government fiscal and economic priority. For various reasons, especially as a result of the too wide interpretation given by the Privy Council to the provinces' powers, the Dominion was not in a position to exercise such a priority, and the result was confusion and uneasiness. It was necessary, therefore, to restore to the Dominion the priority which was its right, and without which it could not ensure the prosperity of the country. The provinces, as a result, had to withdraw from the field of the more important direct taxes and agree to accept federal subsidies according to a national norm. To promote the general welfare of the Canadian people, they were also to recognize without argument the authority of the federal government in the economic life of the country. In regard to some social services, for reasons of uniformity, economy and financial disparity among the provinces, it was decided that these should be entrusted to the Dominion. Thus authorized, the federal government would be able to act swiftly and efficiently in all sectors of the economic field, and meet any crises with much greater chances of success. In short, uniformity and centralization of direction were the prime factors behind Canada's prosperity.

It was not difficult to convince the federal government of the soundness of such reasoning. In the policy which it followed during the war, it went much further and illustrated and confirmed the thesis of the Rowell-Sirois Report. What was said during the Conference on Reconstruction in 1945 implied that during the 1929-1939 depression, when uniformity of control did not exist, the Canadian economy was disorganized. During the war, however, a certain unanimity appeared, and unity of effort became a fact. These last two factors were to bring the war to a victorious conclusion. Therefore, it was inferred that we should remain united under a single control for all post-war tasks.

REQUIREMENTS OF THE "NEW ECONOMICS"

At the time of the writing of the Rowell-Sirois Report, the theories of the English economist, Keynes, had already begun to spread and to influence Canadian minds. Although the Commissioners acknowledged these theories, they did not appear to be too deeply affected by them. There is no doubt that they envisaged public works on a national scale, and public finances in relation to an over-all national revenue. But their social and fiscal recommendations were dictated by considerations of a balanced budget, social welfare and standardization of services, rather than by reasons of economic stabilization.

The War of 1939 and the important role played by Lord Keynes in the economic and financial organization of the British war effort were to bring prominence to his interventionalist doctrines, even within our own government. The federal capital began to swarm with Keynesian economists. It was to these economists that the government was to appeal in its effort to prepare a post-war economic and social programme. They did not fail to include their own ideas in the plans suggested or recommended to the government.

The objective envisaged was the maintenance of economic stability and full employment. But these presuppose that the Canadian people in its entirety (including companies and governments) will be prepared to spend all its cash income for the purchase of all available properties and services, or at least invest such income. Both expenditures and investments, by individuals as well as by companies, should, therefore, be encouraged. Moreover, the government should take a part in this, and co-operate in stabilizing the economy and in ensuring full employment by its own expenditures and investments. This would demand from it an appropriate fiscal and monetary policy, as well as a programme of carefully planned public works.

Fiscal policy would affect enterprise directly by a tax system favouring investment, or by rates of interest which would make it more attractive. It would also influence the available volume of buying power – for investment and consumers' services –

either by modifications in taxation or by provision of social security. The programme of public works would provide employment and restore unused savings to circulation.

Finally, as North American policy in relation to economics has for more than a century been characterized by cyclical variations, the governments would have to learn the art of meeting such variations by means of an elastic policy of taxation which would take into account both economic and fiscal factors.

The new policy necessarily entailed a considerable number of social security measures regarded as indispensable for the correction of variations in the economic cycle. Social security comprised an important group of fiscal instruments which could be employed by all governments for purposes of rehabilitation and stabilization. As a result, certain social security measures were to be regarded as an essential feature of the government's economic policy. This was all the more important since the diverse aspects of a system of social security react on each other, and it was essential that the whole be developed logically under the leadership of one authority having a uniform policy.

For it is on this condition that success rests: the public investment policy must be prompt and flexible, it must be prepared in detail and beforehand, and there must be a co-ordination of government efforts throughout all of Canada.

But these measures of co-ordination would settle only one part of the problem. The governments would have to reach some understanding on the sharing of fiscal powers and economic and social functions. A new Federal-Provincial Conference would also be necessary. This conference would, moreover, take as the basis of its discussions and plans for reform the recommendations of the *Report of the Royal Commission on Dominion-Provincial Relations,* which still commend themselves to the attention of all.

To convince oneself of the fact that the federal government adopted such a programme, one has only to consult the pamphlet entitled *Employment and Income* presented to Parliament by the Minister of Reconstruction in April, 1945.

It was at the Conference held in August, 1945, that the Dominion made its proposals known. They were clearly inspired by the theories of the "new economy." They had the same objective: a high level of employment and profit; the same means: state intervention on a triple scale – economic, fiscal and monetary – to combat cyclical variations; the same importance accorded to governmental budgeting.

These formed the basis of the centralist thesis, and they have constantly reappeared in all subsequent discussions, especially in the first post-war budget speeches.

Critique Of The Economic, Social And Fiscal Theories Of The New Federalism

The centralist argument leads to the conclusion that traditional federalism, because of present-day economic and social necessities, is doomed to disappear in Canada, to be replaced by new structures which will ensure unquestionable preponderance for the central government, together with jurisdictional concurrence – instead of exclusivity – on most subjects of legislation.

1.—The Values At Stake In This Adventure

This adventure involves certain human values which neither economic stability, nor full employment, nor social security can replace. The human values at stake in this adventure are, first, of a political and then of a national order. Some considerations may contribute to a better understanding of the fate which would befall these values through a policy of progressive centralization in Canada.

HUMAN VALUES OF A POLITICAL ORDER

We have described and emphasized at some length the human advantages which federalism, as a system of social organization, allows. As we then said, it is the system which, in practice, best translates the Christian concept of Man and of society, and the idea of the common good as well as the principle of every collectivity's subsidiary function, while, at the same time, it respects the fact of social life's variety and complexity.

These considerations might have appeared somewhat abstract and irrelevant in that context. But they constitute the basic criticism of the centralist thesis. Therefore, we suggest to readers who really desire to inform themselves on the human and political value of true federalism and the dangers of excessive centralization that they refer back to that chapter. Suffice it to say here that one of these dangers is, precisely, that of causing the Canadian state to lose its political character and of being transformed into an economic society which, above all else, would be concerned with material well-being and technical efficiency.

Without a doubt, both these things are necessary, but only as means, as instruments with a view to a higher life – the life of the spirit which is, above all, conscience, liberty, responsibility, initiative, self-determination and self-government. A society of a truly political nature seeks to respect and promote this life of the spirit among its members; it seeks to release and elevate their human qualities by constantly appealing for use of all such qualities which are, precisely, manifestations of the life of the spirit, at all levels of the social and political order.

Centralization carried out in the name of economic theories and with a view to objectives which are, above all, economic, can only culminate in purely economic results, with sacrifice of the citizens' political life, since they would become only a shifting mass of producers and consumers.

The costs of such an adventure would be charged to Man himself and he would pay for them with his dignity and his liberty. In this connection, it is not without interest to here recall remarks made by the head of the Catholic Church, His Holiness Pope Pius XII, on the tendency to organize social life on the model of great modern industrial enterprises. These remarks are of value, not only to Catholics, but to all Christians and to all who seek to safeguard the life of the spirit in Man.

We cannot, said the Sovereign Pontiff, adopt these gigantic modern industrial enterprises as a universal model of social life, whatever their achievements may be, because the question arises whether a world which recognizes only the economic form of an enormous productive organization can ever succeed in exercising a beneficial influence on social life in general and on the three basic institutions of the family, state and private property.

We must answer that the impersonal character of such a world is contrary to the fundamentally personal nature of those institutions which the Creator has given to human society. In fact, marriage and the family, the state and private property tend of their very nature to form man as a person, to protect and render him capable of contributing

through his own voluntary cooperation and personal responsibility to the similarly personal life and development of
human relations. The creative wisdom of God is therefore
alien to that system of impersonal unity which strikes at the
human person, who is origin and end of society, and in the
depths of his being an image of his God.[1]

We shall not, for the moment, pursue the subject further. It
will suffice if we have indicated where we are led by a centralist
adventure entirely directed by economic theories and motives
and which, to ensure its success, begins by destroying regional
and local autonomies. For that, indeed, is the result in which the
centralist thesis culminates, in practice, even if its proponents
make outward professions of respect for our federative system
and advertise their doctrines as "the new federalism".

HUMAN VALUES OF A NATIONAL ORDER

The centralist adventure in which we are invited to participate
by federal economists and politicians also puts at stake human
values of a national order. In this respect, the French-Catholic
population of Quebec is directly and vitally interested because
the cultural and national sacrifices necessary to ensure the project's success would be required of them, and of them alone.

In our historical outline on Confederation, we stressed the
special reasons which led the French-Catholic population of
Lower Canada to demand a federative instead of a legislative
union. In order to induce the French-Catholic population of
Quebec to accept the new system, political leaders and supporters of the scheme repeatedly told them to have no fear for the
future, since Lower Canada was going to regain its autonomy
and would be in a position to exercise the necessary surveillance
over its institutions and its laws to preserve them from any
danger.

That, it should be noted, took place at a time when the state's
role in social and cultural life was a very minor one. Now, the
watchword has changed and the state intervenes in everything.
If, indeed, and according to Macdonald's own testimony, the
people of Lower Canada, because of the fact that they constituted a minority, spoke a different language and professed a
faith different to that of the majority, considered that they could
not, at that time, accept legislative centralization because it was

[1] Christmas radio broadcast, December 24, 1952.

prejudicial to their institutions, laws and national traditions, how much more dangerous must the massive and universal intervention of the state now appear to them?

We pose the fundamental and even crucial question: can a system of legislative centralization give justice to the French-Canadians and promote their interests as such, that is to say, not merely as individuals but also as members of a national group whose culture has a right to live, to expand and to spread throughout this country? In 1867, they considered it too dangerous to entrust the guardianship and promotion of their culture and national interests to the central government. Does a similar danger still exist today? Is the situation of the French-Canadians so improved, or has their influence been so increased, that there is now no more danger to be feared?

Anglo-Canadian Protestants control the governments, not only of the nine other provinces, but of the Canadian federation itself. These latter years have witnessed fiscal and economic centralization, and, to a lesser degree, centralization of social policy. Now, of all the federal measures adopted in these three fields within the past dozen years, how many have drawn their inspiration from the French-Canadian group's philosophy of life, and how many have concerned themselves with safeguarding and promoting the national values which are peculiar to this group?

We would like it well understood that there is no question here of attributing to the federal government sentiments of hostility with respect to the French-Canadian nationality. The question, rather, is to know whether, when the central government makes laws, it can do otherwise than draw its inspiration from the Anglo-Protestant majority's mentality, requirements and philosophy of life. Can it really do otherwise or, in a democratic system, seek its inspiration elsewhere? But, then, how can it adapt its legislation to a different mentality, a different culture and different institutions? From whatever angle we look at it, legislative centralization can mean nothing but levelling and standardization and thus enfeeblement and ruin for the national values special to the French-Canadian group.

Some persons have answered that while it might, perhaps, be reasonable to entertain fears regarding direct interventions by the federal government in the fields of education and culture, it is an exaggeration to believe centralization in social, economic and fiscal affairs threatens French Canada's national values. Those who hold and disseminate opinions of this kind appear to us to have overlooked two essential matters – the value of autonomous political frameworks for the survival of modern nationalities, and the ever-increasing repercussions which legislative measures, in economic, social and fiscal matters, exercise on cultural and national values.

As regards economic, social and fiscal legislation, we believe it would be difficult to deny its present profound repercussions on the people's ways of life and thought and, consequently, on cultural and national values in particular. This fact seems obvious to us, when we consider social policy, that is, the overall legislative and administrative measures relating to the public welfare, to health, to hygiene and to social security. In each of these cases, there are involved particular institutions which are already existent or which are being set up to meet new needs. It is through the institutions it creates that a people translates its philosophy of life and these institutions become, at the same time, the manifestations and guardians of its cultural and national values.

Thus we return to the fundamental and even crucial question: with what philosophy of social life will a centralized social legislation be inspired in Canada – with that of the Anglo-Protestant majority, or with that of the French-Catholic minority? The answer is already known and it is needless to insist upon it further.

However one looks at it, fiscal, social and economic centralization can only be realized by sacrificing higher values, values of a human order, both political and national. To demand such a sacrifice of the Province of Quebec – because, in the end, it would be the only one of whom it would be required – there must be other and more cogent motives than administrative simplification, technical efficiency or even economic stability.

II.—The Scope Of Arguments In Favour Of Centralization

If, again, the arguments in favour of centralization all had convincing and undeniable force, the Province of Quebec might, perhaps, have less reason to oppose the adventure into which it is sought to involve it. But is this actually the case? Can or should it, in the first place, blindly and without debate or correction agree with the arguments of the centralist thesis? In the second place, has it been demonstrated that, in economic, social and fiscal matters, there is no other solution possible in Canada except centralization? Since these two questions go to the very root of the problem, answers to them will go far to provide the problem's solution.

1. THE FEDERAL GOVERNMENT'S HISTORICAL AND JURIDICAL CLAIMS TO DIRECT ECONOMIC LIFE

While the general tenor of this argument is already known, it may, nevertheless, be well to repeat its salient features. The Fathers of Confederation, so it runs, entrusted the main functions and the main powers of government to the Dominion, especially in the financial, fiscal and economic fields; on the other hand, they left to the provinces only powers and functions of a somewhat secondary nature which carried with them only minor obligations not likely to be increased in the future. This school hastens to add that, unfortunately, these wise provisions and expectations were upset through action of three factors: the Privy Council's interpretation of the Canadian Constitution, the claims and activities of the provincial governments, and the federal government's inertia. Since the depression of 1930 demonstrated how badly the mechanism established by the Fathers of Confederation had been deranged, it is suggested that a return to the original provisions of the 1867 Act should be made, that is, to uncontested supremacy of the federal government on the economic, fiscal and financial planes, with gradual effacement of the provincial governments from these same fields.

This argument impels us to make a careful examination of one aspect of the centralist thesis – that of the economic preponderance, in law or principle, which the Fathers of Confederation are supposed to have assigned the Dominion.

The Fathers of Confederation scarcely departed from the liberal tradition. The latter has always agreed that the state's duty is to ensure essential non-profit-making services for general economic development and the governors of Canada did not handle the transport question in any way different from what had been done even in Europe.

It is, certainly, permissible to stress the amplitude of federal powers in economic matters, but it should not be forgotten that the provinces nonetheless have the right to wide initiatives in this same field. When a distribution of powers was made, the provinces in any case got the ownership of the lands and administration of natural resources, both being competences which rather closely affect the country's economic development. In view of that apportionment, may it not be concluded that the Fathers of Confederation confided precise and limited tasks to the central government in the economic field, without attaching thereto any question of principle, and that they foresaw, once these tasks were accomplished, that it would then be the turn of the provinces which, having conceded resources to private interests, would derive from them revenues which would enable them to meet their governments' expenditures?

It seems to us somewhat difficult to admit the validity of the historical and juridical argument perpetrated and defended by partisans of centralization in Canada, when there exists both in Canadian history and law another interpretation which seems to us to conform much more closely to reality and which does not, like the other, tend to ruin genuine federalism in our country.

2. THE PROVINCES' FINANCIAL INCAPACITY

The centralist thesis adds an argument of a financial nature to the historical and juridical one. The provinces, it alleges, are financially unable to meet the charges nowadays incumbent on them because of the insufficiency of a) their fiscal resources; b) inequality in the distribution throughout Canada of industrial, commercial and financial establishments; and c) limitations on their borrowing and credit potential. Is this financial incapacity of the provinces founded in reality and on law? If so, is the only or best solution for this serious defect fiscal centralization at Ottawa?

Primarily, it seems to us an exaggeration to sustain in principle that there is simultaneous financial incapacity of all the provinces. Whether it be the federal or the provincial governments which collect it, the money always comes from the same taxpayer and the federal government does not, in its collection methods, possess any magic touch the others do not have. In other words, the fact of centralizing tax collections does not sensibly increase the yield of such taxes, and if all the provinces are incapable of financially fulfilling their obligations, then it is not by transferring the provinces' revenues and charges to the federal government that the situation can be remedied. It is, therefore, regarding only certain provinces that financial incapacity can be alleged.

The whole question, then, is to know whether, in order to assist the handicapped provinces, it is fair and politically sound to deprive *all* the provinces of the natural exercise of their fiscal powers. In any case, we fail to see the necessity of centralizing the collection of billions of dollars in Ottawa in order to effect the transfer of, let us say, a hundred million dollars.

A re-allocation of taxes and the co-ordination of the provinces' policies between themselves and between the provinces and the federal government, would ensure the maximum equality of services it is possible to achieve between one province and another in a country like Canada, whether it be organized as a unitary or as a federative state.

Finally, it is alleged, the provinces possess only limited borrowing and credit potentials; in the event of a depression, they would find themselves unable to meet their financial obligations and obliged to beg for federal assistance while having recourse to the traditional policy of balanced budgets.

Today, experience forces us to admit that a government cannot get through a major depression without having to borrow from the inflationary methods of deficit financing. We practised such methods in 1930-1934 without either knowing or desiring it; subsequently, we told ourselves that it would be just as well to employ these methods in a deliberate and scientific way. Under these conditions, it is hard to see why the provincial governments could not just as well present themselves to the Bank of Canada and obtain from it, directly, the funds needed to finance their deficit budgets in time of crisis.

From a technical and even constitutional viewpoint, what inconvenience would there be in allowing the provinces free access to the Bank of Canada in order to finance their government policy? If the provinces had free access to the Bank of Canada, they would not only be able to practise an anti-cyclical policy, but they would also bear full responsibility for their financial policy, which would better suit their character as sovereign powers.

3. – THE ECONOMIC ARGUMENT: MAINTENANCE OF ECONOMIC STABILITY

This question of the financial incapacity of the provinces arising from their lack of jurisdiction over money and the banks naturally brings us to undertake a critical examination of the present main argument of the centralist thesis, namely, that centralization is today the primary condition for any effective economic stabilization policy.

What interests us is not the intrinsic value of economic

theories but their political effects, or, more precisely, the political consequences which certain economists draw from them. Keynesianism, for instance, seems to us one of history's great economic theories but if, for its full application in Canada, we must start by destroying our traditional federative system, we feel caution is necessary, and that the circumstances in Canada are such that we do not have any right to throw ourselves into any sort of adventure, in the name of any theory, so long as it has not been proven that centralization is the condition *sine qua non* of Keynesianism's success.

It is in the name of a theory, and of one which is widely controverted, that the Keynesian economists claim to impose centralization on us in Canada. They say, particularly, that there is no economic stability possible unless the main fiscal powers are concentrated in the hands of one and the same authority. It may be well to pause for a moment to examine the validity of this claim.

Let us note, first of all – because it is a significant fact – that a similar claim has never been made in such categoric terms anywhere else than in Canada. The American Keynesians, for example, have been especially impressed by the monetary aspects of the limits of local action. And, despite the fact that multiple tax jurisdictions are more numerous in the United States than in Canada, they have never gone so far as to claim that economic stability required absolute control of fiscal means or surrender of their taxation rights by the various states.

Having made that point, let us proceed to the heart of the argument. The fiscal centralization which is asked for is to allow the federal government to exercise, through taxation, a regulatory and stabilizing action on the economy.

Neither of the two political conclusions of the Keynesian economists seems to us sufficiently proved, namely a) that traditional federalism means the prevalence of economic instability and b) that with fiscal centralization economic stability in Canada is assured.

Practice of federalism appears to us as feasible in the realm of economic control as it is in other fields. Perhaps more than elsewhere, insistence would have to be laid on the need for co-operation between the autonomous governments which every federative system carries within itself. Thus, what is most needed for the moment is the organization of permanent mechanisms of co-ordination and co-operation which are shown to be necessary for the Canadian population's common good.

All governments in Canada should join in this necessary organizing effort and all of them – the federal government as well as the provincial governments – should fully decide to make the sacrifices required to maintain our federative system, which is a system of co-operation with the autonomy of each respected. The Province of Quebec should be ready for such co-operation, but on one condition – that it is not asked to make all the sacrifices alone, or that it should be asked to sacrifice the very reason for its existence, on the pretext that practice of an economic theory could thereby be better effected. History is strewn with learned theories and policies which appeared marvellous to their contemporaries, but which no one takes seriously any more. The provinces which risk little or nothing in the new centralist adventure, sponsored by economic theorists, can afford to join in it or let themselves be swept away by it without undue emotion or alarm, but the Province of Quebec which, for its part, risks all, cannot be too careful. It has the right to ask that economic stability experiments be carried out within the terms of the Canadian Constitution and according to the means which that constitution provides.

4. ARGUMENT OF A SOCIAL ORDER: A CANADIAN SOCIAL
SECURITY PROGRAMME

The centralist thesis brings forward another argument which, moreover, fits in with the preceding ones and especially with the argument regarding requirements of the new economic policy. It is that centralization is necessary to ensure a full and effective programme of social security in Canada. As a matter of fact, the argument does not bring forward much new material and seeks to support itself on the same reasons as the others, namely, that the provinces do not have sufficient resources to fulfil their social obligations; administrative economy and efficiency require, or at least strongly recommend, uniform legislation in this field; and, finally, that social security is now an integral part of governmental economic policy, being a means of ensuring the economy's stability and progress and, as such, it should rest more and more with the government already entrusted with general economic policy, which is to say, with the federal government. In reply we say that if social charges are the most costly today, direct taxes are also the most productive and, provided the federal government leaves the field open, most of the provinces could handle matters alone, while it would be possible to institute a means of financial equalization to help the others, but only the others.

Even if it were shown that centralization of social security would, *ipso facto,* give more economical and efficient results, we should ask ourselves whether the technical and economic advantages are such that the provinces, particularly Quebec, should hand over to Ottawa organization of their social policy. In any case, for Quebec the answer is clear.

We might limit ourselves to these few brief reflections on the scope of the argument of social order which is put forward in favour of centralization but, it seems, we would not then have sufficiently touched the very root of the question, which is the philosophical and vital problem which state social security today presents. Unanimity has by no means been reached on the question of whether massive state intervention is desirable in social security. The question of state intervention in the social and economic field is a matter of philosophic concepts which touch the vital nerve of cultures – the determination as to what Man is, what is his role in society, what are his rights and duties towards society and, reciprocally, what are society's rights and duties towards him.

Consequently, for Quebec the problem is not merely a technical one, but it is one of social philosophy. If the province fears centralization in this field, it is precisely because it knows this is a means of imposing on it social measures which are foreign to its people's own philosophy and way of life. It feels, more or less confusedly, that all this social policy of foreign inspiration constitutes a constant temptation for it to give up its way of life and cannot fail to work towards its assimilation.

The Province of Quebec is far from being convinced that the organizational principles, which it is sought to impose on it through centralization, are superior to its own. On the contrary, it is aware that it is the failure to apply a right concept of the state which is the main cause of constitutional difficulties regarding social security. The Province concludes from this that the confusion of ideas which presently exists, regarding what matters belong to public and private rights respectively, makes it more than ever imperative that the exclusive jurisdictions enacted in the original Constitution be respected.

The principles to which French-Canadian civilization is attached are very difficult to reconcile with statist doctrine. On the one hand, they reject socialism, while being unable to agree with a liberal or pragmatic statism. These principles are not opposed to bold and resolute state intervention in the name of the common good. But such interventions should be of a very definite kind, and must respect human dignity, the chief common good which the state is charged with safeguarding and protecting. They should, over and above all else, condition the initiative of individuals and of their associations, encouraging association where the individual does not succeed, and, in a word, they should stimulate private action but never substitute themselves for it, save in cases where it is impossible to act otherwise or when the common good truly demands direct action by the state.

Such doctrine harmonizes poorly with a statism, even liberal, which prefers direct action by the state rather than efforts to encourage association. It does not harmonize any better with an empirical statism, which does not underestimate private action but which does not attach any special importance to it, and is satisfied to weigh the pros and cons in terms of technical or administrative efficiency. It is only satisfied with a policy oriented towards a definite common good in terms of human destiny, which is not wholly resumed in a vague intellectual or even moral progress, but which also comprises an appeal to super-natural spirituality.

In these perspectives, the state's function is wholly conditioned by the need for preserving the individual's liberty of choice, without which it becomes impossible for the human being to perform these acts which will lead him to that liberty of autonomy or true liberty of which the philosopher, Jacques Maritain, speaks and which consists in learning and succeeding in self-mastery according to an order indicated by the very finality of the human person. The state authority must, like all authority, thereafter be impregenated with that desire to guide the individual towards true liberty and by so arranging the terrestrial world that it will not offer obstacles to personal initiative. In that function, it may have to constrain wills to right action, but it should substitute itself for such wills as little as possible.

Federalism puts forward a principle which may be stated thus: as regards individuals and lower groupings, every community should content itself with exercising a suppletory and subsidiary function and refrain from doing for them whatever they are able to do for themselves, either individually or in association. This principle of federalism wholly corresponds to the concept which the French-Catholic population of Quebec has of the state and of the state's role. The Province of Quebec cannot sacrifice the direction of its social policy for reasons of a technical, administrative or even of an economic nature. In this field, more than in any other, save the field of education and culture, it needs to have the autonomy guaranteed to it by the Constitution of 1867 fully respected.

III. — Possibility of a Truly Federalist Policy

All that we have said regarding the real meaning of arguments favouring centralization gradually leads us to the conclusion that, provided there is good will on both sides, a policy of federalist inspiration on economic, social and fiscal matters is still possible in Canada. And such a policy would not necessarily mean a retrograde and anarchic policy which would be a source of insecurity.

Considered only from its political aspect, federalism is essentially defined as a system in which the governments are both autonomous and co-ordinated. According to needs and circumstances, stress can be laid on the first point or on the second, but never to the extent that the one destroys the other, for then there would be an exit from federalism. So much being said, let us examine the posibility, in Canada, of a truly federalist policy in economic, social and fiscal matters from the dual viewpoint which every authentic federative system connotes — the *autonomy* and *co-ordination* aspect of policies.

1.   AUTONOMY OF POLICIES

Fiscal Policy
Is fiscal autonomy of governments something that is possible in Canada? As a matter of fact, ever since the beginning of the Second World War, a single government has, in this country, enjoyed true fiscal autonomy: that is the central government, and it has enjoyed it to the point of being able to dispose of enormous revenue surpluses which have enabled it to multiply its offers of help to the provincial governments and to create for itself new obligations in fields belonging to the provinces.

We clearly indicated, when discussing the argument that the provinces do not have the desired resources to meet their constitutional obligations, that a settlement is possible. If the federal government, we then said, left them full liberty in the field of income taxes and succession duties, most of the provinces could handle their affairs alone and thus finance themselves out of their own taxes.

But, it will be objected, what would become of the federal government's fiscal autonomy in such a case? It could be preserved, safe and sound, on condition that it contented itself with the charges entrusted to it by the original Constitution.

Economic Policy

The centralist thesis claims for the federal government the quasi-exclusive direction of economic policy in Canada, and it leaves only a very minor trickle of provincial autonomy in that field. According to this thesis, there is no room for two orders of autonomous policy, with federalism having become impracticable and even harmful.

Efficiency, efficacy, administrative savings, stability and security are not supreme values, nor ends in themselves, but only means aimed at aiding the human person to develop himself in conformity with the requirements of his nature. Wherever these things tend to destroy the human, instead of helping to create it, they are to be set aside as being more harmful than useful.

Canadian Keynesians have been so preoccupied with economic policy in general that they have been led to consider it as the sole appanage of the central government and, consequently, they have been led to reject as a dangerous rival any autonomous policy in that direction on the part of the provincial governments. In our opinion, there is nothing to prevent problems of economic policy being, even in the Keynesian view, settled within the framework of our present federative system. In other words, the federal government, in order to put its economic policy into operation, in no way needs to monopolize this field and, as a consequence, despoil the provinces of their prerogatives. It already enjoys important means of elaborating and executing such a policy, among others the exclusive power to decide monetary policy which, after all, is the key to the entire programme. It could, if it so desired, use that power to "live and let live" without losing its right of supervision. It could even use the Bank of Canada as an instrument to dispose the provinces to a true co-operative spirit. The provincial governments, for their part, could then follow their own economic policy.

In short, autonomous policies are still possible even on economic grounds, but that is not to say they should not be co-ordinated. On the contrary, in this field more than elsewhere, co-ordinated policies are required.

Social Policy

Is an autonomous social policy on the part of the provincial governments possible? The centralist thesis brings two factual objections against such a possibility – unemployment and social security. It is necessary to consider both of these objections and to discuss their validity.

The federal government, the partisans of centralization claim, would be more interested in adopting remedial measures against unemployment if it had full responsibility for it. Here we encounter the most important premise of the federal-provincial relations problem in its economic and social aspect, and it is the one which, for a quarter of a century, has given rise to the lengthiest discussions and which has contributed most to the deviation of constitutional policy. To see it clearly, unemployment, which is an economic factor, must be distinguished from the unemployed worker, the product of unemployment, who is a human and social fact.

The unemployed worker, the product of unemployment, is an assistance case and, as such, comes within provincial jurisdiction. It is needless to repeat why, in a country such as Canada, this has to be so. The social is the meeting place of the economic and the cultural and, consequently, the place where a people creates, according to its special genius, the framework of its everyday life, the various institutions which are both the expression and the sustenance of its culture, the communal bond: work system, mutual aid, welfare, assistance, etc. Insurance or assistance are aids to the unemployed worker, and they are necessary aids; but the remedy for unemployment, the only real remedy, is work.

In a period of economic recession, work may itself be considered an aid. But relief work only has its full value if it is included in a more general policy which tends to develop employment through action on the whole economy. This would include trade policy, easing of credit, reduction of taxes and other measures whose consequences would be to multiply means of payment and to stimulate exchanges.

These means of action, of general scope, can only be put into effect if the situation justifies them, that is, if unemployment at any given moment exceeds normal levels and threatens to become general. In a country as extensive as Canada, unemployment does not show itself everywhere at the same time, for the same causes, in the same forms and with the same severity. The public authorities closest to the people and in the most immediate relations with the centres where unemployment is occurring are in the best position to intervene most swiftly and most effectively.

Thus, in our opinion, the distribution of powers effected by the Constitution corresponds today, as it did in 1867, to reality's requirements. Because of its jurisdiction on the economy's primary factors and the diversity of initiatives it may take in order to make work, the provinces (including the municipalities) are in a better position than the federal government to go to the aid of the unemployed and to take steps to overcome unemployment.

The same is true of social security in general. The centralist thesis seems to consider a provincial system of social security as being impossible to realize or, at best, doomed to inefficiency. There is always this search for efficiency first in a profoundly human domain. It might be added that the provinces are better able than the central government to provide social security, by adapting benefits to the conditions suitable to their milieu.

Autonomous policies in fiscal, economic and social matters are not only possible but even desirable in Canada. We admit there might be difficulties in putting such policies into effect. But the inconveniences which they involve are less, and not so harmful as those which derive from centralization in these same matters, and they could be greatly reduced through co-ordination.

2. THE CO-ORDINATION OF POLICIES

If federalism is founded upon the presence of autonomous governments, it also requires, especially in the twentieth century, that these governments should co-ordinate their policies between them on all matters of common interest, and this co-ordination should be effected on the interprovincial as well as on the federal-provincial plane. In this way, and only in this way, will it be permissible to speak of a new orientation to be given Canadian federalism.

The misfortune has been that, in view of the difficulties of organizing such co-operation, in Canada the easiest solution, although it is the least human and the least democratic, has been chosen, namely, centralization. In order to cure the ailment it was decided to suppress the patient who, in this instance, bore the name "provincial government."

All kinds of objections have been made against this co-ordination of policies, among others that differences of opinion between the provinces are too wide and that the co-operation of some of them could not be counted upon, and that past experience has only given unsatisfactory results in this matter.

This is the same obsession with technical efficiency and the same temptation to attain it by treating Man more like a thing or a number than like a person enjoying liberty and capable of responsibility. It is always easier to suppress human resistances than to convince minds of the interest of common action to be undertaken. In other words, the methods of the dictatorial and totalitarian regimes give much speedier results than those of the democratic systems, but which of them has the greater human value?

Some people reject, *a priori*, such a solution on the pretext that it offers insurmountable difficulties and paralyzes provincial action for fear that disadvantageous situations will be created. The thesis of provincial paralysis is largely founded on the depression of 1929 and on the attitudes which the governments of that time adopted towards unemployment. But this can be explained much more fully by the financial concepts of that time. Deficit financing at that time was somewhat unfashionable. However, imbued with the same theories and the same fears, the central government also practised evasions by invoking the Constitution as a reason for not taking action. It was not really the operation of federalism which was under judgment, but many other considerations, even if federalism was used as an excuse for dilatory politics.

The technical problems of insurance equally become false problems when placed on the scale of state interventions and when the law of large numbers which is necessary to insurance is invoked to favour centralization. It is clear that private enterprises accommodate themselves very well with the law of large numbers, without it being necessary for them to reduce the organization of insurance to a single enterprise.

As for the objection that it has become impossible to divide jurisdictions, on pretext that Man, being a well-integrated whole, cannot be subjected to completely separated directives from two different governments on subjects perfectly divided among them, this seems to be one of these hasty generalizations meant to exaggerate the complexity of problems. In reality,

Man, however integrated he may be, does not need two governments to make laws at the same time on education, old age pensions, health insurance, etc.

In conclusion, it seems to us that the supporters of centralization purposely exaggerate the difficulties both of autonomy and of co-ordinating policies in Canada. Since there must be an interventionist policy in the economic domain, a solution for the problems it presents should be sought in the same spirit as presided over the confederative compact, and according to the rules of a democratic federalism. In practice, that means the central government should assume only such control powers as do not produce repercussions on institutional structures, or on the qualitative aspects of a civilization.

From 1945 the fiscal question has engrossed Canadian opinion and many settlement plans have been offered. Formulated in different terms and spirit, these plans have one common pre-occupation – the maintenance and satisfactory functioning of the federative system. Moreover, they share a certain number of ideas which, while not always corresponding to the same notion for all who present them, are nonetheless basic premises of the policy to be put into effect: synchronization of the fiscal systems, co-ordination of federal and provincial politics and financial equalization.

Fiscal theories are in intimate relationship with the political philosophy from which they proceed. They are, at one and the same time, one of its modes of expression and one of its means of realization. It is not, therefore, sufficient that the fiscal system should procure for the Canadian state (federal and provincial governments and municipalities) the funds necessary for its administration. It is required that, in the very first place, this fiscal system by its inspiration and modalities shall be in harmony with the political philosophy from which this state issued and by which it should continue to live.

The fiscal theories of the federal government have closely followed changes in its economic and social doctrine; it has not made an effort to adapt its fiscal concepts to constitutional law as a juridical expression of a certain philosophy of the state, but it has, on the contrary, applied itself to interpret constitutional law according to its economic and social concepts. This has accounted for the level and modalities of its personal income tax, its succession duties, etc., and, in a general way, the importance given to taxation and especially to the direct tax as instruments for regulating economic and social life.

To the extent that the federal government assumes responsibilities which the Constitution does not impose upon it, it appropriates to itself an increasing share of the direct tax. It imposes its standards everywhere and assigns to itself a social and cultural influence which the Constitution does not assign to it. Through its draining away of funds available for taxes, the federal fiscal system deprives the provinces, municipalities and school commissions of the funds which they should have at their disposal in order to fulfil their functions. Directly, insofar as it expresses itself in laws, and indirectly insofar as it is an instrument of various social laws, this fiscal system exerts a social and cultural influence for which neither the letter nor the spirit of the Constitution leaves the initiative to the federal government.

Thus, the theory of maximum taxation as a means of controlling the economy transforms the family's living conditions, in the home itself and also in its relations with the complementary institutions: education, health, welfare. Whether it be a question of living accommodation, of having his children taught, of getting medical care, of protecting himself and his family against the risks inherent in all human existence, of providing for his old age, man is forced to depend more and more upon the state and particularly upon the federal government which, although devoid of constitutional competence, has none the less taken the initiative in most of these domains. It takes advantage of this to impose its social standards which, most of the time, are foreign to the population's social traditions. Thus, little by little and chiefly among the rising generations, there spreads a mentality of dependence closely akin to that which would develop from the practice of socialism itself. From that point to winning their minds to the socialist concept of order is only a single step and institutional action will ensure that that step will not be long delayed.

The phenomenon is particularly noticeable in the Province of Quebec because of the traditional attachments of a population to personal initiative, individual and communal property, and family, as well as a certain retardation in economic evolution. Thus any undermining of these customs and institutions is particularly critical.

Without a doubt, technical and economic evolution has prepared the social movement of which we have just mentioned some aspects, and the federal government may claim that it is only adapting its legislation to the new conditions. But there, precisely, is the question. The state's role is not to allow the policy it puts or will put into effect to be imposed upon by the facts, but its role is to control the movement of facts and regulate it for the purposes of its policy, and therefore to order it according to a certain concept of Man. A philosophical choice is implicit in every political action. The rest is a matter of administrative technique.

In short, through the combined interaction of its social policy and its fiscal system, the federal government is proceeding to remodel and render uniform the sociological framework of culture from one end of the country to the other. If the two cultural groups which gave Canada its social, juridical and political institutions allow it to impose the policy in which, during the past thirty years, it has gradually engaged itself, they doom themselves to assimilation, that is to say, fusion into a new whole, whose characteristics cannot be predicted in advance. Perhaps these two groups are satisfied with this policy; it is for them to decide. But at least they should be aware of its deep implications and they should know where it is leading them.

Therefore, it is in the overall perspective which we have just sketched that the fiscal problem should be studied and solutions sought. The Province of Quebec in particular which, of all the Canadian provinces, is the one which risks most in the federalist adventure, has every interest to see that the horizons in which the country's policy is being developed are not narrowed.

Solution of the fiscal problem requires above all else a return to the Constitution and to the philosophy from which it proceeds. This is because, let us repeat, in regard to the state's purposes, the fiscal system is only a means and, in a country as complex and differentiated as Canada, only a policy respectful of regional and human particularisms and, therefore, itself decentralized and differentiated, can ensure harmonious development of the whole. What is required is to take a steady look at the problem, as the Canadian reality presents it, and then to seek its solution according to the spirit of the Constitution, itself taken as a juridical expression of a certain general concept of life.

PART FOUR:
RECOMMENDATIONS

19. GENERAL OUTLINE AND SUMMARY OF RECOMMENDATIONS

The constitutional imbroglio which has played a dominant part in Canada's recent history, has appeared to be mainly fiscal and its most outstanding episodes have been in regard to taxes. But it has its origin in a fundamental divergence of opinion on the interpretation of Canadian federalism.

The situation which has gradually developed in this country, especially since the last war, is one whose control and remedy requires a re-examination of our attitudes towards the foundations of our constitutional and political system. There is not and there cannot be any question (despite suggestions from certain quarters) of a mere redistribution, through one method or another, of the funds required for the public administration. The real need is for a re-appraisal of the socio-political reality's lasting requirements, with a re-adjustment of the fiscal system made consequent thereto.

Therefore, we ourselves have sought to grasp the problem in its entirety. We are firmly of the belief that the entire constitutional system is bound up with the questions of taxes and of the allocation of taxes which, in turn, also involves the fundamental liberties and political lot both of the individual as a citizen, and of the two great cultural communities which make up our population.

To encompass the present situation in its true dimensions and in its profound causes, we have considered it our duty to study it first of all in the perspectives of history and according to the basic principles of political philosophy. For every human society is, in fact, a constantly evolving living complex whose state, at any given point of time, can only be understood by reference to the past and to a certain concept of order.

History

The time originally placed at our disposal did not allow us, as we would have considered useful, to re-tell the history of the Province of Quebec since Confederation, particularly from the economic and social angle. But, in the present state of research and historical labours, realization of such an undertaking would take years and would require the aid of numerous specialized groups. We have, therefore, limited ourselves to the aspect which most closely touches the object of our inquiry – constitutional history envisaged in a provincial perspective.

The constitutional policy of the Province of Quebec has never, since 1867, departed from the strict federalist interpretation of the constitution, nor from the proper juridical status and mutual relations of the parties constituting the Canadian state. It is its own best witness that it has taken seriously the agreement reached in 1867 and, in every circumstance, has done what was necessary to promote the spirit of that agreement in Canadian political life.

This fidelity to the federative principle it asserted resoundingly, and at the cost of heavy sacrifice, with regard to taxation and, notably, on the question of subsidies which is the central issue in the present federal-provincial controversy.

The Province of Quebec, like all the other provinces, accepts the statutory subsidies provided by the constitution. In 1887 and in 1907 it even requested their revision. These subsidies were established as compensation for taxes whose surrender by the provinces was compulsory, for without their surrender Confederation would not have been possible. So it is scarcely surprising that the provinces periodically seek to have the compensation adjusted to the sacrifice involved, to the extent that the latter's amplitude reveals itself. There is nothing in such procedures which contradicts the federative pact of 1867.

But the case is not the same with regard to conditional subsidies and fiscal subsidies which the federal government, especially within the last twenty years, has made the instruments of its constitutional policy. Fiscal subsidies are being offered in compensation for taxes whose surrender by the provinces is in no way necessary to the state's stability. Indeed, the contrary is true, for so long as the federative system is not abolished, the proper functioning of the state requires that the provinces conserve taxes proportionate to the extent of their constitutional obligations. The Province of Quebec has preferred to deprive itself of important revenues rather than consent to a mode of subsidization which would imply a diminution of its autonomy and a surrender of its prerogatives.

As regards conditional subsidies, if the Province of Quebec consented thereto, as it did in the case of technical education and of old age pensions, it was because of the false position in which the provinces were placed by reason of the federal government's interventions in fields not within its jurisdiction. By refusing federal subsidies, as it did on various occasions, the Province not only deprived itself of the sums offered it, but, through federal taxes, contributed to the amounts of which other provinces, less scrupulously faithful to federalism, were the beneficiaries.

In a word – and this is the salient point to be gleaned from these pages of history – the attitude of the Province of Quebec in fiscal matters, as in all other matters of a constitutional nature, has never changed. It holds to an interpretation, according to the spirit of federalism, of the agreement reached in 1867.

THE PROBLEM OF CULTURE AND FEDERALISM

The Basic Question

Federalism and the problem of cultures are, to some degree, correlative. Here we touch the very root of the debate which has agitated Canadian opinion for years. The duality of cultures is the central premise of the Canadian political problem, no matter from what angle it may be approached. If the population were homogeneous, with the same religion, the same language, the same traditions and the same concept of order and of life, Canada might, especially in these days of swift and easy communications, satisfy the geographic and economic diversity of its vast territory with a modified federalism and even, in certain fields, with a fairly wide measure of administrative decentralization.

But such is not the case. Two great communities of differing origin and culture constitute its human components and each of them intends to live according to its own concepts and to preserve its own identity from one generation to another. The phenomenon is all the more ineradicable inasmuch as the difference in cultures almost exactly corresponds to the difference in religion. This fact has dominated the country's history for almost two centuries and it has conditioned all main stages of its constitutional evolution.

The Idea of Culture

Since this duality of cultures is the principle premise of the Canadian political problem, we have endeavoured to deal with it in its primary elements. We have therefore taken up and analyzed the basic ideas of culture, nation, society and state both *per se* and in their reciprocal relationships. We have attempted to isolate the predominating features of the two great Canadian cultures: what it is that distinguishes them and even what places them in opposition to each other. We have recalled the social consequences resulting from the opposition of cultures ever since the conquest in the province of Quebec; and, finally, we have sought to define Quebec's special role within the Canadian Confederation, insofar as it constitutes the national focus of French- Canadian culture.

Federalism

Only federalism as a political system permits two cultures to live and develop side by side within a single state: that was the real reason for the Canadian state's federative form. Therefore we have studied federalism, first as a system of social organization resting on the four sociological and philosophical bases: the Christian concept of Man and society; the variety and complexity in social life, the idea of the common good, and the principle of every society's complementary functions. In the second place, we have studied federalism as a political and juridical system.

Competing Theses

According to the ideas held regarding the two major matters just mentioned, one either reaches the centralizing position habitually taken by the federal government or else one reaches the autonomist position which is traditionally that of the Province of Quebec.

As regards taxes, political economy, social policy and educational subsidies, these are the two theses which stand opposed. The federal government looks at Canada as a whole; it talks about *"Canadian unity"* without specifying whether it will be the product of group fusions or of their voluntary co-operation; of *"Canadian culture"* as if culture, which has Man himself as its object and has reference to a certain general concept of life, will allow no differentiation of inspiration or ways of life as between one group and another, of the *"Canadian nation,"* as if the nation were not primarily and essentially a community of culture. Starting from there it considers it normal that, throughout the country, Canadians of every group should, for example, be subjected to the same system of social security and that the constitution should be interpreted in the most centralizing way. Our chapters on the federal government's theories

THE TREMBLAY REPORT

and practices on constitutional matters, with respect to education as well as in regard to economic, social and fiscal subjects
clearly illustrate what we have just written. These bring to
light the eminently practical effects of a whole series of concepts which, at first glance, might be considered essentially
theoretical and speculative. As a matter of fact, the interpretation given, at the state level, to concepts such as culture, nation,
society and citizenship expresses itself in laws, institutions and
ways of life and thus tends either towards the conservation of
a particular culture and the stimulation of its development or
else it tends to undermine its capacity to perpetuate itself and,
eventually, impoverishes its sources.

Federalism, as a political system, may vary according to the
purposes for which it is intended. When its sole objective is to
adapt the political system to the geographical and economic
diversity of any given country, it can be more or less flexible
and relaxed. On the contrary, if, within the framework of a
single state, it aims at ensuring the parallel development of
distinctive cultures, it is extensive and rigid.

Culture and the Sociological Milieu
Every particular culture needs a focus wherein to maintain
and renew itself from generation to generation. That is to say,
it requires a centre where each of its particulars, including
language, traditions and ways of life must be currently necessary and a requisite for success to every person making up
the collectivity. Thus, the required centre is one wherein the
people who embody it may live according to their concepts,
where they may express themselves freely according to their
spirit and where they themselves may erect, according to their
idea, the institutions necessary for the full expansion of individual and collective life. To fulfil its purpose and allow the
cultural groups present within a single state to develop themselves according to their respective particularisms and thereby
contribute to the prosperity of the whole, federalism must be
broad enough to assure to each of them the political initiative
in such functions of collective life as lie closest to the ideological, intellectual and social exigencies of the culture itself.
By these we mean education, public charities, mutual assistance, labor and family organization, etc.

Despite the ambiguity of some of its sections, that is precisely what the constitution of 1867 sought to bring about in
Canada. Through its method of distributing powers, it assigned

to the two orders of government those prerogatives which correspond to the objectives of cultural federalism. Since 1867, the Canadian reality has grown. It has become articulated and integrated but it has not changed insofar as its cultural components and its political requirements are concerned. And it is to these we must revert, no matter from what angle the state's structure and functioning may be studied. Without such a reference to the heart of the matter, technically efficient solutions may be found for this or that problem, but none will be found which will be politically just.

The Province of Quebec and French-Canadian Culture

If Anglo-Canadian culture is today spread throughout nine of the ten Canadian provinces and if it can count upon their organized life for its diffusion and renewal, French-Canadian culture on the other hand has only one real focus, and that is the Province of Quebec. This, then, is how the case of French Canada and of the Province of Quebec rests with regard to English Canada and the Canadian state. If, as is its legitimate ambition, Canada should eventually give birth to an authentic "nation" in whose midst the two groups will live in friendship, finding their full flowering in a co-operation made all the more fruitful because it is based on mutual trust, the role of the Province of Quebec, as national focus and primary political centre of one of the two groups, will be a truly great one, and one of which it must itself become aware, while the rest of the country has every interest not to under-estimate the importance of its role.

Canadian Culture and American Culture

Within the question of cultures, there also lies the problem of Canada as a whole in relation to other countries and, notably in relation to the United States and the powerful cultural centre which that country has now become. If Canada, lying within the immediate influence of American culture, must assert its own personality, French Canada, without a doubt, is its principal element of originality and its most vigorous resistance centre.

The problem of cultures which we have just raised, however specifically Canadian it may appear, is only the local application of the same kind of problem which today faces all peoples of the same cultural filiation: that of knowing whether, in a world transformed by technical progress, a humanist civilization is still possible, and on what terms. If, in the transition phase through which the world is now passing, Canada desires to be an authentic factor of renewal, it has every reason, not only to refrain from ruining federalism, but, in fact, to deepen its federalist experience and to garner its full fruits.

Recommendations

FEDERAL-PROVINCIAL RELATIONS

The Problem

In order to give a better idea of the direction and scope of our recommendations, we think it may be useful to re-state our problem's main elements. On the one hand:

1. The primary purpose of Canadian federalism is to allow the two great cultural communities which made up our population a) to live and develop themselves according to their respective particularisms and b) to co-operate in the building and progress of a common fatherland;

2. With regard to French-Canadian culture, the Province of Quebec assumes alone the responsibilities which the other provinces jointly assume with regard to Anglo-Canadian culture;

3. The Canadian reality, both economic and sociological, has undergone a profound transformation since 1867, but its cultural elements have not changed, so that the basic problem still remains the same.

Furthermore:

4. a) Transformation and integration of the economic and social complex have made economic stability one of the major political goals; b) ideas regarding the state's economic and social role have also evolved, with intervention by the state in the economy's functioning being today admissible, both in theory and in practice, while a new school of economists claims it can give it a scientific basis and standards;

5. Industrial concentration has created fiscal inequalities as between the provinces, and these should be remedied, as far as possible.

In the third place:

6. Control of the economy and equalization of fiscal conditions as between the provinces are the main reasons today invoked by the federal government as justifying its social as well

as its fiscal policy. It considers both of these, over and above their special purposes, as being indispensable instruments of economic control. The federal government, moreover, relies on an interpretation of the Constitution according to which it is vested with the main economic powers, and possesses "unlimited" power to tax and "absolute" power to spend. Thus, it concludes that it alone can exercise all initiatives needed to control the economy, to maintain employment, and to equalize fiscal resources between the provinces. As a consequence, it seems to think that pursuit of economic and social goals has, in some way, priority over cultural objectives, and also that the federal government itself has similar priority over the provinces.

Such is the basic conflict of which the fiscal problem is the most visible manifestation. In short, it arises from a unitary and non-federative interpretation of the Constitution and of the very notion of a state, and it arises also from a technically administrative but non-political concept of the state's role in economic and social affairs.

For our part, we hold that there is no opposition between the state's economic and social goals and its cultural objectives, and we believe that both of them can be effectively realized in a federative system, provided there is an awareness of the political nature of the problem and of the steps that must be taken in order to ensure a harmonious solution in a country as differentiated as Canada.

1. Politics, in the best sense of the word, has for its objective not merely welfare but good living, that is, the hierarchic totality of conditions needed for full assertion of human individuality. If it is true that the citizen serves the state, it is equally true that the state is in Man's service.

2. In a federative system, the state is composed of two orders, and not merely one single order of government, each of them acting by its own authority within its special domain but in coordination within the framework of constitutional law. Autonomy for the component parts and co-ordination of policies are the conditions required to make this type of state efficacious, particularly in these days when the various functions of collective life are so fully integrated.

3. The institutions of communal life are the sociological expression of the culture, and one of its modes of renewal. Cultural policy and social policy are, therefore, only extensions of each other; they must have the same inspiration and they must be entrusted to the government which, being itself a participant

in the culture, can best grasp its spirit and express it through laws.

4.   The various kinds of taxes are in a qualitative relationship to the functions of collective life. In a federative state of the cultural type, they should be distributed between the orders of government according to the functions with which the latter are vested. Thus, since taxes on incomes have a direct incidence on persons and institutions, they should belong to the government on which cultural and social responsibility is incumbent. Since taxes on business operations and on the circulation of goods have a direct economic incidence and, if employed on the regional and local level, would tend to raise barriers within the same country, they should logically belong to that government which is vested with the larger economic responsibility and whose jurisdiction extends over the whole territory.

5.   If equality of services between the several parts of a federative state is desirable, it cannot, however, be considered an absolute. Consequently, it cannot be established as a permanent system for the redistribution of funds nor, more especially, can it be sought to the detriment of the higher interests of one or more groups.

General Solution

RETURN TO THE CONSTITUTION

In our opinion, only a frank return to the Constitution can conciliate the principles enumerated above with the practical exigencies of Canadian politics today. We, therefore, recommend to the government of the Province of Quebec that it should invite the federal government and the governments of the other provinces, as constituent parts of the state, to undertake jointly a re-adaptation of the public administration according to the spirit of federalism. This re-shaping, carried out within the framework of the Constitution, would aim at re-interpreting its master-ideas in the four major provisions which a fiscal policy for our times, conforming both to federalism and to the state's general needs, ought to provide.

Two of these provisions, in their choice and arrangement of fiscal structures, imply options as to the principles from which Canadian policy should proceed.

I The Fiscal System and the Citizen's Personal Freedom

The first of these options would consist of an agreement between the governments regarding the percentage of the national product which, with regard to present conditions and foreseeable changes, might be considered the maximum limit of taxation. This percentage would, therefore, be set at such a rate that the taxpayer could preserve the initiative and responsibility for his own existence to the full extent that, in view of the present integration of the social economy, the service of the common good allows him.

II The Fiscal System and Constitutional Order

Once agreement is reached on the general level of taxation, the governments could proceed to a division of the tax-fields according to a method which would put each of them in a position to procure permanently, by its own authority and on its own responsibility, the resources needed for the free exercise of its jurisdictions. In such case, the option would be one respecting the state's form. Is the Canadian state in future to be unitary, frankly, federal, or will it continue to practise the halting and unaware federalism which carries with it all the inconveniences and none of the advantages of true federalism, and in which current constitutional practises threaten to engulf it? In a country such as Canada, this option lies at the very heart of the state's functioning and of the harmony of relations between the different parts of the population and of the country. So, therefore, there can be no federalism without autonomy of the state's constituent parts, and no sovereignty of the various governments without fiscal and financial autonomy.

Parallel Action on the Social and Fiscal Planes

Since the financial imbroglio whose solution is now being sought developed through parallel action on the social and fiscal planes, a return to the spirit of the Constitution and to federalism consequently requires action on the same two planes. It is useless to pretend that the fiscal problem can be solved according to the intent of the Constitution's authors, if there is not restored to the two orders of government the functions which the sociological reality respectively assigns to them today, just as it did in 1867. Considered outside of the political perspectives in which the Canadian state was given form and spirit, the fiscal problem is a matter lying well within the scope of the experts' skill and subject only to the criteria of simplicity and efficacy.

Rule for Sharing Direct Taxes

Since indirect taxes (within the meaning of constitutional jurisprudence) are assigned to the federal government by the Constitution, any agreement that may be made would only affect
direct taxes. With the federal government itself having access to
this category of taxes, any settlement between the governments
assumes there would be definition and acceptance of a rule of
sharing which would suppress the ambiguities from which the
constitutional practices of the past thirty years have resulted,
and which have also given rise to the present confusion. We
have already formulated this rule of sharing and it is deducible
from the Constitution's general aims and purposes. Inasmuch
as taxes have a qualitative relationship with the functions of
collective life, (such relationship becoming more apparent as
taxation becomes more onerous), they should be assigned, in a
federative state, to the two orders of government according to
the functions respectively vested in them. Thus, taxes on incomes affecting individuals and institutions should be reserved
to the provinces, upon which devolves jurisdiction in cultural
and social matters. On the other hand, since the federal government, for its part, is vested with the wider economic responsibilities, it should have sole access to taxes on goods and on the
circulation of goods.

Return of Social Security to the Provinces

A return to the spirit of the Constitution in fiscal matters
implies, as we have already noted, a parallel return in social
matters. In the first place, the transfers of taxes which we have
just mentioned demand a corresponding lightening of the
federal government's charges. The original text of the Constitution particularly reserved to the provinces all that field which
is today termed "social security", and this includes veterans'
assistance, family allowances, old age pensions, unemployment
insurance, etc. Having in view the higher aims of Canadian
federalism, it is necessary this should be so. If the provinces
have sufficient resources at their disposal – and such would be
the case if the re-distribution here proposed is effected – nothing
would stand in the way of their assuming full responsibility in
these matters. To the Province of Quebec, bearing in mind its
special rôle in the Canadian Confederation, the plenary exercise
of its jurisdiction in social matters is of primary importance.

It would certainly be surprising if the transfers which we
have just mentioned were to translate themselves immediately

into a perfect balancing of budgets. Certain adjustments would, therefore, be necessary. However, it is worth noting that the five largest provinces, representing about 80% of the Canadian population, would immediately have at their disposal the resources necessary for the administration of their affairs, (including social security maintained as a state service at its present level), as well as an excess for future developments.

Federal Finances

The federal government would have to envisage a gap of $409 million between its revenues and expenditures at their present level, which, now includes a military budget of $1,850 million.

Two solutions are possible:

a) Either the federal government reduces its expenditures to that extent and thereby brings its budget into balance;

b) Or, the provinces reduce taxes on individual incomes by 25%, so as to permit the federal government to increase its own levies in proportion to its revenue shortage.

Without compromising their financial positions the provinces could also reduce their taxes on individual incomes. The 25% reduction on individual incomes and a corresponding increase by the federal government in its taxes on consumption, according to a well-calculated scale, would leave the Canadian fiscal system in almost perfect equilibrium as between taxes on incomes and taxes on business operations, with each of them producing approximately 50%.

The first solution appears to have much more to recommend it. As we have already pointed out, the drainage of public funds by the federal fiscal system seriously hampers the provinces, and especially municipalities and school corporations throughout the whole country, while the high level of taxation rules out any possibility of remedying these conditions by an increase in local levies. Moreover, the Province of Quebec foresees a need for heavy expenditures both by the Province and by local communities within the next few years, in order to keep pace with industrial expansion. The excess which would be left to it by the transfers suggested above would barely suffice for its present and immediately foreseeable needs. Therefore, it would be reasonable that the federal government should finally consent to leave a sufficient portion of tax-available funds to be used for the purposes of the provinces and municipalities, whose stability and progress are the key to the progress and stability of the entire Canadian community.

"Poor" Provinces and Financial Equalization

With these transfers effected, Saskatchewan and the Maritime Provinces would remain with deficits – to a large extent because of the concentration of industry which prevents them from obtaining full benefit from their own taxes. The situation can only be remedied by a good financial equalization organism. However, the distinction must be made between *fiscal equalization,* whose object is to restore to each province the revenues to which it is entitled, and *social equalization,* whose object is to assure the really handicapped provinces of social services in conformity with the minimum standards of the country as a whole.

Fiscal equalization, if well organized, would improve the finances of all the less rich provinces and would allow all provinces, excepting the Maritimes, to balance their budgets, even at the high levels at which many of them have established their provincial services. This form of equalization could be established through agreement among the provinces, with each of them undertaking to tax only revenues earned within its limits while co-operating with the others regarding taxes to be levied on that portion of revenues derived from inter-provincial trade.

Only the Maritime Provinces would need a certain measure of social equalization, with one hundred million dollars needed to assure them the same services as the rest of the country. This form of equalization can be organized by agreement among the provinces themselves which, according to Ontario's proposals at the Federal-Provincial Conference of 1945, would set up a fund for that purpose, or it could be assured by the federal government acting as their agent. In either case, an amendment to the Constitution would be required, since the latter makes no provision for equalization in any form. At the present time, the federal government claims to provide therefor, but this is through an interpretation of its powers which, in our opinion, is inadmissible, (the "unlimited" taxing power and the "absolute" spending power). It is essential that this situation be regularized.

It would, therefore, require a social equalization operation involving a hundred million dollars to assure the budgetary equilibrium of all the country's governments. It is quite evident that completion of such a relatively small financial operation would not necessitate all the provinces being deprived of the fiscal prerogatives conferred on them by the Constitution.

III – Organic Policy of Economic Control

The social philosophy from which the Province of Quebec derives its inspiration is not opposed to state intervention in economic and social life, and it even provides for it, on certain conditions, notably on condition that such intervention carries no risk of destroying individual initiative and responsibility.

The fiscal re-arrangement which we have proposed meets one of the main concerns of our era, particularly in industrialized countries, and that is control of the economy and maintenance of employment – to the extent that taxation and social security are instruments in the hands of the state for that purpose. Our proposal, in fact, commits to each order of government means of action corresponding to its economic powers and responsibilities. To the federal government, on which the most extensive of these powers and responsibilities devolves, it attributes exclusive use of taxes whose incidence on business operations and on the movements of economic life is the most direct and the most effective. To the provinces which, through natural resources, enter into the primary phase of the economy, and which, through their cultural and social functions, respond to the collectivity's stable needs, it assigns the taxes which the most recent interpreters of current economic theories consider subject to minimum variation. For there can be no question of changing income tax rates or social security benefits according to the more or less sudden fluctuations of economic activity.

To ensure the efficacy of the policy of economic intervention and control, two conditions have to be met:

(1) New Federal Tax Structures

That the federal government revise its tax structure so as to lighten its social and economic incidence. At uniform rates, taxes on goods and the circulation of goods bear heavily on the small consumer, and have a regressive effect on the economy. But this "regressivity" is due to the methods of applying such taxes and not to their nature. To correct their social incidence and to make them an effective instrument of economic control, they would have to be established on a progressive scale, in the same way as has long been done with taxes on incomes. Experience with the *Purchase Tax,* now applied in Great Britain, and whose results, from this viewpoint, appear very interesting, may guide research by the fiscal experts.

(2) Organic Participation of the Provinces

That the provinces' participation in the anti-cyclical policy be organized according to the requirements of their constitutional functions, on the one hand, and of the socio-economic reality on the other. Control of the economy has, for its purpose, the prevention or alleviation of unemployment. A distinction must be drawn between unemployment which is an economic phenomenon and, as such, incumbent on the responsibility of governments according to the extent of their respective powers in economic affairs; and the jobless worker, who is the human product of unemployment and as such, a charity case, incumbent upon the provinces' responsibility. In a country as differentiated as Canada, unemployment does not make its appearance everywhere at the same time, for the same causes, and with the same severity. But whatever may cause unemployment, the unemployed person stands in need of aid. If the federal government alone has initiative and authority on the subject, it will have to wait until unemployment is sufficiently prevalent to justify putting into action the major mechanisms of which it holds the control, such as credit, currency and trade policies. During this interval, the jobless suffer. The experience of recent years is enlightening in this respect.

In the interests of the unemployed and of general economic stability, it is of the greatest importance that the provincial and local public authorities should be able to intervene effectively at the first signs of declining employment, even if the phenomenon is not sufficiently widespread to justify use of the major means at the federal government's disposal. Now, the remedy for unemployment is work – and even by virtue of their constitutional powers the provinces have, from this viewpoint, much more varied opportunities for initiative than has the federal government, and these are considerably more in line with the community's current needs, viz., roads, bridges, hospitals, schools, opening up of new areas, etc. But intervention of the provinces to the desired extent is only possible on two conditions:

a) Sufficient Fiscal Resources
That they have at their disposal financial resources both sufficient and as stable as possible which, let us repeat, would be the case if the fiscal re-arrangement we propose were put into effect;

b) Access to Credit
That they have access, in periods of depression, to credit. In

practice, this means the provinces should, like the federal government itself, be able to sell their bonds to the Bank of Canada. Nothing, either technically, juridically or economically prevents the provinces, within the lines of the economic policy put into execution by the federal government, from having access to the Bank of Canada and of being able to count upon its assistance in case of need and according to the extent of such needs. The provinces are constituent parts of the state as much as is the federal government itself, and, in a federative system, they should have at their disposal the resources necessary for the exercise of their functions.

IV Co-ordination of Policies

In our era of integrated economic and social functions and of constant expansion of the state's role, co-ordination of policies within a federative state is a necessity which would become even more imperative, if, as we propose, the Canadian provinces assumed the full responsibility for their jurisdictions in economic and social matters. Now, this co-ordination cannot be obtained without a special effort being made towards that end. It requires suitable organizations.

Secretariat of Federal-Provincial Conferences

The general or special federal-provincial Conferences have, at least partly, brought it about, insofar as federal and provincial policies are concerned. It has been proposed that a permanent Committee of Federal-Provincial Conferences be created. However, such an organization might be accused, as the Conferences themselves have been, of constituting a sort of super-Parliament, and, in a country of English public law, any institution which lays itself open to such a reproach has little chance of being accepted. But a permanent secretariat of Federal-Provincial Conferences would perform just as effective service without suffering from the same objections. It would ensure continuity in the work started by the Conferences themselves; it would bring together documentation; establish permanent contact between the experts of the federal administration and those of the provincial governments; and it would prepare and facilitate the usual exchange of views between the two orders of government. Constitution of such a secretariat would be highly desirable.

Permanent Council of the Provinces

At present, there is no organization which ensures co-ordination of provincial policies. Yet the provinces should discuss among themselves, without the federal government's participation, the problems which are properly within their resort. That is the only means of working out a provincial policy, suited to each province but still Canadian in nature. Creation of a permanent Council of the Provinces on the model of the American *Council of State Governments* would fill a great need. Such an organization seems to us necessary for the preservation of Canadian federalism. If the provinces do not agree to co-operate among themselves, the country's own interest will finally require the federal government to take over the supreme command.

Intermediate Solution

The foregoing plan of re-arrangement proposes an integral return to the Constitution in social and fiscal matters. But, taking into account the *de facto* situation perhaps there is occasion to envisage a less complete settlement, which would lead, sooner or later, to the final solution. This intermediate settlement would call, on the whole, for the same provisions as the general plan but it would allow for a certain participation by the federal government in social security and, consequently, in the taxes devolved to the provinces. Two cases may be imagined: (1) Since long-established opinion is that the federal government, being responsible for defence, should also be responsible for war's social consequences, it should keep Veterans' Aid. To cover the costs thereof, approximately 15% on corporation incomes would be allowed. (2) Besides Veterans' Aid, the federal government would keep the social security measures consigned to it or in whose administration it has been authorized to participate by amendments to the Constitution, viz., unemployment insurance and old age assistance. In that case, at least 50% of the tax on corporation incomes should be left to it.

If it is truly desired to return to the spirit of Canadian federalism, one cannot go beyond the two foregoing hypotheses.

Temporary Solution

Such far-reaching reforms obviously cannot be brought about immediately. As we have said, *de facto* situations and habits of thought have been created which must be corrected. In addition, the transfers we have suggested pose technical problems which would have to be solved – in the proper spirit. While awaiting these solutions, the very serious situation, which has already lasted too long, should be remedied.

As a temporary solution, therefore, we recommend the form of settlement proposed in 1947 by the Chambre de Commerce of Montreal, later taken up by the Chambre de Commerce of the Province of Quebec. This plan is the most comprehensive yet proposed. As a temporary solution, it offers very great advantages. Its principal provisions are:

(1) Agreement between the governments as to a maximum level of taxation, and, consequently, as to the limits of the fiscal system, with regard to the citizen's personal liberty;

(2) Sharing of taxes between the two orders of government according to needs – with freedom for each government to utilize, fully or not, the margin of taxation assigned to it;

(3) Provincial exclusivity in the taxing of estates;

(4) Concurrent levying of income taxes;

(5) Deduction of the provincial income tax from income taxable for federal purposes;

(6) Financial equalization in co-ordination of policies;

(7) Agreement for periodic revision as, for example, every five years. An urgency clause in favour of the federal government.

REPARATION FOR PREJUDICE SUFFERED THROUGH THE TAX AGREEMENTS

Our Report is conceived entirely in terms of the present and of the future. However, we do not forget the past.

It appears from our studies that the Province of Quebec, by refusing to traffic with the rights conferred on it by the Constitution, has suffered, by reason of the policy put in force by the federal government, and especially since 1947, losses which can be valued at more than $300 million.

It rests with the government of the Province to decide whether it should claim reparation for the damage suffered.

SUGGESTIONS FOR
FURTHER READING

I. HISTORY

The French Regime (to 1759)
G. Frégault, *La civilisation de la Nouvelle-France* (Montréal, 1944)

————, La Société canadienne sous le régime français (Canadian Historical Association, Booklet No. 3, Ottawa, 1954)
Lionel Groulx, *Histoire des Canadiens-Français, I, Le Régime français* (Montréal, 1950)
————, *Notre maître, le passé*
Jean Hamelin, *Economie et société en Nouvelle-France* (Québec, 1960)
R. C. Harris, *The Seigneurial System in Early Canada* (Québec, 1966)
W. A. Riddell, *The Rise of Ecclesiastical Control in Quebec* (New York, 1916)
Marcel Trudel, *The Seigneurial Regime* (Canadian Historical Association Booklet No. 6, Ottawa, 1956)
Mason Wade, *The French Canadians 1760-1967*, 2 vols (Toronto, 1966)

The British Regime (1759-1867)
J. C. Bracq, *The Evolution of French Canada* (New York, 1924)
Michel Brunet, *La présence anglaise et les Canadiens* (Montréal, 1958)
————, *Canadians et Canadiens* (Montréal, 1955)
Thomas Chapais, *Cours d'histoire du Canada* Vol. I, 1760-1791; Vol. II, 1791-1814; Vol. III, 1815-1833 (Québec, 1919-1921)
Donald G. Creighton, *The Commercial Empire of the St. Lawrence* (Toronto 1937)
————, *The Road to Confederation* (Toronto, 1964)
L. O. David, *Les Patriotes de 1837-8* (Montréal, 1930)
A. DeCelles, *The "Patriotes" of 1837* (Toronto, 1916)
G. Filteau, *Histoire des patriotes*, 3 vols. (Montréal, 1938-42)
Auguste Gosselin, *L'Eglise au Canada après la Conquête*, 2 vols. (Québec, 1916-17)

Lionel Groulx, *Nos luttes constitutionelles* (Montréal, 1916)
_____, *Lendemains de Conquête* (Montréal, 1919-20)
Arthur Maheux, *Ton histoire est une épopée: Nos débuts sous le régime anglais* (Québec, 1941)
Helen T. Manning, *The Revolt of French Canada 1800-1835* (Toronto, 1962)
Hilda Neatby, *Quebec: The Revolutionary Age 1760-1791* (Toronto, 1966)
Fernand Ouellet, *Histoire économique et sociale du Québec, 1760-1850* (Montréal, 1966)
_____, *Louis Joseph Papineau: A Divided Soul* (Canadian Historical Association Booklet No. 11, Ottawa, 1960)
Mason Wade, *The French Canadians 1760-1967,* 2 vols. (Toronto, 1966)

POST CONFEDERATION

Lionel Groulx, *La Confédération Canadienne* (Montréal, 1918)
Robert Rumilly, *Histoire de la province de Québec,* 41 vols. (Montréal, 1940-1969)
_____, *Histoire du Canada* (Paris, 1951)
Stanley Ryerson, *French Canada* (Toronto, 1943)
André Siegfried, *The Race Question in Canada* (Carleton Library, Toronto, 1968)
Goldwin Smith, *Canada and The Canadian Problem* (London, 1891)
Mason Wade, *The French Canadians 1760-1967*, 2 vols. (Toronto, 1966)

II. SOCIAL STUCTURE AND EVOLUTION

Albert Breton, "The Economics of Nationalism," *Journal of Political Economy*, LXXII, 1964, p. 376-86
Maxwell Cohen, "The Unquiet Revolution", *University of Manitoba Alumni Journal*, XXIII, 1963, p. 19-22
J. P. Desbiens, *Les Insolences de Frère Untel* (Montréal, 1960)
F. Dumont, *Le Pouvoir dans la société canadienne-française*
J. C. Falardeau, "L'origne et l'ascension des hommes d'affaires

dans la société canadienne-française", *Recherches Sociographiques* VI, 1965, p. 33-45

J. C. Falardeau, "Réflexions sur nos classes sociales," *Nouvelle Revue Canadienne* June-July 1951, p. 1-9

_____, *Essais sur le Québec contemporain* (Québec, 1953)

Hubert Guindon, "The Social Evolution of Quebec Reconsidered", *Canadian Journal of Economics and Political Science*, XXVI, 1960, p. 533-51

_____, "Social Unrest, Social Class and Quebec's Bureaucratic Revolution", *Queen's Quarterly*, LXXI, 1964, p. 150-62

David Kwavnick, "The Roots of French-Canadian Discontent", *Canadian Journal of Economics and Political Science*, XXXI, 1965, p. 509-23

H. Miner, *St. Denis: A French Canadian Parish* (Chicago, 1939)

Esdras Minville, *Le Citoyen canadien-français*, 2 vols. (Montréal, 1946)

J. Melançon, "L'Entreprise canadienne-française", *Actualité Economique*, XXXI, 1956, p. 503-22

L. J. Rogers, "Duplessis and Labour", *Canadian Forum*, XXVII, 1947, p. 151-2

Ringuet (Dr. Panneton) *30 Arpents* (Montréal, 1939) also available in English as *Thirty Acres* (New Canadian Library, Toronto, 1960)

Claude Ryan, "Les classes moyennes au Canada français", *Action Nationale*, XXXV, 1950, p. 207-28

Pierre E. Trudeau, *La grève de l'amiante* (Montréal, 1956)

III. POLITICAL DEVELOPMENT

G. Bergeron, "Political Parties in Quebec", *University of Toronto Quarterly*, XXVII, 1958, p. 352-67

G. Dion & L. O'Neill, *Political Immorality in the Province of Quebec* (Montréal, 1957)

J & M Hamelin, *Les moeurs électorales dans le Québec de 1791 à nos jours* (Québec, 1960)

Pierre Laporte, *The True Face of Duplessis* (Montréal, 1960)

Michael K. Oliver, "Quebec and Canadian Democracy", *Canadian Journal of Economics and Political Science*, XXIII, 1957, p. 504-15

Herbert F. Quinn, *The Union Nationale: A Study in Quebec Nationalism* (Toronto, 1963)

Marcel Rioux, "La démocratie et la culture canadienne-française", *Cité Libre*, June-July 1960, p. 3-4, 13

Pierre E. Trudeau, "Some Obstacles to Democracy in Quebec", *Canadian Journal of Economics and Political Science*, XXIV, 1958, p. 297-311

_____, "Reflexions sur la politique au Canada français", *Cité Libre*, II, December 1952, p. 53-70

IV. NATIONALISM

Jacques Bobet, "Laïcité, nationalisme, sentiment national", *Liberté*, V, 1963, p. 189-92

G. Boulet, *Nationalisme et séparatisme* (Trois Rivières, Qué., 1962)

Michel Brunet, "L'évolution du nationalisme au Canada français de la conquête à 1961," *Le Magazine Maclean*, March 1961, p. 19, 54-62.

J. C. Bonenfant and J. C. Falardeau, "Cultural and Political Implications of French-Canadian Nationalism", *Canadian Historical Association Report*, 1946, p. 56-73

Henri Bourassa, "Le patriotisme canadien-français", *Revue Canadienne*, XLI, 1902, p. 423-48

_____, *La langue, gardienne de la foi* (Montréal, 1919)

_____, *Réligion, langue, nationalité* (Montréal, 1910)

_____, *La langue française et l'avenir de notre race* (Québec, 1913)

Ramsay Cook, *French-Canadian Nationalism* (Toronto, 1969)

Lionel Groulx, *Vers l'émancipation* (Montréal, 1921)

_____, *Vers l'indépendence*

_____, *Notre mission française*

_____, *Nos positions*

_____, *La naissance d'une race* (Montréal, 1919)

_____, "Notre doctrine", *Action Canadienne Française*, V, 1921, p. 24-33

_____, "Langue et survivance", *Action Nationale*, IV, 1934, p. 46-62

_____, "Une politique nationale – notre destin français", *Action Nationale*, X, 1937, p. 130-43

_____, "Pour un commencement de libération", *Action Nationale*, XVI, 1940, p. 115-22

_____, "Nos raisons de survivre", *Action Nationale*, XLV, 1956, p. 441-48

R. Jones, *Community in Crisis: French-Canadian Nationalism in Perspective*, (Carleton Library, Toronto, 1972)

J. M. Leger, "Aspects of French-Canadian Nationalism", *University of Toronto Quarterly*, XXVII, 1957-58, p. 310-29

Arthur Maheux, "Le nationalisme canadien-français à l'aurore du XXe siècle", *Canadian Historical Association Report*, 1945, p. 58-74

Fernand Ouellet, "Le nationalisme canadien-français de ses origines à l'insurrection de 1837", *Canadian Historical Review*, XLV, 1964, p. 277-92

————, "Nationalisme canadien-français et laïcisme au XIXe siècle", *Recherches Sociographiques*, IV, 1963, p. 47-70

————, "Les fondements historiques de l'option séparatiste dans le Québec", *Canadian Historical Review*, XLIII, 1962, p. 185-203

W. H. Paradis, "Le nationalisme canadien dans le domaine religieux", *Revue de l'histoire d'Amérique française*, VII, 1953-54, p. 465-82 and VIII, 1954-55, p. 3-24

M. Tremblay, "Réflexions sur le nationalisme", *Ecrits du Canada Français*, V, 1959, p. 9-44

Pierre E. Trudeau, "L'alienation nationaliste", *Cité Libre*, XII, March 1961, p. 3-5

V. SOCIAL PHILOSOPHY

The most comprehensive source for traditional French-Canadian social philosophy is the *Semaine Sociale du Canada* series. Initiated in 1920, it now numbers over 40 volumes.

F. A. Angers, "Le corporatisme devant le démocratie et le problème de la liberté", *Action Nationale*, XX, 1942, p. 175-196

————, "Les Canadiens français et la securité sociale", *Action Nationale*, XXIII, 1944, p. 416-37

————, "Naissance de la pensée économique au Canada français", *Revue de l'histoire d'Amérique Française*, XV, 1961, p. 204-29

————, "Le problème économique au Canada français", *Action Nationale*, XLIX, 1959, p. 171-83

R. Ares, "L'âme de la corporation", *Action Nationale*, XII, 1938, p. 239-56

Michel Brunet, "Trois dominants de la pensée canadienne-française", *Ecrits du Canada Français*, III, 1957, p. 31-118

A. Dagenais, "Mission spirituelle de la nation", *Action Nationale*, XXXV, 1950, p. 121-29

J. Genest, "Qu'est – ce que l'éducation chrétienne?", *Action Nationale*, LIV, 1964, p. 120-43

_____, "Réflexions chrétiennes sur l'éducation", *Action Nationale*, LIV, 1964, p. 255-69

P. Garigue, "Organisation sociale et valeurs culturelles canadiennes-françaises", *Canadian Journal of Economics and Political Science*, XXVIII, 1962, p. 189-203

E. Lacroix, "Le syndicat catholique et national", *Action Canadienne Française*, IV, 1920, p. 64-70

Mgr. L. F. R. Laflèche, *Quelques considérations sur les rapports de la société civile avec la réligion et la famille* (Montréal, 1866)

H. G. Lemieux, "Essai d'orientation de la pensée syndical", *Action Nationale*, XX, 1942, p. 248-65.

Esdras Minville, "L'organisation corporative sur le plan national canadien-français", *Action Nationale*, VIII, 1936, p. 24-34

_____, "Réformer la régime industriel", *Action Nationale*, XXX, 1947, p. 164-71

_____, "Les conditions de l'autonomie économique des Canadiens français", *Action Nationale*, XXXVII, 1951, p. 260-85

_____, "Economic and social tendencies of French Canada", *University of Toronto Quarterly*, XIX, 1950, p. 141-57

M. Tanusier, "La question de l'école et les peuples catholiques", *Revue Canadienne*, XLVIII, 1905, p. 487-92

J. P. Tardivel and C. J. Magnan, *Polémique à propos d'enseignement entre J. P. Tardivel et C. J. Magnan* (Montréal, 1894)

THE CARLETON LIBRARY